Report of the Committee of Enquiry into Mental Handicap Nursing and Care

Chairman: PEGGY JAY

Volume II

OPCS Survey of Nurses and Residential Care Staff

*Presented to Parliament by the Secretary of State
for Social Services, the Secretary of State for Scotland
and the Secretary of State for Wales
by Command of Her Majesty
March 1979*

LONDON

HER MAJESTY'S STATIONERY OFFICE
£4 net

Cmnd. 7468 - II

910173

ISBN 0 10 174681 4

ACKNOWLEDGEMENTS

This volume presents the results of the survey carried out by the Office of Population Censuses and Surveys on behalf of the Committee of Enquiry. As the research officer and author of this report, I should like to thank all those who have helped to make this project possible. Special thanks are due to all the nurses and hostel staff who took part in the survey and especially to the staff who assisted the interviewers in planning their work within the hospitals and hostels.

I am most grateful for advice on the questionnaire design from members of the Jay Committee, particularly Derek Thomas, Nicholas Bosanquet and Rolf Olsen, and also from Professor J Tizard from the Thomas Coram Research Institute and Dr A Kushlick from the Wessex Health Care Evaluation Research Team.

A project of this complexity is essentially a team effort and I should particularly like to thank Denise Lievesley, Bernadette McCarron, Lorraine Polley, Bob Jones and the other staff from OPCS Sampling, Field, Primary Analysis and Computing Branches who have contributed to the survey's design and execution. In addition the interviewers must be thanked for their invaluable work.

I should also like to thank those members of Research and Reprographics Branches who assisted with the preparation of the questionnaire and text of this report.

Finally, I am particularly indebted to Margaret Bone and Roma Morton-Williams for their guidance and assistance on this survey.

PAUL WILSON,
Social Survey Division,
Office of Population
Censuses and Surveys

CONTENTS

v

TABLE CONTENTS

SUMMARY

Chapter 1   Introduction

1. This volume presents the OPCS report of their survey which was commissioned by the Committee of Enquiry into Mental Handicap Nursing and Care (Jay Committee). The survey's purpose was to provide information from a representative sample of nursing and hostel staff on their present and future roles, training and career structures. A principal objective was to find what emphasis staff placed on the social aspects of caring, that is on developing their residents' individual abilities and enabling them to live as independently as possible.

2. Interviews were carried out with 967 nurses from 56 hospitals for the mentally handicapped and with 390 care staff from 103 local authority hostels. In addition, information was obtained on the present abilities of the residents and staff ratios within a representative sample of 297 wards in these hospitals and within all the hostels. Almost all of the hospitals and hostels which were approached agreed to take part in the survey and interviews were conducted with about 95% of the selected individuals.

Chapter 2   Characteristics of the staff

3. Although the majority of staff were women (70% of the nurses and 82% of the hostel staff) almost half or more of the staff in the more senior grades were men.

4. Half of the nursing and care assistants, but less than a tenth of the more senior staff, worked part-time; the part-time staff mainly being married women.

5. About a quarter of the staff had obtained at least one A level or five O levels but almost two thirds had no O levels (or equivalent qualifications).

6. Very few of the nurses had ever worked in a hostel for the mentally handicapped but 40% of the hostel staff had previously been nurses, including 20% with experience of subnormality nursing.

7. About three quarters of the nurses in each of the trained nursing grades were qualified in subnormality nursing; the remainder were qualified in general or psychiatric nursing. Most of the officers in charge of the hostels were qualified either in nursing or in social work (or both in a few cases) but a third of them held no formal qualifications.

8. Twenty-seven per cent of all the nurses were born outside the United Kingdom and about half of these nurses had come from a developing country. However, a much higher proportion than this of the trainee nurses and of the younger trained nurses were born in developing countries (about 30%). Only a tenth of the hostel staff were born outside the UK and most of these had come from Eire.

Chapter 3 The wards and hostels and their residents

9. Almost 90% of the wards and 75% of the hostels were for adults and these units were classified into four ability groups:—

High ability—(36% of the adult wards) with residents who generally seemed to be able to look after themselves with a minimum of supervision.

Average ability—(34% of the adult wards) most of these residents were considered to need some help with their basic care (especially in washing or dressing).

Low ability—(19% of the adult wards) with residents who needed considerable assistance with their basic care and were often incontinent or considered to have a behaviour problem (for example being aggressive).

Non-ambulant—very low ability—(10% of the adult wards) three quarters of these residents could not walk by themselves and most of them needed assistance with feeding as well as in washing and dressing.

Almost all of the adult hostels were in the high ability group. A much higher proportion of patients in the non-ambulant and children's wards, than in the other units, suffered from various physical handicaps or illnesses—in particular two thirds of the former suffered from cerebral palsy (spasticity).

10. There was a lower average number of residents in the hostels than in the wards and the hostels had better staff ratios (calculated as the average number of residents that each staff member was looking after during the day-time), particularly in comparison with the high ability adult wards. In the hospitals the staff ratios were related to the ability level of the patients in that there were fewer patients per nurse in the low ability and non-ambulant wards than in the others.

11. Two factors which contributed to the hostels having relatively better staff ratios than the hospitals were firstly that more of the hostel residents attended an occupational centre and secondly that the hostel staff worked more overtime.

Chapter 4 The work carried out by the nursing and care staff

12. The proportion of the staff who, on their last working day, had spent over an hour on one of four tasks which form part of their social caring role (teaching, playing with residents, going on outings or encouraging them to organise their own activities) was similar in the adult wards and hostels (about 44%), but rather lower in the children's wards (35%) than in the children's hostels (55%).

13. Nurses working with the lower ability patients or in wards with relatively poor staff ratios spent more time, than staff in the other units, on providing basic care for their patients. Conversely staff working with higher ability residents or in wards with relatively good staff ratios seemed to be able to place more emphasis on helping their residents to do tasks like feeding, washing and dressing themselves.

14.	According to the staff, behaviour modification programmes were used in a third of the wards and a fifth of the hostels; the ward or hostel staff usually being involved in carrying out the programmes.

15.	The question of whether the nursing and care staff spend too much time on domestic and administrative work is discussed. Only a few of the staff expressed dissatisfaction with the domestic side of their work but a third of the more senior ward and hostel staff were dissatisfied with their administrative work.

## Chapter 5	The way the wards and hostels were run

16.	In general fewer restrictions or routines were adopted in the hostels than in the hospitals but there were only minor differences between the adult hostels and the high ability wards. There appeared to be some scope for allowing the residents to live more independently in some of the hostels and wards in each ability group and particularly within a few wards which seemed to be run on traditional institutional lines.

17.	There was slightly more stability in the staffing of the hostels than of the wards in that, for example, 80% of the officers in charge of hostels compared with 70% of the ward sisters or charge nurses had worked in their unit for a year or longer.

18.	Half of the nurses, but hardly any of the hostel staff, were obliged to wear uniforms. The wards in which the nurses wore uniforms tended to be run in a more institutional way than the other wards.

19.	The arrangements for and frequency of contacts with relatives and voluntary workers were similar in the hospitals and hostels. During the previous week almost a fifth of the residents had been visited by relatives and voluntary workers had assisted in activities with the residents in about half of the units.

## Chapter 6	Contact with staff in other professions and influence over decisions on individual residents

20.	Most, but not all, of the more senior ward and hostel staff had frequent discussions with staff from their residents' occupational centres or with the school teachers. However, about half of the more junior staff had never taken part in this type of discussion.

21.	The vast majority of the ward sisters/charge nurses, but only half of the officers in charge, had discussed the progress of at least one of their residents with a consultant for the mentally handicapped within the last six months. Conversely almost all of the officers in charge, but only two-thirds of the ward sisters/charge nurses had had this type of discussion with a social worker within the same period.

22.	Just over a third of the ward sisters and a fifth of the officers in charge said that case conferences were never held on their residents. Within the hospitals this seemed to be linked to many of the ward sisters and nursing officers feeling that their views were not fully taken into account in making decisions concerning their patients, for example with respect to admitting new patients or transferring them. The ward sisters who were rarely involved in making these decisions tended to have more limited objectives for their patients and to have a more pessimistic view of the scope for developing the potential abilities of the mentally handicapped.

Chapter 7   The staff's general attitudes towards mentally handicapped people

23.   In general both the nurses and the hostel staff seemed to appreciate the value of developing the individual potential of mentally handicapped people. The hostel staff were generally in favour of community provision and integration of the mentally handicapped whereas more of the nurses were sceptical about the quality of care at present provided for discharged patients who lived in hostels.

24.   The staff's attitudes towards the questions of sterilisation and of whether to discourage or encourage sexual relationships amongst the mentally handicapped suggested that this was an area which presents them with difficulties. About 40% of both groups of staff felt that more mentally handicapped patients or residents should be sterilised.

Chapter 8   The staff's view of their present aims

25.   The staff's aims for their residents were related to some extent to the ability level of the residents. However, more of the staff from the adult hostels, than from the high ability adult wards, considered that their most important aim was to enable their residents to live independently in society. About a quarter of the nurses in the lower ability wards felt that their main objective was to provide (rather than teach) basic care or to give medical attention.

26.   The senior nursing staff tended to have a more optimistic view, than the ward nurses, of the present aims for the hospital patients.

27.   The staff's aims and general attitudes towards the mentally handicapped did not appear to depend on whether their unit had a relatively good or poor staff ratio (after taking into account the ability levels of their residents).

Chapter 9   The staff's views on their work at present and in the future

28.   Of various tasks that they carried out at present almost half of the nurses and three quarters of the hostel staff liked part of their social caring role the best. But an appreciable proportion of the nurses (22%) most preferred their clinical nursing work.

29.   The majority of both staff groups felt that in the future they should place a greater emphasis on their social role either by helping their residents to develop to their full potential or by providing a more homelike, family atmosphere. About a third of the staff suggested that more community services or community care should be developed, including half of the nursing officers who thought that their nurses should give more domiciliary support or advice to parents.

Chapter 10   The staff's views on their relationship with other professional staff

30.   At least half of the nursing and hostel staff would have preferred to have had more contact with staff in all but one of the professions covered by the survey. The exception was ward doctors or GPs with whom most of the staff felt they had sufficient contact at present.

31. Two factors which were found to be related to dissatisfaction amongst the nursing or hostel staff with the present role or service provided by other professional staff were, firstly, a lack of influence over decisions on individual residents from their units and, secondly, a lack of regular discussions with the other professional staff (especially with respect to staff from the training centres and psychologists).

Chapter 11   The staff's views on their careers

32. In many ways the careers of the nurses seemed to be more closely linked to providing social care for the mentally handicapped than to doing clinical nursing. Recently recruited nurses had mainly been attracted by the opportunity to do a caring job rather than by the opportunity to become, or continue to be, a nurse. Similarly most of the nurses thought they would still be working with the mentally handicapped in five years time. Nevertheless, an appreciable proportion of the nurses had previously worked with other types of patients (41%) or thought they would like to transfer to other types of nursing in the future (32%).

33. A lack of career opportunities for the enrolled nurses, nursing and care assistants seemed to lead to a relatively higher proportion of these staff feeling that chances of promotion were inapplicable to them or to dissatisfaction with their prospects.

Chapter 12   Training in the care of the mentally handicapped

34. It is questionable whether the nursing and care assistants or enrolled nurses receive sufficient training on the scope for developing the full potential of their residents. With respect to nursing or care assistants this seems to be related to a general lack of training for staff in their grades in that, for example, almost half of them said they had not received any training or advice on ways of dealing with behaviour problems. The enrolled nurses seemed to be more attached to their clinical nursing role than the registered nurses which may stem partly from their formal training placing undue emphasis on the clinical and medical aspects of their work.

35. The changes in the syllabus for student nurses in 1970 appear to have led to recently trained nurses having a rather more optimistic view of the scope for developing their residents' abilities but, in practice, they do not seem to spend more time on teaching their patients or encouraging them to be more independent. Almost half of the senior nursing staff who expressed a view on this issue felt that the students' syllabus placed too much emphasis on clinical nursing.

36. There was no evidence to suggest that the type of care provided in the hostels depended on whether or not the officers in charge had obtained a recognised training qualification, or on whether they were qualified in nursing or social work. About half of the hostel staff who had recently attended a social work course felt that the educational side of their work and the type of activities they could do with the residents had not been covered on their course.

1 INTRODUCTION

1.1 Background to the survey

The Committee of Enquiry into Mental Handicap Nursing and Care (Jay Committee) was appointed by the Secretary of State for Social Services in February 1975 to examine the roles, training and career structure of nurses and residential care staff required for the care of mentally handicapped adults and children. The Committee's full terms of reference were:

> "To consider recommendation 74 of the *Report of the Committee on Nursing* (Briggs Committee), in particular to enquire into the nursing and care of the mentally handicapped in the light of developing policies, to examine the roles and aims of nurses and residential care staff required by the health and personal social services for the care of mentally handicapped adults and children; the inter-relationship between them and other health and personal social services staff; how existing staff can best fulfil these roles and aims; in the interest of making the best use of available skills and experience, the possibilities of the career movement of staff from one sector or category to another; the implications for recruitment and training; and to make recommendations."

Recommendation 74 of the Briggs Committee (1972) was that:

> "A new caring profession for the mentally handicapped should emerge gradually. In the meantime in the training of nurses in the field of mental handicap, increased emphasis should be placed on the social aspects of care."

The Jay Committee asked Social Survey Division of the Office of Population Censuses and Surveys to carry out a survey of the nursing staff in hospitals and care staff in local authority hostels for the mentally handicapped in order to help them in this task by supplementing other evidence presented to the Committee.

1.2 Objectives of the survey

The survey was intended to provide information on the present role of the nursing and residential care staff and their views on some issues relating to their possible future role. It is convenient to think of there being several possible roles for the staff of which the main ones to be considered in the survey can be summarised as:

(a) **Teaching:** enabling their residents to feed, wash and dress themselves and providing appropriate social training and education. This could involve working towards the rehabilitation of some of the residents.

(b) **Providing an informal, homelike environment for the residents:** this would include taking part in games and other activities with the residents and would involve recognition of the residents' individuality.

(c) **Providing basic care for the residents:** that is ensuring that they are properly fed, washed, clothed and so on.

1

(*d*) **Clinical nursing**: for residents who have physical (or mental) illnesses or physical handicaps.

(*e*) **Custodial**: preventing residents from causing trouble to themselves or to others.

A principal objective of the survey was to find out the relative emphasis placed on roles (*a*) and (*b*) which can be considered together as providing the social aspects of caring, and the way the emphasis on this type of care is related to the residents' abilities, the staff ratios, the staff's attitudes and the staff's training. Interest in the emphasis placed on the social aspects of caring stems from some of the evidence to the Briggs Committee which argued that nurses place too much emphasis on the medical and health aspects of care and too little on the social development of the mentally handicapped person as an individual.

A second objective of the survey was to examine the extent to which the nurses and hostel staff work as part of a team in co-operation with staff from other professions and to obtain the staff's views on their relationship with other professional staff. In addition, the staff's views were to be sought on their careers, particularly considering any links with other types of nursing, and some information was required on the adequacy of the training received by the staff.

1.3 Method

The survey was based on nationally representative samples of all grades of nursing staff working in hospitals for the mentally handicapped and of all levels of care staff working in local authority hostels for the mentally handicapped. Although the Committee was also interested in the views of other groups, including for example, staff in homes run by voluntary societies and staff in other professions it was not possible to include them in the time available.

All the information was obtained from individual interviews with the selected members of staff using the structured questionnaires which are reproduced in Appendix C. One limitation of the survey is that the information on factual questions, such as the abilities of the residents, the way the wards or hostels are run and the time spent on tasks, has been derived from answers given by the staff and not from observational studies which would have been too complex to have been carried out within the survey timetable.

1.4 The sample

It was decided to select nationally representative samples of hospital wards[1] and local authority hostels for the mentally handicapped, and representative samples of nurses and care staff working within these units. This enabled information on the abilities of the patients and residents to be linked to information on the work carried out in their units and to the views of their staff. To make the sample representative of all hospital nurses with responsibilities for mentally handicapped patients, an additional sample was selected of nurses who were not based on wards including, for example, nurses working in recreational units and senior nursing staff.

_____
[1] "Wards" is used to refer to all the wards and other types of residential units in the hospitals.

The selection of wards and hostels was derived from lists provided by the Department of Health and Social Security which covered all the NHS hospitals in Great Britain which were known to have wards for mentally handicapped patients and all local authority hostels[2] for the mentally handicapped.

The sample was selected using a multi-stage random sample design which is described in detail in Appendix A. Briefly the design involved initially selecting a sample of hospitals taking into account their size and regional location and then selecting a sample of wards and nurses from within these hospitals. One of the advantages of this design was that several of the larger hospitals were selected so that the wards and nurses from larger hospitals were not drawn from only one or two examples of such hospitals. The hostels were selected in conjunction with the initial selection of hospitals using a method which ensured that most of the selected hostels were within a reasonable travelling distance of other selected hostel(s) or hospital(s) thereby reducing the interviewing costs. The number of hospitals and hostels within the sample are shown by region in Figure (1).

A total of 57 hospitals and 108 hostels were initially selected of which all except one hospital and five hostels agreed to take part in the survey.

A sample of 299 wards was drawn from the 56 remaining hospitals and information was obtained on the patients in all except two of these wards. A total of 967 individual interviews were carried out with nurses and 390 with hostel staff and it is estimated that within the hospitals and hostels which participated in the survey 94% of the selected nursing staff were interviewed and 97% of the selected hostel staff. The response rates and the number of interviews carried out with various grades of staff are shown in table 1.

Table 1   Numbers of staff of each grade interviewed

	Numbers interviewed	Response rate (interviews obtained as a percentage of the initial sample)
(a) Nursing staff		%
Senior nursing staff (ie above the grade of ward sister)	95	93
Ward sisters/charge nurses	264	96
Staff nurses (including deputy sisters/charge nurses)	97	93
Enrolled nurses (including senior enrolled nurses)	123	93
Student nurses	89	99
Pupil nurses	64	99
Nursing assistants	235	94
All nursing staff	*967*	*94*
(b) Hostel staff		
Officers in charge	115	98
Deputy officers in charge	59	94
Other care staff	216	97
All hostel staff	*390*	*97*

In order to include sufficient numbers of trained nurses and officers in charge, the probability of selecting individuals varied according to their grade

[2] A checking procedure was adopted to ensure that the sample included hostels which had recently opened (see appendix A.3).

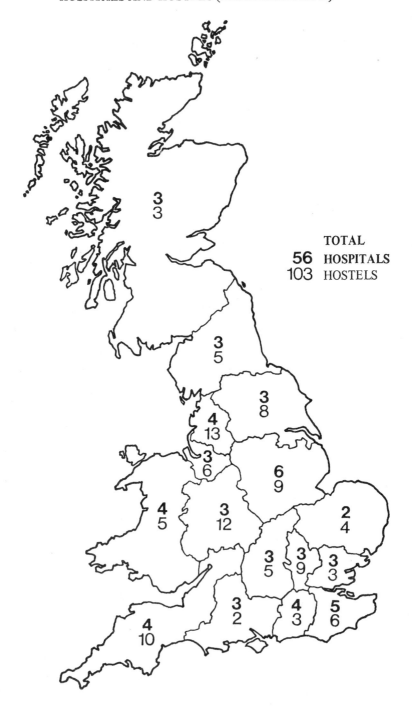

TOTAL

56 HOSPITALS

103 HOSTELS

so that, for example, within the selected hostels all the officers in charge were included in the sample but only three in seven of the deputies and other care staff. It was therefore necessary to apply a reweighting procedure to any tables which combined results for grades of staff with differing probabilities of selection. In addition, because of the way that hospital size was taken into account in the sample design it was necessary to apply a separate reweighting factor to the wards, ward sisters and senior nursing staff in the seven smallest hospitals. As a result of these procedures the reweighted total numbers in the hospital samples are 563 nurses and 311 wards and the reweighted total number of hostel staff is 324 individuals.

1.5 Interviewing

The interviewing was carried out in July 1976 by Social Survey Division interviewers. Senior staff in the hospitals and hostels provided valuable help to the interviewers by making arrangements for most of the interviewing to take place in private offices out of the hearing of other staff or residents. The information was obtained in three ways: (a) by individual interviews with the selected nursing and hostel staff (b) by interviews with the ward sister or officer in charge of the selected wards and hostels (c) from a short self-completion questionnaire which was left with the ward sister or officer in charge of the selected wards and hostels.

The individual staff interviews covered the staff's present work and their views on their work, and usually lasted from 30 minutes to $1\frac{1}{4}$ hours. The additional interviews with the ward sisters and officers in charge usually lasted for 15 minutes and concerned the abilities of residents on the selected wards and hostels and the number of staff on duty. The self-completion questionnaires covered the extent of chronic physical illnesses and handicaps amongst the residents of the selected wards and hostels. These questionnaires were left with the ward sister or officer in charge to be returned after completion to the interviewer or to Social Survey Division.

General notes on terminology and on the tables in the report

1. **"Ward sisters"** is used to refer to both ward sisters and charge nurses except where their sex is explicitly mentioned.
2. **"Wards"** is used to refer to all the wards and other residential units in the hospitals.
3. **"Staff nurses"** is used to refer to both staff nurses and deputy sisters or deputy charge nurses.
4. **"Enrolled nurses"** is used to refer to both enrolled nurses and senior enrolled nurses.
5. **"Care assistants"** is used to refer to both care assistants and senior care assistants.
6. All percentages have been rounded to the nearest whole number so that the percentages in the tables do not always add up to exactly 100. Percentages of less than 0·5 are shown as zeros.
7. The small number of individuals for whom there were "no answers" to a particular question have been excluded from the appropriate tables except where they may affect the interpretation of the results.

5

2. CHARACTERISTICS OF THE STAFF

This chapter describes the basic demographic characteristics of the staff, their normal working hours and shifts, previous nursing experience and educational and professional qualifications. The main objective of the chapter is to provide information on the characteristics of the staff which need to be taken into account when considering their role, career structure and training requirements in later chapters. An indication of the link between subnormality nursing and other nursing specialities is given in an analysis of the staff's previous experience of other types of nursing.

2.1 The staff grades

Nurses The most senior nursing staff are in the nursing officer grades which are mainly administrative and supervisory. The ward sisters (females) and charge nurses (males) are usually responsible for the day to day running of the wards under the supervision of a nursing officer. Almost all of the nursing officers and ward sisters/charge nurses were state registered nurses although a quarter were not registered in subnormality nursing. The other trained nurses are: staff nurses (including deputy sisters/charge nurses) who are almost all registered nurses; and enrolled nurses who have received a less academic training.

Forty-five per cent of the nurses were in one of the trained nursing grades described above and 42% were untrained nurses in the nursing assistant grade (see table 2). The remaining 14% of the nurses were in one of the training grades either as student nurses who are usually in training for three years to become registered in subnormality nursing, or as pupil nurses who are in training for two years to become enrolled nurses in subnormality nursing.

Table 2   Grade distributions of the nursing and hostel staff

Nursing staff	All nursing staff	Hostel staff	All hostel staff
	%		%
Senior nursing officers (including divisional and principal NOs)	1	Officers in charge	15
		Deputy officers in charge	18
		Care assistants (including	67
Nursing officers	4	senior care assistants)	
Ward sisters or charge nurses	13		___
Staff nurses (including deputy sisters and deputy charge nurses)	9		100
Enrolled nurses (including senior enrolled nurses)	18	*Base for percentages: all hostel staff (reweighted)*	324
Nursing assistants	42		
Students	8		
Pupils	6		
	___		
	100		
Base for percentages: all nursing staff (reweighted)	563		

Hostel staff The most senior grade covered in the survey was officer in charge, often referred to as the warden or matron. The officers in charge direct

6

the day to day running of the hostels and are responsible to more senior local authority staff who are not based in the hostels and were not included in the survey. All but 15 of the 103 hostels had one officer in charge whilst the 15 exceptions had a warden and a matron, usually a married couple, who were both designated as officers in charge.

Table 2 shows that a third of the hostel staff were either officers in charge or deputies and the other staff were all care assistants or senior care assistants.

2.2 Sex, age, marital and family situation

Sex It can be seen in table 3 that the majority of the nursing and hostel staff were female but that the proportions of males were highest in the more senior grades and amongst student nurses.

These results suggest that the men were more likely to make a career out of nursing than the women. This is supported (a) by the finding given later in this chapter, that approximately a third of the female nurses were working part-time whereas almost all the men worked full-time and (b) by previous research (Sadler et al 1975) which showed that only 52% of the women, aged under 50, who were qualified in nursing were still working in the NHS compared with 70% of male qualified nurses.

Age Previous research for the Briggs Committee (1972) found that 29% of all types of NHS nurses were aged under 25 which is appreciably more than the 19% of nurses for the mentally handicapped found to be under 25 in this survey.

The nursing staff tended to be slightly younger, on average, than the hostel staff. As was to be expected the greatest proportion of young people were found amongst the student and pupil nurses, of whom over half were under 25 compared with less than a fifth of any of the other nursing grades. A noticeably higher proportion of the officers in charge (71%), than of the ward sisters (43%), were aged over 40 although it will be seen later in this chapter that the staff in these two grades had a similar number of years experience of working with the mentally handicapped. The average age of the ward sisters in this survey (39) was about 5 years younger than that of ward sisters in subnormality hospitals in a survey carried out for the Prices and Incomes Board in 1967 prior to the introduction of the senior nursing structure and posts recommended by the Salmon Committee (1966).

Marital status and family situation In both the hospitals and hostels, approximately three quarters of the staff in all the grades, apart from the trainee nurses, were married and over a half were married with at least one child. Table 4 gives separate demographic information for the female staff and shows that about 40% of all the female nurses and care staff had children aged under 16, including about 10% who had children aged under 5. Possibly because many of the female staff had worked part-time or had stopped working while bringing up their families they tended to be slightly older, on average, than the male staff in the same grades, except for the trainees and staff nurses.

7

Table 3 The nursing and hostel staff analysed by sex, age and marital status

	All nursing staff	All hostel staff	Senior nursing staff	Ward sisters	Staff nurses	Enrolled nurses	Nursing assistants	Students	Pupils	Officers in charge	Deputies	Care assistants
	%	%	%	%	%	%	%	%	%	%	%	%
Sex												
Male	30	18	70	50	44	22	16	46	34	45	32	7
Female	70	82	30	50	56	78	84	54	66	54	68	93
	100	100	100	100	100	100	100	100	100	100	100	100
Age												
16–24	19	17	0	3	10	13	16	58	70	0	8	24
25–29	15	11	3	25	23	11	13	26	14	8	19	10
30–39	25	18	35	30	25	16	29	13	13	21	17	17
40–49	19	28	29	20	21	23	22	3	2	38	29	26
50–59	16	21	24	18	13	28	16	0	2	28	15	21
60+	5	5	9	5	8	10	4	0	0	5	12	2
	100	100	100	100	100	100	100	100	100	100	100	100
Average age	37	39	44	39	38	43	37	25	24	45	41	38
Marital and family situation												
Single	25	22	7	17	13	22	20	64	72	6	27	24
Married with at least one child	55	61	69	58	64	54	66	15	9	71	53	62
Married without any children	11	10	12	16	16	15	6	14	14	13	14	8
Widowed, divorced or separated	9	7	12	10	8	10	8	8	5	10	7	6
	100	100	100	100	100	100	100	100	100	100	100	100
Base for percentages: all staff (reweighted)	*563*	*324*	*113*	*290*	*97*	*123*	*235*	*89*	*64*	*115*	*59*	*216*

8

Table 4 The marital and family situation of female staff by grades

	All female hospital staff	All female hostel staff	Senior nursing staff	Ward sisters	Staff nurses	Enrolled nurses	Nursing assistants	Students/ pupils	Officers in charge	Deputy officers in charge	Care assistants
	%	%	%	%	%	%	%	%	%	%	%
Marital situation											
Single	20	21	24	17	11	17	14	63	8	25	22
Married	69	71	50	71	78	71	77	28	78	68	71
Widowed, divorced or separated	11	7	26	12	11	12	9	9	14	8	7
	100	100	100	100	100	100	100	100	100	100	100
Average age	38	40	48	41	38	44	38	24	47	43	38
Family situation											
Single	20	21	24	17	11	17	14	63	8	25	22
Married, widowed, divorced or separated and:—											
Without any children	12	10	23	20	11	16	4	20	10	15	10
With youngest child aged 16 or older	26	32	41	23	32	39	25	2	40	45	28
With youngest child aged from 5 to 15	31	28	12	31	18	21	43	12	33	8	31
With youngest child aged under 5	11	9	0	10	28	7	13	2	10	8	9
	100	100	100	100	100	100	100	100	100	100	100
Base for percentages: all female staff (reweighted)	*393*	*267*	*34*	*144*	*54*	*96*	*197*	*90*	*63*	*40*	*200*

9

2.3 Hours of work, shifts and staff accommodation

Hours of work Over 90% of the nursing officers, ward sisters, trainee nurses, officers in charge and deputies worked full-time, that is at least 40 hours a week (see table 5). In the other grades the proportion of full-time staff varied from 70% of the enrolled nurses to approximately 50% of the nursing and care assistants. For this survey the views and work carried out by the part-time staff were given the same weight as that of the full-time staff except that staff who were working for less than 10 hours a week were excluded. This affects some comparisons, for example of grade and sex distributions, between the results from this survey and figures from other statistical sources based on the "equivalent numbers" of whole time staff.

Over 85% of the male staff and single female staff worked full-time in both the hospitals and hostels. Slightly over half of the married women worked part-time and they comprised almost 80% of the past-time staff. Half of these married women who were working part-time had a child aged under 16.

Table 5 Usual hours* of work per week by grade (excluding overtime)

	Nursing officers	Ward sisters	Staff nurses	Enrolled nurses	Nursing assistants	Students /pupils	Officers in charge	Deputy officers in charge	Care assistants
	%	%	%	%	%	%	%	%	%
Less than 19 hours*	0	0	5	3	2	0	0	0	6
20–29 hours	0	2	23	11	23	4	0	2	32
30–39 hours	6	7	14	16	25	2	5	2	15
40 or more hours	94	91	58	69	51	94	95	97	47
	100	100	100	100	100	100	100	100	100
Base for percentages: all staff (reweighted)	77	290	97	123	235	134	115	59	216

*Staff who were expected to be working for less than 10 hours a week were excluded from the survey.

Overtime A higher proportion of the hostel staff (43%) than of the nurses (17%) had worked some paid or unpaid overtime during their last working week (see table 6). Considerably more overtime was worked by the officers in charge, of whom about half had worked for more than 10 hours of overtime (often unpaid), than by staff in the other grades. It may be worthwhile carrying out a fuller investigation of the causes of the relatively high amount of overtime worked in the hostels because this could deter other people, including suitably qualified nurses, from working in hostels.

Shifts Three-quarters of the nurses and 88% of the hostel staff were working on day shifts. There was a considerable variation in the arrangements for the shift systems within the wards and hostels. Half of the nurses and hostel staff knew their shifts at least 6 months in advance but about a fifth of the staff in each grade had less than a fortnight's advance notice. Except for the trainee nurses almost all of the nursing staff on duty at night were permanently on night shifts.

The proportion of trained nurses working on the night shifts was similar to that on the day shifts but slightly more of the trained nurses on the night shifts were enrolled nurses and there were fewer ward sisters (see table 7).

10

Table 6 The amount and type of overtime worked analysed by grade

Overtime worked in their previous working week	All nurses*	All hostel staff	Nursing officers	Ward sisters	Staff nurses	Enrolled nurses	Nursing assistants	Students/ pupils	Officers in charge	Deputies	Care assistants
Any overtime worked	17	43	43	24	14	15	15	16	77	54	32
Paid overtime worked:											
less than 10 hours	6	15	10	9	2	5	5	4	14	15	13
10 hours or more	5	11	0	3	6	7	6	2	22	15	8
Unpaid overtime worked:											
less than 10 hours	5	13	23	9	2	6	3	5	26	17	8
10 hours or more	1	8	8	0	0	0	1	3	26	15	2
Unpaid overtime but will take time off in lieu	2	3	12	2	1	2	2	1	10	2	2
Base for percentages: all staff* (reweighted)	544	324	77	290	97	123	235	134	115	59	216

*Excluding senior nursing officers and trainee nurses who were studying full-time.

11

Table 7 The grade distribution of the nursing ward staff and hostel staff on day and night shifts.

Nursing staff	Nurses, ward staff on day shifts	Nurses, ward staff on night shifts
	%	%
Ward sisters	16	8
Staff nurses	9	9
Enrolled nurses	19	25
Nursing assistants	40	56
Students	8	1
Pupils	7	1
	100	100
Base for percentages: (reweighted)	*324*	*148*

Hostel staff	Hostel staff on day shifts	Hostel staff on night shifts
	%	%
Officers in charge	17	0
Deputies	21	0
Care assistants	62	100
	100	100
Base for percentages: (reweighted)	*285*	*39*

The night staff in the hostels were all care assistants but 80% of the officers in charge and deputies were on call at least two nights a week.

A higher proportion of the staff on night shifts than on day shifts worked part-time and relatively more of the night staff were females (see table 8).

Table 8 Sex and hours of work of staff on day and night shifts

	Nurses— ward staff on day shifts	Hostel staff day shifts	Nurses— ward staff on night shifts	Hostel staff night shifts
	%	%	%	%
Male staff working 40 or more hours	29	19	17	3
Male staff working less than 40 hours	3	1	3	0
Female staff working 40 or more hours	46	49	28	24
Female staff working less than 40 hours	22	31	52	73
	100	100	100	100
Base for percentages: all ward and hostel staff (reweighted)	*324*	*285*	*148*	*39*

Accommodation Staff accommodation for the nursing and hostel staff differed in that less than a quarter of the trained nurses lived within the grounds of their hospital whereas 90% of the officers in charge and over half of the deputies were living within their hostel's grounds. This is no doubt related to the arrangements for the senior hostel staff to be on call during the night.

Although only 20% of all the nursing staff lived in accommodation provided by the hospital, this proportion was much higher among the trainee nurses of whom a half were in accommodation which was provided for them, mainly within the hospital grounds. Of the hostel staff who were living within the hostel grounds, 40% were in accommodation which had an entrance separate from that used by the residents (see table 9).

Table 9   Staff's accommodation by grade

Hospital staff	All hospital staff	Senior nursing staff	Ward sisters	Staff nurses	Enrolled nurses	Nursing assistants	Students/ pupils
	%	%	%	%	%	%	%
Living in accommodation provided by the hospital							
—within the hospital grounds	17	26	22	20	15	6	46
—outside the hospital grounds	5	9	12	10	2	1	6
Living in own accommodation (not provided by the hospital)	78	66	65	70	84	93	48
	100	100	100	100	100	100	100
Base for percentages: all nursing staff (reweighted)	*563*	*113*	*290*	*97*	*123*	*235*	*153*

Hostel staff	All hostel staff	Officers in charge	Deputies	Care assistants
	%	%	%	%
Living in accommodation provided by the hostel				
—within the hostel grounds	32	88	58	13
—outside the hostel grounds	0	1	0	0
Living in own accommodation (not provided by the hostel)	67	11	42	87
	100	100	100	100
Base for percentages: all hostel staff (reweighted)	*324*	*115*	*59*	*216*

2.4   Education

The educational qualifications and average school leaving ages of the nurses taken as a single group were broadly similar to those of the hostel staff (see table 10). In considering the staff's educational attainments it is important to bear in mind that within the population as a whole younger people are more likely to have passed examinations than older people as they have generally had more educational opportunities (as shown, for example, in the reports of the General Household Survey 1971–76).

Consequently it is not surprising to find that the student nurses, who were mainly aged under 30, had a higher educational level, on average, than the present registered nurses who were older. A similar result applied to pupil nurses in comparison with enrolled nurses.

Approximately 40% of the registered nurses had obtained at least one O level or equivalent compared with slightly less than a fifth of the enrolled nurses (see table 10). This is to be expected as nurses training for registration are required to have a higher educational level and are given a more academic training than nurses training for enrolment. Similarly a higher proportion (54%) of the student nurses than of the pupil nurses (34%) had obtained at least 5 O levels or 1 A level.

The Briggs Committee recommended that special attention should be devoted to the recruitment of nurses with higher academic qualifications. It is therefore interesting to examine the qualifications of the staff who have been recruited fairly recently and are now registered or student nurses, or officers in charge or deputies. For this purpose we analysed the educational qualifications of all the staff in these grades who had worked with the mentally handicapped for less than 6 years and were aged under 40. About a quarter of the 26 officers in charge or deputies had a university degree or a teaching qualification which compares with 3% or less of the staff in each of the nursing grades. This implies that the hostels are more likely than hospitals to recruit staff with higher academic qualifications.

2.5 The staff's experience of working with the mentally handicapped and of other types of nursing

The nursing staff tended to have had more years' experience of working with the mentally handicapped than the hostel staff (see table 11).

Two-thirds of the senior nursing staff had spent over 10 years (not necessarily continuously) working with the mentally handicapped which was higher than the proportion in any of the other grades. However, 16% of the senior nursing staff had worked with mentally handicapped patients for less than four years, although most of these nursing officers were also responsible for other types of patients within the same hospital. The number of years' experience of working with the mentally handicapped was similar for the ward sisters and the officers in charge and in both groups half the staff had over 10 years' experience. Compared with the enrolled nurses and nursing assistants relatively few (29%) of the care assistants had over four years' experience which explains why on average the hostel staff had fewer years of experience than the nurses. This is probably related to finding that a third of the hostels had been open for less than five years (see chapter 3) and may have recruited care assistants locally who had not previously worked with the mentally handicapped.

Table 12 shows that almost all the nursing staff started working with the mentally handicapped within a hospital and, in fact, less than 3% of the nurses had at any time worked in a hostel for the mentally handicapped run by a local authority or voluntary society. This compares with 20% of the hostel staff who had previously been nurses in hospitals for the mentally handicapped, which had usually provided their first experience of working with the mentally handicapped.

Approximately 40% of the nursing staff had earlier experience of nursing other types of patients, particularly in general nursing, psychiatric or geriatric nursing (see table 13). The proportion with other nursing experience was

Table 10 The staff's highest educational qualification and age when completed full-time education by grade

	All nursing staff	All hostel staff	Senior nursing staff	Ward sisters	Staff nurses	Enrolled nurses	Nursing assistants	Students	Pupils	Officers in charge	Deputies	Care assistants
	%	%	%	%	%	%	%	%	%	%	%	%
Highest educational qualification												
University degree	0	2	0	0	1	0	0	1	0	2	5	1
Teaching* qualification (or university diploma)	0	2	3	1	1	0	0	1	0	3	5	1
At least 1 A level or 5 O+ levels	23	20	29	27	30	17	14	52	34	21	12	22
3 or 4 O+ levels	3	4	9	5	6	0	2	6	3	7	7	3
1 or 2 O+ levels	4	4	2	6	6	2	5	3	9	3	9	1
Any foreign qualification	8	3	8	11	7	10	4	16	16	4	2	3
None of the above	61	65	49	50	48	71	75	21	38	60	60	67
	100	100	100	100	100	100	100	100	100	100	100	100
Age when completed full-time education												
19 or older	8	6	1	11	7	9	4	16	17	5	9	5
17 or 18	18	15	25	25	28	13	10	40	27	17	14	15
16	20	23	30	23	25	19	17	26	25	22	29	21
15	54	56	45	42	40	59	69	18	31	56	49	59
	100	100	100	100	100	100	100	100	100	100	100	100
Base: all staff (reweighted)	563	324	113	290	97	123	235	89	64	115	59	216

*Excluding a qualification in teaching the mentally handicapped.

†Or equivalent qualification.

15

Table 11 The number of years the staff have worked with the mentally handicapped by grade

Hospital staff	All hospital staff	Senior nursing staff	Ward sisters	Staff nurses	Enrolled nurses	Nursing assistants	Students/pupils
	%	%	%	%	%	%	%
Less than 2 years	25	8	4	6	6	38	50
2 years but less than 4 years	19	8	7	16	15	21	37
4 years but less than 10 years	29	18	36	35	29	33	12
10 years or longer	27	66	53	43	50	9	1
	100	100	100	100	100	100	100
Base for percentages: all nursing staff (reweighted)	*563*	*113*	*290*	*97*	*123*	*235*	*153*

Hostel staff	All hostel staff	Officers in charge	Deputies	Care assistants
	%	%	%	%
Less than 2 years	34	3	19	46
2 years but less than 4 years	22	9	22	26
4 years but less than 10 years	26	35	36	22
10 years or longer	17	53	24	7
	100	100	100	100
Base for percentages: all hostel staff (reweighted)	*324*	*115*	*59*	*216*

Table 12 The staff's first paid job working with the mentally handicapped

	All nursing staff	All hostel staff
	%	%
In a hospital for the mentally handicapped (or hospital unit for the mentally handicapped)	98	19
In a hostel for mentally handicapped adults	0	50
In a hostel for mentally handicapped children	1	26
In any other type of unit	1	5
	100	100
Base for percentages: all staff (reweighted)	*563*	*324*

highest for the senior nursing staff (79%) and lowest for the students and pupils (25%). 40% of all the hostel staff had previous experience of any type of nursing and this proportion was highest amongst the officers in charge of whom 60% had earlier nursing experience including 43% who had been nurses with the mentally handicapped (see table 14).

Table 13 Previous experience of other types of nursing for nurses by grade

	All hospital staff	Senior nursing staff	Ward sisters	Staff nurses	Enrolled nurses	Nursing assistants	Students/ pupils
	%	%	%	%	%	%	%
Previous experience of:							
general nursing	27	66	43	39	30	18	14
psychiatric nursing	15	43	36	27	20	4	8
geriatric nursing	15	22	19	14	22	13	7
sick children's nursing	5	9	8	8	8	2	2
other specialised types of nursing	5	14	9	7	5	3	3
Has only had experience of nursing the mentally handicapped	59	22	36	44	52	72	75
Base for percentages*: all nurses (reweighted)	*563*	*113*	*290*	*97*	*123*	*235*	*153*

* *These percentages do not add up to 100 as some of the nurses had previously worked in more than one type of nursing.*

Table 14 Previous experience of any types of nursing for hostel staff by grade

	All hostel staff	Officers in charge	Deputies	Care assistants
Previous experience of:	%	%	%	%
subnormality nursing	20	43	29	13
general nursing	23	29	24	22
psychiatric nursing	13	30	15	8
geriatric nursing	16	17	14	16
sick children's nursing	7	8	9	6
other specialised types of nursing	8	8	14	7
No previous nursing experience	60	40	59	67
Base for percentages*: all hostel staff (reweighted)	*324*	*115*	*59*	*216*

**These percentages do not add up to 100 as some of the staff had previously worked in more than one type of nursing.*

2.6 Qualifications held in nursing and social work

Approximately three-quarters of the nurses in each of the trained nursing grades were qualified in subnormality nursing (see table 15). Of the remaining quarter about half were qualified in general and half in psychiatric nursing. A higher proportion of the senior nursing staff, than of the ward sisters or staff nurses, had been registered in subnormality nursing for at least five years. 35% of the senior nursing staff were registered in both subnormality nursing and another nursing speciality; this was higher than the proportion of ward sisters (20%) or staff nurses (7%). This is consistent with the previous finding that more of the senior nurses had had exprience of other types of nursing.

About a half of the enrolled nurses who were qualified in subnormality nursing had been enrolled after training as a pupil nurse. The remainder had been enrolled by experience which is only possible for staff who worked as nursing

17

Table 15 Nursing and social work qualifications of nurses in the trained nursing grades

	Senior nursing staff	Ward sisters	Staff nurses	Enrolled nurses
	%	%	%	%
Qualifications in mental handicap nursing				
Registered Nurse for the Mentally Subnormal (RNMS)* and:—				
Qualified from 1971–76	9	27	37	0
Qualified prior to 1971	64	49	30	0
State Enrolled Nurse for the Mentally Subnormal (SEN(MS))* obtzined:—				
After being a pupil nurse	0	1	2	34
By experience†	0	1	2	38
Not qualified in mental handicap nursing	27	23	29	28
	100	100	100	100
Qualifications in other types of nursing				
State Registered Nurse (SRN)*	52	19	19	2
Registered Mental Nurse (RMN)*	35	27	13	0
Reigstered nurse in other specialised types of nursing	2	2	3	0
State Enrolled Nurse (SEN)*	3	3	2	15
State Enrolled Mental Nurse (SEN(M))*				
Has obtained any social work qualifications (listed in table 2.14)	2	0	0	0
Base for percentages: all nurses in specified grades (reweighted)	*113*	*290*	*97*	*123*

Or the equivalent Scottish qualifications.
†*See text.*

assistants with the mentally handicapped, full-time, for at least two years prior to 1968. This partly explains why half of the enrolled nurses had worked with the mentally handicapped for at least 10 years compared with less than a tenth of the nursing assistants (table 11).

From table 16 it can be seen that the hostel staff were more likely to be qualified in nursing than in social work. A third of the officers in charge did not hold any formal social work or nursing qualifications, a third had a social work qualification and slightly more, 41%, held a nursing qualification including 10% who were qualified in both nursing and social work. The most frequently held social work qualifications were the CRSW[1] for residential work with adults or the equivalent qualification for residential work in children's homes (CRCCYP[2]). A quarter of the officers in charge were qualified in subnormality nursing and a quarter were qualified in either psychiatric or general nursing. The type of qualifications held by the deputies were similar to those of the officers in charge although a lower proportion of the deputies were qualified.

[1]Certificate in Residential Social Work.
[2]Certificate in the Residential Care of Children and Young People.

18

Table 16 Nursing and social work qualifications of hostel staff by grade

	All hostel staff	Officers in charge	Deputies	Other care staff
	%	%	%	%
Summary of qualifications:				
Has obtained qualifications in both social work and nursing	2	10	5	0
Has obtained qualification(s) only in social work	10	25	15	6
Has obtained qualification(s) only in nursing	15	31	24	10
Has no formal qualifications in nursing or social work	73	35	56	84
	100	100	100	100
Type of social work qualifications obtained:				
CQSW—professional social work qualification (Certificate of Qualification in Social Work)	1	2	2	1
CRSW—(Certificate in Residential Social Work)	5	17	5	2
CRCCYP or SCRCCYP—(Certificate or Senior Certificate in the Residential Care of Children and Young People)	5	9	12	3
DipTMHA—(Diploma in the Training and Further Education of Mentally Handicapped People)	1	4	2	0
NNEB—(Nursery Nurse Education Board Certificate)	2	4	3	1
Type of nursing qualification obtained:				
RNMS* (Registered Nurse for the Mentally Subnormal)	5	15	10	1
SEN(MS)* (State Enrolled Nurse for the Mentally Subnormal)	3	10	3	1
SRN* (State Registered Nurse)	3	9	7	1
RMN* (Registered Mental Nurse)	5	17	7	2
SEN(M)* or SEN* (State Enrolled Mental Nurse or State Enrolled Nurse)	5	3	5	6
Base for percentages: all hostel staff	*324*	*15*	*59*	*216*

Or equivalent Scottish qualification.

2.7 Country of birth and nurses from developing countries

Table 17 shows that 27% of the nurses were born outside the UK including 14% who were born in developing countries.[1] Compared with the other nurses, a higher proportion of those born in developing countries were male, aged under 40, and were either trained nurses or trainees (see table 18). The proportion of nursing assistants born in developing countries was relatively low, perhaps partly because nurses applying from overseas often do so in order to obtain a nursing qualification. Only 11% of the hostel staff were born outside the UK and most of these had come from Eire.

Further information on the recruitment of the nurses from developing countries is given in table 19 as this was of special concern at the time of the

[1]Developing countries refers to any country in Asia (excluding Japan), the West Indies, South America, or Africa (excluding South Africa and Rhodesia).

Briggs Committee (see Thomas et al 1972). Almost all of these nurses were likely to have completed their full-time education before coming to the UK and 45% of them had applied from abroad for their first nursing post with the mentally handicapped in the UK. It was not feasible to ask for detailed information which would have established their nationality or whether they required work permits but table 19 shows that these nurses had mainly come from New Commonwealth countries and the majority of them had lived in the UK for over five years.

Table 17 Country of birth of staff by grade

Hospital staff	All nursing staff	Senior nursing staff	Ward sisters	Staff nurses	Enrolled nurses	Nursing assistants	Students	Pupils
	%	%	%	%	%	%	%	%
England	60	52	49	61	56	66	64	50
Scotland	7	11	7	5	7	8	0	3
Wales	5	8	9	3	4	5	2	3
N Ireland	2	9	3	1	2	2	0	2
Eire	6	11	8	5	7	5	3	5
Other European country	5	3	2	3	7	6	1	3
Other developed country*	2	1	2	1	2	2	2	3
Developing country*	14	6	19	21	15	7	27	31
	100	100	100	100	100	100	100	100
Base for percentage: all nurses (reweighted)	*563*	*113*	*290*	*97*	*123*	*235*	*89*	*64*

Hostel staff	All hostel staff	Officers in charge	Deputies	Other care staff
	%	%	%	%
England	78	76	83	77
Scotland	4	8	2	4
Wales	5	4	3	6
N Ireland	2	3	2	1
Eire	7	6	9	7
Other European country	1	3	2	1
Other developed country*	0	1	0	1
Developing country*	3	1	0	4
	100	100	100	100
Base for percentages: all hostel staff (reweighted)	*324*	*115*	*59*	*216*

Developing countries refers to any country in Asia (excluding Japan), the West Indies, South America or Africa (excluding South Africa or Rhodesia).

20

Table 18 Characteristics of nurses born in developing countries

	All nurses born in developing countries	All nurses born in the UK
	%	%
Sex		
Male	54	25
Female	46	75
	100	100
Age		
16–24 yrs	21	20
25–29 yrs	39	12
30–39 yrs	28	25
40 yrs or older	12	44
	100	100
Interviewers assessment of "colour"		
"White"	4	99
"Non-white"	96	1
	100	100
Base for percentages: all nurses born in the specified countries (reweighted)	*77*	*416*

Proportion of the trained nurses and trainees who were born in developing countries analysed by age and sex

	All ages	16–24	25–29	30–39	40 or older
Proportion of the trained nurses and trainees who were born in a developing country:					
Males	28%	28%	57%	29%	2%
Base (reweighted)	*157*	*28*	*35*	*47*	*47*
Females	13%	17%	35%	16%	2%
Base (reweighted)	*235*	*53*	*32*	*36*	*112*

Table 19　Recruitment of nurses born in developing countries

	All nurses born in developing countries
	%
Country of birth	
Africa (mainly Mauritius)	40
West Indies	27
South East Asia	19
India, Pakistan, Bangladesh or Ceylon	13
	100
Age when arrived to live in the UK	
Under 16	5
16 or over	95
	100
Number of years living in the UK	
Less than 18 months	4
From 18 months to 4 years	35
From 5 to 10 years	25
10 years or longer	36
	100
Initially applied for their first job in the UK with the mentally handicapped when living:	
Abroad	45
In the UK	55
	100
Base for percentages: all nurses born in developing countries (reweighted)	77

22

3 THE WARDS AND HOSTELS AND THEIR RESIDENTS

The aim of this chapter is to describe the wards and hostels in terms of the kind of residents who lived in them and their staff ratios. This information was required primarily to provide the context for examining the role of the staff but it is also directly relevant to considering the training that the staff need.

3.1 The hospitals, wards and hostels

The hospitals differ from the hostels in that they are much larger and are rarely situated in towns or cities whereas the hostels are usually single units within residential areas. Most of the hospitals for the mentally handicapped were opened at least 40 years ago whereas a third of the hostels in the sample had been open for less than five years reflecting the general increase in provision of local authority hostels for the mentally handicapped over this period (see table 20). Other reserch has pointed to the inaccessibility of some of the hospitals affecting the amount of contact that the patients have with the outside community including contact with their own relatives (eg Jones 1975). Also partly because of the size of the hospitals compared with the hostels, the nurses generally have less direct influence over the work carried out by the catering and domestic staff.

Table 20   The length of time that the hostels had been open for mentally handicapped residents

	All hostels*
	%
Less than a year	8
One year but less than 5 years	27
5 years or longer	64
	100
*Base for percentages: all hostels**	95

Excluding the hostels with 3 or more residents who were not mentally handicapped (see page 24).

It can be seen from table 21 that 94% of the selected wards were in hospitals providing only for the mentally handicapped, including 49% in subnormality hospitals with over 500 beds. Most of the wards were part of the main hospital complex although a few were residential units which were geographically separate.

Table 22 shows the extent to which the wards or hostels were for special types of patients or residents. Children's units were defined as being wards or hostels in which more than half of the residents were aged under 16. It can be seen that a higher proportion of the hostels (24%) than of the wards (11%) were for children. It was found that 17% of the patients in the children's wards and 8% of the residents in the children's hostels were in fact aged 16 or older. Similarly 4% of the patients in the adult wards and less than 1% of the residents in the adult hostels were in fact aged under 16.

23

Table 21 The overall type and size of hospitals within which the selected wards were located

	All wards
	%
In hospitals solely for mentally handicapped patients of estimated size*	
less than 100 beds	4
100 to 299 beds	18
300 to 499 beds	22
500 to 999 beds	24
1,000 to 1,499 beds	13
1,500 to 1,750 beds	12
In units attached to hospitals which also contained other types of patients	6
	100
Base: all sampled wards (reweighted)	*311*

Estimated from the number of beds in 1974.

Table 22 Special types of wards and hostels

	All wards
	%
Wards	
Children's wards	11
Acute sickness wards	3
Adult wards for:	
predischarge patients	5
short stay patients	1
geriatric patients	6
adolescents	1
psychopathic patients	4
other adult wards	69
	100
Base: all sampled wards (reweighted)	*311*

	All hostels
	%
Hostels	
Children's hostels	
short stay	3
long stay	21
Adult hostels:	
short stay	1
long stay	67
Hostels containing 3 or more residents who were not mentally handicapped	8
	100
Base: all sampled hostels	*103*

Three per cent of the sampled wards were for acutely sick patients who needed general medical treatment and consequently the patients in these wards have been excluded from the subsequent analyses in this chapter. Also, as the survey was primarily concerned with hostels which were solely for mentally handicapped residents, eight hostels have been excluded from the other tables in

24

this chapter because they contained three or more residents who were not mentally handicapped (most of these residents were considered to be mentally ill or disturbed).

Table 23 shows that the hostels generally contained fewer residents than the wards; the hostels having an average of 18 residents compared with an average of 28 patients in the hospital wards. In both the hostels and hospitals the children's units tended to be smaller than adult units with averages of 13 and 19 children respectively. It is possible that the size of the units influences the staff's work independently of the staff ratios which are discussed later in this chapter.

Table 23   The number of patients or residents* in adult and children's units

Number of patients or residents	All wards†	All hostels†	Adult wards	Adult hostels	Children's wards	Children's hostels
	%	%	%	%	%	%
10 or fewer	2	20	1	11	9	44
11–20	22	41	19	40	46	44
21–30	44	33	44	41	43	8
31–40	16	3	18	3	3	4
over 40	15	3	17	4	0	0
	100	100	100	100	100	100
Average number	27·9	18·5	29·0	20·5	19·2	13·0
Base: all sampled wards and hostels (reweighted)†	302	95	266	70	35	25

This refers to the number of patients or residents living in the units at the time of the interviews and not to the number of beds.
†Excluding acute sickness wards and hostels with 3 or more residents who were not mentally handicapped.

3.2   The classification of the wards and hostels

The wards and hostels included in the survey were classified according to the abilities and extent of physical handicaps or chronic illnesses of the residents in them at the time of the survey. It is important to note firstly that the assessments of the residents' abilities and physical handicaps were made by the ward sisters and officers in charge and not from direct observations and, secondly, that the aim of these assessments was to describe the present abilities of the residents and not their potential capabilities.

The main purpose of classifying the units was to provide a way of relating the staff's roles and views to the type of residents with whom they were working. The classification was also needed to identify a group of wards which had patients with similar abilities to the hostel residents. The role of the staff working in these wards could then be directly compared with the role of the staff working in the hostels without needing to take into account differences in the type of residents.

25

In order to save time the information on the residents' abilities was collected for the entire ward or hostel and not for individual residents, so the ward sisters or officers in charge were asked how many of their residents had each of a list of abilities or handicaps. The classification was derived by a statistical technique known as cluster analysis which classifies units into groups with a similar type of resident. This technique produced several classifications using different statistical criteria and the selection of the most useful result was based partly on statistical grounds and partly on the judgment of the researcher. The cluster analysis[1] was carried out with all the selected wards and hostels (except for acute sickness wards and hostels with three or more residents who were not mentally handicapped), using 13 variables which were expected to reflect the basic workload for the staff. The classification adopted was considered to be the most useful way of describing the types of units for this survey, but other classifications would be preferable for other purposes.

The classification distinguished four groups which can be described as high ability, average ability, low ability and non-ambulant with very low ability. In general the wards or hostels did not have residents who were all of the same ability level and so the descriptions refer to the majority but not to all the residents within each type of unit. The high ability group contained about a third of the adult wards and all apart from three of the adult hostels. A third of the adult wards were in the average ability group and a fifth in the low ability group. A tenth of the adult wards were in the group described as non-ambulant with very low ability which for the sake of brevity will be referred to as "non-ambulant" although it will be seen that a quarter of the patients in these wards were able to walk by themselves. The exact proportions and numbers of adult wards in each group are shown in table 24 together with the way the adult hostels and children's units were allocated to these groups. As there were only a few children's units in each group they have not been separately analysed within ability groups in the subsequent tables.

[8]Fuller technical details of the cluster analysis are given in appendix B.

Table 24 The allocation of wards and hostels to the classification derived from the cluster analysis

	High ability	Average ability	Low ability	Non-ambulant —very low ability
Percentage of the adult wards allocated to each group*	36%	34%	19%	10%
Number of adult wards* allocated to each group (reweighted)	97	90	52	28
Number of adult hostels* allocated to each group	67	2	1	0
Number of children's wards allocated to each group (reweighted)	0	9	13	13
Number of children's hostels allocated to each group	6	14	4	1

Excluding acute sickness wards and hostels with more than 3 residents who were not mentally handicapped.

26

Table 25 shows the characteristics of the patients and residents in the different ability groups. The high ability groups in the wards and hostels were very similar in all the characteristics except for the proportion of residents who were allowed to go out alone, which was higher in hostels than wards. As these proportions may depend on the policy of the hospitals or hostels as well as on the residents' abilities it was not considered essential that they should be equal.

Almost all the patients and residents in the high ability groups were able to feed, wash and dress themselves and there were only a few with problems of behaviour or incontinence. All of the adult wards which were described as being predischarge or short stay were in the high ability group and these comprised one-fifth of the wards in the group.

In comparison with the high ability group the adult wards in the average ability group have a smaller proportion of patients who were able to wash and dress themselves (about a third) and very few who were allowed to go out alone.

In the low ability adult wards about half of the patients were reported to have behaviour problems, for example being aggressive, destructive or overactive, which was higher than the proportion in any other group. The patients in this group generally needed more assistance with basic care than patients in the average group as one-third of them could not feed themselves, 90% could not wash and dress themselves and about a half were doubly incontinent (wetting and soiling) during the daytime.

Most of the adult wards which were described as being for patients with disturbed behaviour or psychopaths were in the average or low ability groups and they comprised slightly over a tenth of the wards in each of these groups.

Relatively few of the patients in the high, average or low ability groups were severely affected by any of the specified physical handicaps or chronic illnesses. Within these three groups the highest proportion affected by any of these handicaps or illnesses was 17% of the patients in the low ability group who had had at least one epileptic fit in the previous month.

In the non-ambulant group a quarter of the patients were able to walk by themselves including those who used walking aids but who did not need assistance from the staff. The patients in this group were generally of very low ability with only a third able to feed themselves and three-quarters were doubly incontinent during the daytime. A higher proportion of the patients in this group were also reported to have each of the physical handicaps (apart from deafness) or longstanding illnesses which were included in the cluster analysis. Of these physical handicaps or illnesses, cerebral palsy (spasticity) occurred the most frequently and affected two-thirds of the patients in the non-ambulant group, almost all of whom were bedridden or had difficulty in walking up stairs.

In general compared with the hostel children those in the hospitals were reported as having fewer basic skills, a higher frequency of behaviour and incontinence problems, and were more likely to be reported as suffering from each of the physical handicaps (apart from deafness) or chronic illnesses. The general ability level of the children's wards is slightly lower than the level of the adult wards in the low ability group. As shown in table 24 the cluster analysis allocated 15 of the 37 children's wards to the low ability group. The general ability level of the children's hostels is similar to the level of the adult wards in the average ability group and 14 of the 25 children's hostels were allocated to this group.

Table 25 The final classification of the wards and hostels derived from the cluster analysis

Average percentage* of the patients or residents in each type of unit who:	Adult hostels high ability	Adult wards high ability	Adult wards average ability	Adult wards low ability	Adult wards non-ambulant—very low ability	Child-ren's hostels	Child-ren's wards
	%	%	%	%	%	%	%
were able to walk by themselves (possibly using walking aids)	100	98	90	83	25	89	64
were able to feed themselves	99	97	93	64	33	76	53
were able to wash and dress themselves	87	85	37	12	10	51	20
were allowed out of the hospital or hostel grounds on their own	84	57	9	12	2	8	1
were double incontinent during the day	1	2	9	47	74	18	55
were singly or doubly incontinent during the night	5	8	21	66	76	31	68
had any other behaviour problems (for example being aggressive, destructive or overactive)	6	9	35	49	27	38	49
had at least one epileptic fit in the previous month	4	7	10	17	20	8	18
were blind (or partially sighted)	2	3	4	9	13	5	10
were deaf (and could not use a hearing aid)	3	4	4	6	5	4	4
suffered from cerebral palsy (or arthritis) *and* were bedridden or had difficulty walking up stairs	2	3	6	14	65	7	25
had a respiratory illness or heart condition *and* were bedridden or had difficulty walking up stairs	1	3	4	4	10	2	8
needed a special diet for health reasons	3	7	7	7	18	4	10
TOTAL number of units in each group (unweighted)	68	84	87	51	29	25	35

*The percentages given in this table were based on the unweighted sample of wards and hostels included in the cluster analysis (see appendix B).

3.3 The abilities of the residents and extent of specified physical illnesses and handicaps in more detail

The characteristics of the patients and residents are covered in greater detail in this section partly to enable comparisons to be made with other research and partly to present comparable results for the hospital and hostel residents which can be taken into account in planning training programmes for the staff. In order to be compatible with other sources the percentages in tables 26–28 are based on the total number of patients or residents whereas the percentages in table 25 were based on the total number of wards and hostels.

Table 26 compares the results from the survey with results from (i) the censuses of mentally handicapped patients and of residential accommodation for the mentally handicapped (DHSS 1970 (a) and (b)) and (ii) the national survey of hospitals for the mentally handicapped which was conducted in 1965 by Morris (1969). Exact comparisons of specific characteristics can rarely be made because the definitions and the classifications used vary. For example the hospital census would have classified a patient who needed helping with washing but could feed and dress himself as not needing assistance which probably explains why the percentage classified as not needing assistance with feeding, washing or dressing in the census (58%) is higher than the percentage classified as being able to wash and dress themselves (without any assistance) in this survey (46%).

In addition to the results shown in table 26 separate comparisons were made for the children's and adult units as far as possible, and also with the results for three hospital regions reported by Bone et al (1972). After taking into account the differences in definitions it appears that, except in the children's hostels, the ability levels of the patients and residents in the present survey are similar to those previously reported. The differences in the children's hostels are not in a consistent direction in that we found that 76% of the children could feed themselves and 56% could wash and dress themselves whereas the 1970 census found that 90% could feed themselves but only 47% could wash themselves (and probably not all of these could also dress themselves). The results from previous research on the extent of physical handicaps and illnesses in hospital patients are also generally similar to the results in this survey but there is no comparable research on hostel residents on a national basis.

Table 27 compares the abilities of the hospital patients with the hostel residents and confirms the results from the cluster analysis in showing that the hospital patients were generally reported to have a lower ability level than the hostel residents. The extent to which this may be related to differences in the potential capacities of the residents of the 2 types of unit is discussed at the end of this chapter.

This survey did not cover the residents' ability to speak or degree of literacy as these were not expected to be closely related to the basic workload for the staff (but these are covered in the 1970 hospital census). Mental illness was excluded from the survey because it was felt that this could not be assessed reliably. However it is likely that many of the residents who were reported to have behaviour problems would be considered to be psychiatrically disturbed. In the pilot stage of this survey the staff were asked to describe the behaviour

29

Table 26 Comparisons of the patients' and residents' characteristics with some results from previous research

Comparisons with the 1970 census of mentally handicapped hospital patients (DHSS)*	1970 Census all hospital patients England and Wales	Comparable† survey results 1976, hospital patients England, Wales and Scotland	
	%	%	
Non-ambulant (severely)	13	16	(excluding people who could use aids)
Needs asistance to feed, wash or dress**	42	54	(needs assistance with washing or dressing)
Incontinent—severely	20	22	(doubly incontinent in the day time)
Incontinent—severely or to a lesser degree	30	29	(singly or doubly incontinent in the day time)
Behaviour difficulty—severe or to a lesser degree	32	27	
Blind or almost blind	4	5	
Deaf—severely or almost severely	3	4	
Base: all hospital patients (reweighted)	*63,385*	*8,441*	

Comparisons with the national survey of hospital patients carried out in 1965 by Morris (1969)	1965 survey of hospital patients (Morris)	Comparable† survey results 1976, hospital patients	
	%	%	
Non-ambulant	17	16	(excluding people who could use aids)
Needs assistance with dressing	34	54	(needs assistance with washing or dressing)
Suffers from cerebral palsy	12	14	
Suffers from epilepsy (severely or moderately)	21	19	(had at least one fit in the previous month)
Base: all hospital patients reweighted)	*3,038*	*8,441*	

Comparisons with the 1970 Census of residential accommodation for the mentally handicapped (DHSS)	1970 Census all residents of local authority hostels England and Wales	Comparable† survey results 1976, hostel residents England, Wales and Scotland	
	%	%	
Able to feed themselves	97	94	
Able to wash themselves	82	⎰81	(able to wash and dress themselves)
Able to dress themselves	84	⎱	
Singly or doubly incontinent	11	9	(in the night)
Doubly incontinent	4	4	(in the day)
Base: all hostel residents	*3,691*	*1,760*	

Notes:
  *The precise definitions of the characteristics used in the hospital census depend on cumulating scores on scales which are specified in the report of the census.
  †The precise definitions used in the survey are shown in tables 27 and 28 and are rarely identical with those of other sources. A brief description of the survey's definition is shown in brackets where differences in the definitions are particularly likely to affect the Comparisons.
  **The hospital census defines a patient as not needing assistance with feeding, washing or dressing when help is needed with only one of the three tasks.

problems involved and the analysis showed that in over 90% of the cases there were serious problems which were likely to need immediate staff action. The most frequently occurring problems were aggression directed at people or property, "hygiene" problems connected with food or toilet habits and self-destructive behaviour. This highlights the difficult task faced by staff in the low ability group of wards where half the patients were reported to have a behaviour problem.

Table 27 The present abilities of the patients and residents

Proportion of the patients or residents who:	All wards*	All hostels†	Children's wards	Children's hostels
	%	%	%	%
(a) were able to walk by themselves (possibly using walking aids)	84	98	66	92
(b) were able to feed themselves	80	94	49	76
(c) were able to wash and dress themselves	46	81	21	56
(d) were allowed out of the hospital or hostel grounds on their own	25	68	3	8
(e) had behaviour problems (for example, being aggressive, destructive or overactive)	27	12	50	34
(f) were singly or doubly incontinent at least twice a week during the day	29	6	61	22
(g) were doubly incontinent at least twice a week during the day	22	4	55	15
(h) were singly or doubly incontinent at least twice a week during the night	32	9	67	26
(i) were doubly incontinent at least twice a week during the night	21	3	55	12
Base for percentages: Total number of residents	8,441	1,760	673	325

Excluding acute sickness wards.
†Excluding hostels with 3 or more residents who were not mentally handicapped.

Table 28 shows that a higher proportion of the hospital patients than of the hostel residents suffered from each of the specified physical handicaps or illnesses (apart from respiratory illnesses). These proportions were often considerably higher in the non-ambulant group of adult wards and in the children's wards. The extent of physical handicaps or illnesses in the adult hostels is similar to that of the high ability adult wards and slightly less than that of the average ability adult wards.

The most frequently occurring of the handicaps and illnesses were cerebral palsy (in 14% of all hospital patients) and epilepsy (in 29% of all patients although only 11% had had a fit in the previous month). Most of the patients with cerebral palsy were also bedridden or had difficulty walking up stairs although we do not know if this was caused by their cerebral palsy as it was felt that the ward sisters may not have been able to make such an assessment. The last row of table 28 shows that overall 2% of the hospital patients and 1% of the hostel residents had had to stay indoors on the previous weekday because of a physical illness. This gives an upper limit on the percentage of the patients who were not in acute sickness wards but who required bedside nursing for acute physical illnesses, although this may increase during the winter months.

31

Table 28 The extent of specified physical illnesses and handicaps

Proportion of the patients and residents who:	All wards*	All hostels†	Adult hostels high ability	Adult wards high ability	Adult wards average ability	Adult wards low ability	Adult wards non-ambu-ant—very low ability	Child-ren's hostels	Child-ren's wards
	%	%	%	%	%	%	%	%	%
were blind (or partially sighted)	5	2	2	2	4	7	14	4	11
were deaf (and could not use a hearing aid)	4	2	2	4	4	5	4	3	5
suffered from cerebral palsy (spasticity)	14	5	4	4	7	16	67	10	28
suffered from cerebral palsy and were bedridden or had difficulty walking up stairs	12	2	1	3	5	12	67	4	25
suffered from a heart condition	5	3	2	5	5	6	5	4	4
suffered from a heart condition and were bedridden or had difficulty walking up stairs	2	1	1	2	2	2	4	0	2
suffered from asthma, bronchitis or any other respiratory illness	6	7	5	4	6	5	8	17	10
suffered from asthma, bronchitis or any other respiratory illness and were bedridden or had difficulty in walking up stairs	2	1	1	1	2	2	5	1	6
suffered from arthritis	2	1	2	2	2	2	3	0	0
suffered from arthritis and were bedridden or had difficulty walking up stairs	1	1	1	1	1	1	2	0	0
suffered from epilepsy (including controlled epileptics)	29	13	12	18	27	36	52	18	44
had at least one epileptic fit in the previous year	19	8	7	10	17	24	33	12	33
had at least one epileptic fit in the previous month	11	5	4	7	9	14	20	8	18
needed a special diet for health reasons	8	3	3	7	6	6	17	4	9
were confined indoors on the previous weekday because of a physical illness	2	1	1	1	2	2	5	1	3
Base for percentages: total number of patients (reweighted)	8,441	1,760	1,416	2,983	2,699	1,347	742	325	673

*Excluding acute sickness wards.
†Excluding hostels with 3 or more residents who were not mentally handicapped.

Implications for staff training of the extent of physical handicaps and illnesses

There were hostel residents with each of the specified physical handicaps and illnesses which implies that at least some of the hostel staff require some training in looking after residents with these handicaps and illnesses and shows that the hostel staff with nursing training would be able to make use of their nursing knowledge. The nursing staff in the non-ambulant and children's wards were working with patients of whom at least half had an associated physical handicap which is much higher than the proportions in the other wards. Consequently these nurses would need more extensive training, than nurses in the other wards, on ways of caring for groups of patients with physical handicaps or illnesses. These two groups of wards also had the highest proportion of patients who were confined indoors because of a physical illness (5% in the non-ambulant wards and 3% in the children's wards) and who may have needed bedside nursing.

3.4 Staff ratio

When considering the staff's present role it is essential to take into account the staffing ratio within their units as this could be a crucial constraint on the sort of activities that can be carried out. The staff ratios in the various types of wards and hostels will be shown in this section and later chapters will examine the relationship between the staff's work and the staffing ratio in their unit.

The ratios were calculated so that they referred to the average number of residents per staff member over the whole of the daytime on a weekday. This calculation was made by cumulating the total number of hours that each resident was in the care of the ward or hostel staff and then dividing this by the total number of hours worked by the day nursing or care staff. The hours were totalled for the whole of the daytime (ie while the day staff were on duty) and were derived from information provided by ward sisters or officers in charge relating to their last weekday on duty. A general limitation of this method is that the resulting ratios only show what the staffing levels would be throughout the daytime if the staff's shifts were arranged to provide the same staff ratio at all times. In practice the staff ratios are likely to be worse, that is with more residents per staff member, during the peak periods immediately after the residents get up and after they return from their training centres or schools.

Any method of assessing staff ratios has some technical limitations which in our case, as well as the general limitation mentioned above, were that (a) the staff ratios relate to one day only and there may be considerable fluctuations from day to day, for example because a staff member is off sick. However the effects of these fluctuations would be expected to cancel each other out when a group of wards or hostels are considered. (b) We relied on the memories of the sisters or officers in charge and in several cases found minor inconsistencies in the way they had accounted for the staff or residents. The effects of these inconsistencies would also be expected to be cancelled out in comparisons between groups of units. (c) The interviewing for this survey was carried out in July when the ratios may be slightly worse than normal because more of the staff are on holiday and a few of the schools and training centres may have been closed, although the interviewers were asked to interview staff from children's units before their schools were closed. The overall effect of these limitations should not invalidate comparisons between groups of units although they do imply that there is little value in quoting the staff ratios obtained for individual units and that the staff ratios for the rest of the year may be slightly better than those we obtained in July.

In general the staff ratios were better in the hostels, where over half the units had a ratio below 5:1, that is an average of less than five residents for each staff member, whereas in the hospitals over half the wards had a ratio which was worse than 7:1 (see table 29). The children's units generally had better staff ratios than the adult units in that in both the hospitals and hostels the median[2] number of children per staff member was about half the median number of adults per staff member in the adult units. Within the adult wards the staff ratios varied according to the type of ward, with the highest number of patients

---

[2]The median staff ratio in a group of units is defined as being the ratio in the middle unit when the units are ranked according to their staff ratios. It is used here in preference to the average ratio because the average may be distorted by a few units with a very high ratio.

per nurse in the high ability group (median 9·7:1) and the fewest patients per nurse in the low ability and non-ambulant groups (both with medians of 6·6:1). Because of this variation, the staff ratios in the high ability adult wards, 45% of which had 11 or more patients per staff member, were much worse than in the adult hostels of which only 6% had 11 or more residents per staff member.

The relatively better staff ratios in the hostels than in the hospitals resulted partly from the greater amount of overtime worked by the hostel staff (see chapter 2) and partly from a relatively higher proportion of the hostel residents leaving the hostel to attend an occupational centre during the day (see chapter 6). However, the day staff in the hostels who were usually on duty between about 7.30 a.m. and 10.30 p.m. did cover a slightly longer period than the day-time nursing staff who were usually on duty between about 7 a.m. and 8.30 p.m.

Compared with the hospital staff ratios in this survey, a national survey in 1965 found appreciably worse ratios with averages of 15·8:1 for all wards and 11·1:1 for childrens' wards (Morris, 1969). These were based on observing the actual ratios in a representative sample of wards which were visited between 9.00 a.m. and 6.00 p.m. It is more difficult to make comparisons with the ratios reported by King et al (1972) as they calculated their ratios in a different way, but from approximate comparisons it appears that the ratios in their childrens, wards were worse than those found here but the ratios in their childrens, hostels were similar. These differences may be partly due to the different methods

Table 29   The staff ratios analysed by the type of unit

The ratio is equal to the average number of patients or residents in the care of one staff member over the whole of the daytime.

Average number of residents per staff member*	All wards†	All hostels**	Adult hostels high ability	Adult wards high ability	Adult wards average ability	Adult wards low ability	Adult wards non-ambulant —very low ability	Child-ren's hostels	Child-ren's wards
	%	%	%	%	%	%	%	%	%
3:1 or fewer	8	33	18	3	1	4	7	72	44
4:1–5:1	21	24	25	21	17	20	14	20	38
6:1–7:1	23	24	33	6	28	39	57	4	9
8:1–10:1	24	13	16	25	27	31	18	4	9
11:1 or more	23	6	8	45	27	6	4	0	0
	100	100	100	100	100	100	100	100	100
Medium staff: resident ratio	7·3	4·7	6·3	9·7	8·0	6·6	6·6	2·8	3·8
Base: all units for which information on the staff ratio was available†† (reweighted)	282	91	63	89	82	49	28	25	34

Decimal fractions in the number of residents per staff member have been rounded to the nearest whole number.
†*Excluding acute sickness wards.*
**Excluding hostels with 3 or more residents who were not mentally handicapped.*
††*The staff ratios could not be calculated in 7% of the wards and 4% of the hostels because of insufficient or inconsistent information.*

of assessing the staff ratios but it is also clear that in general the effective hospital staff ratios have improved since 1965. This is linked to an increase in the total number of nursing staff per 100 patients from 23·1 in 1966 to 48·5 in 1976 recorded in the official statistics on hospital facilities for the mentally handicapped (DHSS 1976).

Other researchers who have assessed the staffing ratios in children's units have not agreed on their relative importance. Kushlick (1973) argued that it would be impossible to redeploy the existing staff resources in children's wards towards more child-oriented patterns of management whereas King et al (1971) and King (1973), while agreeing that the staff resources were often inadequate, felt that several improvements towards more child-oriented patterns could be achieved with the existing staff resources. This disagreement is no longer directly relevant as it was based on the hospital staff ratios found by Morris and by King et al which were worse than the ratios reported here. However, later chapters will present some evidence on the underlying issue of whether the hospitals are prevented from providing the most suitable care for their patients primarily because of a lack of staff resources.

3.5 Discussion on the potential abilities of the patients and residents

In general the present ability level of the hostel residents was found to be higher than that of the hospital patients. This survey can only give speculative indications of the relationship between this and differences in the potential capacities of the residents of the two types of units, or of the way this relates to the amount or quality of training that the residents have received. Clear indications of the results of giving extra or improved training to hospital patients could only be obtained from experimental studies (for example from research on the experimental units set up in Wessex which is described by Kushlick et al (1977)).

A third of the adult patients were in the low ability and non-ambulant wards which had higher proportions of patients suffering from each of the specified physical handicaps and illnesses which may make it more difficult for them to acquire some of the basic skills. Consequently the ability level of the patients in these groups seems to be lower than that of the hostel residents partly because of additional constraints on their capacity to learn which are related to physical handicaps or illnesses.

Two-thirds of the adult patients were in the average and high ability groups of wards where the extent of physical handicaps and illnesses was similar to that in the adult hostels. Patients in the average ability wards generally had a lower ability level than hostel residents in that for example only 37% of these patients could wash and dress themselves compared with 87% of the hostel residents. It is possible that these patients were more severely mentally handicapped than the hostel residents but it is also possible that they have lower ability levels partly because the staffing ratios in their wards are worse than in the hostels so the nurses may be unable to spend so much time on teaching them.

In the basic skills covered in the survey patients in the high ability wards generally had similar ability levels to residents in the adult hostels. The survey did not attempt to assess fully whether these patients (or residents) had acquired other social skills which are likely to be needed to enable them to live more independently. There were two indications that these social skills were more likely to have been acquired by the hostel residents. Firstly a higher proportion of them were allowed out of their hostel grounds alone, and secondly, as will be seen later a higher proportion of the hostel residents were in paid employment outside the hostel. The staff ratios in the adult hostels were generally better than the ratios in the high ability wards so the hostels are more likely to be able to devote staff resources to providing social training for their residents. Also in comparison with the hostels it is likely that the larger hospitals would have more difficulty in providing social training for the majority of the patients in the high ability wards as they may need to be more cautious about allowing a large number of patients out of the hospital and may have access to proportionally fewer local employment opportunities. Later chapters compare the relative emphasis placed on social training by staff in the adult hostels and nurses in the high ability wards.

Compared with the children's hostels the children's wards were more likely to have children who suffered from a physical handicap or illness which may make it more difficult for them to acquire basic skills. The staff ratios in the children's hostels were slightly better than in the children's wards and so the ability level of the children in the hostels may be higher partly because the staff are able to spend more time on teaching them these skills. Further information is provided on this in chapters 4–8 in comparisons of the relative emphasis placed on social aspects of care by the staff in the children's units.

4 THE WORK CARRIED OUT BY THE NURSING AND CARE STAFF

The main objective of this chapter is to look at the type of work carried out by the staff, particularly at the emphasis placed on the residents' social development and the way this is related to the type of ward or hostel. The information on the work carried out was derived from answers given by the staff about their preceding day at work and it was not possible to check on its accuracy or to evaluate the way the work had been done. A fuller account of the staff's work could only have been obtained from observational studies (such as those carried out by King et al (1971), Durwood et al (1975) and Grant et al (1976)) or by asking the staff to complete detailed time budgets showing the tasks they had been carrying out over short periods of time. These methods would have been too complex and time-consuming to have been included in the present study.

4.1 The residents' contact with the staff during the day

Before examining the work carried out by the staff in more detail it is important to take into account the proportions of residents who were in the care of the ward or hostel staff throughout the day. This is because staff who have several residents in their care throughout the day may have the opportunity to spend more time on recreational or teaching activities than the staff who only have one or two, or no residents throughout the day.

Table 30   The residents' contact with the nursing and care staff on the previous weekday

The percentage of the residents who:—	All wards*	All hostels*	Adult hostels high ability	Adult wards high ability	Adult wards average ability	Adult wards low ability	Adult wards non-ambulant —very low ability	Child-ren's hostels	Child-ren's wards
were in the care of the nursing or hostel staff all the day	51	15	13	43	49	64	76	17	39
were not in the care of the nursing or hostel staff all the day	49	85	87	57	36	36	24	83	61
	100	100	100	100	100	100	100	100	100
Base for percentages: total number of residents (reweighted)	8,441	1,760	1,416	2,983	2,699	1,347	742	325	673

*Excluding acute sickness wards and hostels with three or more residents who were not mentally handicapped.

Table 30 shows that half of the hospital patients compared with only 15% of the hostel residents had been in the care of the ward or hostel staff throughout the day. In the adult wards this proportion varied with the ability level of the patients so that a lower proportion of the patients in the high ability wards (43%) than in the non-ambulant wards (76%) were in the care of the nurses all the day.

4.2 The work carried out by the day staff

On their previous day at work 60% of the nurses and 88% of the hostel staff were on day shifts (see table 31). This chapter is mainly concerned with the work carried out by the day staff although the night staff's work is briefly discussed at the end of the chapter. The nursing day staff had worked for an average of 8.2 hours on their last day at work and the hostel day staff for an average of 7.9 hours.

Table 31   The staff's present type of work and shifts

	All nursing staff (excluding the senior nursing staff)	All hostel staff
	%	%
Working on day shifts:		
in one ward or hostel	55	88
in two wards	2	—
in three or more wards	3	—
Working on night shifts:		
in one ward or hostel	15	12
in two wards	1	—
in three or more wards	11	—
Nurses working in:		
acute sickness wards or medical centres	3	Not applicable
any type of occupational, recreational or training centre*	5	Not applicable
the patients' school	1	Not applicable
studying full-time	2	Not applicable
other type of work	1	Not applicable
	100	100
Base: all staff excluding the nursing officer grades (reweighted)	*535*	*324*

*Because of the small number of nurses who were working in training centres or schools it was not possible to analyse their worth or views separately.

The ward and hostel staff were asked to select from a set of 14 cards those which described tasks they had carried out on the preceding day at work and then to say whether they had spent more or less than an hour on each task. Table 32 shows the proportion of the ward and hostel staff who had spent over an hour on any of the main types of work included in the survey. 44% of the nursing and hostel staff had spent over an hour on at least one of 4 tasks connected with providing "social care" for their residents involving either supervising handicrafts or games, taking the residents on walks or outings, teaching, or encouraging the residents to organise their own activities. A much higher proportion (56%) of the nurses than of the hostel staff (27%) had spent over an hour on one of the tasks connected with providing basic care for the residents such as assisting with washing or feeding the residents, or helping to put them

38

to bed. The following sections of this chapter examine in greater detail the work the staff carried out and relate it to the type of ward or hostel on which they worked, the staff ratio, and their grade.

Table 32   The proportion of the day staff who had spent over an hour on various types of task.

The percentage of the day staff who had spent over an hour on:	All nursing day staff	All hostel day staff
	%	%
at least one of 4 **social aspects of care** (involving taking part in recreational activities, teaching the residents or encouraging them to organise their own activities)	44	44
at least one of 2 tasks involving **providing basic care** for the residents (involving getting the residents out of or into bed, or assisting with feeding or washing etc)...	56	27
giving **medical attention or treatment** (eg giving out drugs or injections or looking after residents who are physically ill)	13	4
dealing with behaviour problems (eg restraining aggressive, destructive or noisy residents)	22	12
at least one of 2 tasks involving **domestic work** (making beds or putting out clothes, or preparing or clearing up meals etc)	34	34
routine administrative work	15	24
at least one of 3 other **miscellaneous professional tasks** (involving training other staff, writing reports on individual residents or advising parents)	18	22
Base for percentages: all day nursing or care staff (reweighted)	*324*	*285*

4.3   The relationship between the type of ward or hostel and the work the staff carried out

The proportion of the staff who had spent over an hour on at least one of the four social tasks was slightly greater in the high and average ability adult wards than in the other adult wards. These proportions were similar in the adult hostels and high ability adult wards but higher (55%) in the children's hostels than in the children's wards (35%) (see table 33).

In adult wards, the proportion of the staff who had spent over an hour on teaching the residents to do domestic work or teaching reading, writing or understanding money was greatest amongst staff from the high ability wards (21%) and lowest amongst staff from the low ability (7%) and non-ambulant wards (0%). Except for the time spent on this teaching task there were no consistent relationships between the type of social tasks carried out for more than an hour and the ability levels of the patients from the adult wards.

The proportion of the staff who had spent over an hour on assisting with basic care was related to the ability level of the adult wards and was much lower in the high ability wards than in the others. Even so, nurses on the high ability wards were more likely than staff from the adult hostels to have spent over an hour on basic care.

All the staff who said they had spent some time assisting with feeding, washing or dressing were asked whether for most of this time they had been encouraging the residents to do these tasks for themselves, actually doing the

39

Table 33 Proportion of the day staff who have spent over an hour on various tasks involving direct contact with the residents on their last day at work analysed by their type of unit.

STAFFIN*

Percentage of the day staff who spent over an hour on:—	All wards nursing day staff	All hostel day staff	Adult hostels high ability	Adult wards high ability	Adult wards average ability	Adult wards low ability	Adult wards non-ambulant —very low ability	Children's hostels	Children wards
	%	%	%	%	%	%	%	%	%
1. Social aspects of care:—									
playing games or supervising art or handicrafts	23	18	11	14	27	21	16	38	31
taking the residents out on walks, shopping or outings etc	16	14	12	18	14	13	24	22	9
teaching or encouraging the residents to do domestic tasks, reading, writing or understanding money	15	16	19	21	17	7	0	16	7
encouraging the residents to organise their own activities	13	19	15	17	13	9	9	30	12
at least one of the four social aspects of caring listed above	44	44	42	45	48	37	36	55	35
2. Providing basic care:—									
assisting with feeding, washing, dressing or toileting	52	25	18	30	56	51	68	43	52
getting residents out of bed or putting them to bed	20	9	6	7	17	13	57	19	20
at least one of these two tasks involving providing basic care	56	27	21	34	60	56	78	45	55
3. Giving medical attention or treatment (eg giving out drugs or injections or looking after residents who are physically ill)	13	4	5	16	16	7	14	2	8
4. Dealing with behaviour problems (eg restraining aggressive, destructive or noisy residents)	22	12	9	16	32	21	10	21	26
Base for percentages: all day staff (reweighted)*	324	285	174	71	77	42	33	76	41

tasks for them or supervising while the residents did the tasks. The answers showed that in the adult wards the proportion of the staff who had spent most of the time in actually doing the tasks was related to the ability level of the patients in that it was highest (82%) in the wards with patients of the lowest ability (see table 34). The overall proportion of staff who devoted most of this time to encouraging the residents to help themselves with these tasks did not vary consistently with the ability level of the unit but was lowest in the non-ambulant wards (5%) and highest in the children's hostels (45%). However, if attention is confined to the staff who were either doing the tasks or encouraging the residents to help themselves (ie excluding staff who were supervising residents who were already able to do these tasks and staff who could not say how they had spent most of their time), it is only in the hostels and the high ability wards that the majority were mainly encouraging the residents rather than actually doing the tasks. These results suggest that the staff in the hostels and high ability adult wards were able to place more emphasis than the other nurses on encouraging their residents, perhaps because they had residents who were generally more able, and this additional encouragement may have further improved the abilities of their residents.

A slightly higher proportion of the nurses (13%) than of the hostel staff (4%) had spent over an hour on providing medical attention, for example by giving out drugs or injections or looking after residents who were physically ill. This proportion did not vary consistently with the type of ward.

The proportion of the staff who had spent over an hour on the tasks included in the survey which did not involve direct contact with the residents (ie domestic, administrative and miscellaneous professional tasks) showed only slight variations within the different types of units and therefore are not included in table 33.

In summary it appears that staff in the lower ability units devoted more time than the other staff to providing basic care for the residents. The proportion of the staff who spent over an hour on the social tasks was only slightly greater in the higher ability adult units than in the other adult units but was higher in the children's hostels than in the children's wards. There were no clear indications from the survey as to how the staff in the high ability wards and adult hostels spent the additional time which staff in the lower ability units devoted to basic care. It is possible that they spent much longer than an hour on some of the specified tasks or they may have spent more time on work which was not covered by the specified tasks (for example at meetings with staff from other professions).

4.4 The relationship between the staff ratios and the work the staff carried out

The differences between the units in the work the staff carried out may be related to differences in the staff ratios as well as to differences in the abilities of the residents. In order to assess the influence of the staff ratios the wards in each ability group and the children's wards were separated into those which had a better and those which had a worse staff ratio than the median for their ability group. This divided the wards into two equal sized groups which had relatively good and relatively poor staff ratios but which each contained patients

41

Table 34 Staff who had assisted with providing basic care analysed by whether they said they spent most of this time in encouraging the residents to do these tasks for themselves, actually doing the tasks for them, or supervising.

The staff said that for most of the time they had assisted with basic care they were:	All wards day nursing staff	All hostel day staff	STAFF IN							
			Adult hostels high ability	Adult wards high ability	Adult wards average ability	Adult wards low ability	Adult wards non-ambulant —very low ability	Children's hostels	Children's wards
	%	%	%	%	%	%	%	%	%
encouraging the residents to do these tasks for themselves	22	34	29	32	19	25	5	45	28
actually feeding, washing, dressing or bathing the residents	45	16	14	23	36	55	82	19	48
supervising while the residents did these tasks themselves	19	44	50	37	23	9	1	31	16
unable to say in which way they had spent most of the time	13	6	7	8	22	11	12	5	8
	100	100	100	100	100	100	100	100	100
Base for percentages: day staff who had assisted with basic care on their previous day at work (reweighted)	297	185	104	55	73	41	33	69	39

42

of similar ability levels. The same procedure was applied to the adult and children's hostels in order to divide them into hostels with "good" and "poor" staff ratios.

A separate analysis of staff in the wards with "good" and "poor" staff ratios suggested that the proportion of the nurses' time which has to be devoted to providing basic care for the patients increases with the pressures which result from relatively poor staff ratios (see table 35 (a)). Conversely the nurses in the wards with "poor" staff ratios seemed to have less time to spend on encouraging their patients to help themselves (see table 35 (b)). On the other hand the staffing ratios did not seem to affect the amount of time the nurses (or hostel staff) spent on the social tasks.

Staff in the adult hostels were compared with staff in the high ability wards with "good" staff ratios as these groups had residents of similar ability levels and also similar staff ratios. The number of staff who were interviewed from these wards is small, but it appears that there were only minor differences between these two groups of staff in the proportion who spent over an hour on various tasks (see table 36). It is therefore possible that the differences between the activities of staff in the high ability adult wards and in the adult hostels were mainly related to differences in the staff ratios.

Table 35 Separate analyses for units with relatively "good" or "poor" staff ratios for their type of unit, showing (a) the proportion of time the day staff spent on various tasks and (b) the way they assisted in providing basic care

	STAFF IN			
	All wards with "good" staff ratios for their type of unit	All wards with "poor" staff ratios for their type of unit	All hostels with "good" staff ratios for their type of unit	All hostels with "poor" staff ratios for their type of unit
Percentage of the day staff who spent over an hour on:	%	%	%	%
1. At least one of the four social aspects of care (listed in Table 4.5)	40	46	46	41
2. Providing basic care: Assisting with feeding, washing, dressing or toileting	40	59	26	25
Getting residents out of bed or putting them to bed	17	25	10	11
at least one of these two tasks involving providing basic care	45	63	30	27
3. Giving medical attention or treatment (eg giving out drugs or injections or looking after residents who are physically ill)	11	15	2	6
4. Dealing with behaviour problems (eg restraining aggressive, destructive or noisy residents)	20	24	12	13
Base for percentages: all day nursing or care staff (reweighted)*	125	119	129	120
The staff said that for the most of the time that they had spent on assisting with basic care they were:				
1. Encouraging the residents to do these tasks for themselves	28	13	42	26
2. Actually feeding, washing, dressing or bathing the residents	42	50	14	17
3. Supervising while the residents did these tasks themselves	20	19	39	51
4. Could not say in which way they had spent most of the time	10	18	6	6
	100	100	100	100
Base for percentages: all day staff who had assisted with basic care on their previous day at work	113	110	93	83

*These percentages are based on all staff from the sampled wards and hostels excluding a few units in which the staff ratio was not known.

43

Table 36   The proportion of the day staff who spent over an hour on various tasks in the high ability wards with "good" staff ratios and the adult hostels with high ability residents

Percentage of the day staff who spent over an hour on:	High ability wards with "good" staff ratios	Adult hostels high ability
	%	%
1. At least one of the 4 social aspects of care (listed in table 4.5)	49	42
2. Providing basic care: assisting with feeding, washing, dressing or toileting	20	18
getting residents out of bed or putting them to bed	6	6
3. Giving medical attention or treatment (eg giving out drugs or injections or looking after residents who are physically ill)	6	5
4. Dealing with behaviour problems (eg restraining aggressive, destructive or noisy residents)	13	9
Base for percentages: all day nursing or care staff (reweighted)	*36*	*174*

4.5   The relationship between the way the staff's time was spent and their grade

Table 37 shows the proportion of the day staff who had spent over an hour on each of the tasks covered in the survey. Approximately 44% of the staff in each of the nursing grades and of the officers in charge had spent at least an hour on any of the social tasks but this proportion was higher among the deputy officers in charge (57%) and lower among the care assistants (38%). As was to be expected a higher proportion of the enrolled nurses and nursing or care assistants than of the more senior staff had spent over an hour on the domestic tasks, whilst a higher proportion of the more senior staff than of the junior staff had spent over an hour on routine administrative work (eg filling out bed returns) and on the miscellaneous professional tasks (eg writing reports on individual residents, training junior staff or advising relatives).

A third of all the ward and hostel staff had spent over an hour on various domestic tasks involving clearing away meals, washing clothes, tidying the unit, making beds or putting out clothes. It is perhaps surprising that the proportions of the enrolled nurses and nursing and care assistants who had spent over an hour on one of the domestic tasks were approximately the same as the proportions who had spent over an hour on one of the social tasks (about 40%). Although the proportion of the more senior staff who had spent over an hour on one of the domestic tasks was lower, it was slightly over 20% amongst the ward sisters, staff nurses, officers in charge and deputies.

Less than a quarter of all the nurses and hostel staff had spent over an hour on routine administrative work but this proportion was much higher among the ward sisters (40%), the officers in charge (66%) and the deputy officers in charge (43%). It is likely that the hostel staff are obliged to spend more time than the ward staff on administrative work partly because the nursing officers carry out some of the comparable administrative work for the wards, and partly because the hostel staff are responsible for more of the administrative work connected with their cooks and other domestic staff. It is worth noting that the proportion of the officers in charge who had spent over an hour on routine

Table 37 Proportion of the daytime staff who spent at least an hour on various tasks on their last day at work analysed by their grade.

Percentage of the staff who spent over an hour on:	All nursing day staff	All hostel day staff	Ward sisters	Staff nurses	Enrolled nurses	Nursing assistants	Students/ pupils	Officers in charge	Deputy officers in charge	Care assistants
	%	%	%	%	%	%	%	%	%	%
1. Tasks that involve working directly with the residents:										
at least one of the 4 social aspects of care (listed in table 4.4)	44	44	41	48	42	45	42	48	57	38
at least one of the 2 tasks that involved providing basic care for the residents (listed in table 4.4)	56	27	44	49	61	57	64	18	24	31
Giving medical attention or treatment (eg giving out drugs or injections, or looking after residents who are physically ill)	13	4	24	17	20	3	16	5	5	3
Dealing with behaviour problems (eg restraining aggressive, destructive or noisy residents)	22	12	26	22	26	23	13	10	19	11
2. Routine administrative work	15	24	40	29	17	3	11	66	43	6
3. Domestic work										
making beds or putting out clothes	16	11	13	10	23	18	12	4	3	15
preparing or clearing away meals, mending or washing clothes or tidying their ward or hostel	26	27	20	10	30	28	32	22	17	32
at least one of the 2 domestic tasks listed above	34	34	22	22	39	39	32	24	21	40
4. Miscellaneous professional tasks:										
briefing or training other staff or discussing the residents with other nursing or care staff	13	12	29	17	10	5	10	22	22	6
writing reports on individual residents	6	8	21	9	3	1	6	23	12	3
advising or dealing with residents' parents or relatives	2	5	3	3	3	1	1	13	7	2
at least one of the 3 miscellaneous professional tasks listed above	18	22	44	25	21	5	12	44	36	10
Base for percentages: all day nursing or care staff (reweighted)	*324*	*285*	*213*	*58*	*75*	*129*	*101*	*115*	*59*	*177*

45

administrative work was higher than the proportion who had spent over an hour on one of the social tasks and ward sisters were equally likely to have spent over an hour on the one task as on the other.

About a fifth of all the nursing and hostel staff had spent over an hour on at least one of the three miscellaneous professional tasks but this proportion was much higher among the ward sisters and officers in charge (44%) than among the other staff grades.

4.6 Work carried out by the night staff

The night staff usually came on duty between 8 pm and 10 pm and went off duty between 7 am and 9 am. It was therefore not surprising to find that hardly any of the night staff had spent over an hour on any of the four social tasks (listed in table 33) on their previous night at work. Half of the nurses on night duty and a third of the hostel night staff had spent over an hour helping to put residents to bed or to get them out of bed. A higher proportion of the night staff than day staff had spent over an hour on domestic tasks including 27% of the nurses on night duty who had spent over an hour on making beds or putting out clothes and 39% of the hostel staff on night duty who had spent over an hour on other types of domestic work.

40% of the night staff in the hospitals and hostels would have liked more contact with the day staff and the remainder were happy with the amount of contact they already had. There was some circumstantial evidence suggesting that it would be desirable for some of the night nursing staff to have more contact with the day staff in that, of the night nurses who had worked on the same ward for more than 3 months, 10% did not know whether any of their patients attended occupational centres and 7% of the night nurses in wards containing children did not know whether any of the children went to school. As the night staff have the opportunity to talk to and generally encourage the patients, while helping to put them to bed or get them up, it would seem to be important that they should know about their patients' occupation during the day. In addition the night nursing staff were less likely than the day nurses to have attended meetings of nurses from their ward to discuss individual patients. 27% of the night nurses, below ward sister level, who had worked in their ward for at least 3 months had attended this type of meeting in the previous 3 months as compared with 55% of the day nursing staff (see chapter 6).

4.7 The use of behaviour modification programmes

The use of behaviour modification programmes is considered here because it is relevant to the earlier discussion of the time the staff spent on teaching and encouraging their residents.

Behaviour modification programmes are methods of teaching which involve splitting the task to be learnt into its basic components and reinforcing the process of learning each component with an appropriate reward. For example a patient might be taught to feed himself with a spoon by initially learning to hold the spoon close to his mouth and being rewarded for doing that success-fully, and then learning to raise the spoon etc. These techniques are derived

Table 38 The proportion of the wards and hostels in which behaviour modification programmes are used

Behaviour modification programmes *	All wards	All hostels	Adult hostels high ability	Adult wards high ability	Adult wards average ability	Adult wards low ability	Adult wards non-ambulant —very low ability	Children's hostels	Children's wards
	%	%	%	%	%	%	%	%	%
are used	31	19	18	31	32	34	19	22	43
are not used	60	69	74	65	62	62	77	67	51
staff did not know whether they were used	8	12	9	5	6	4	4	11	6
	100	100	100	100	100	100	100	100	100
Base: all sampled wards and hostels in which interviews were carried out with day staff who had worked for over three months in their unit (reweighted)	248	100	65	77	74	40	24	24	33

*If the staff queried the interpretation of "behaviour modification programmes" the interviewers referred them to the example of a programme for teaching a resident to feed himself with a spoon as described in the text.

47

from experimental work on learning processes carried out by behavioural psychologists and are generally considered to be potentially of great value in teaching the mentally handicapped (see for example Kiernan et al, 1975).

According to the staff, behaviour modification programmes were used in almost a third of the wards and a fifth of the hostels (table 38) and in most of these units the ward or hostel staff were involved in carrying out the programmes. The results in chapter 6 on the staff's contact with other professions suggest that it is unusual for them to have regular discussions (ie on a weekly or monthly basis) with psychologists on the residents' progress with these programmes.

4.8 The extent of staff satisfaction with their domestic work

The staff's views on their role, in general, and particularly on work involving direct contact with the residents is discussed in detail in chapter 9. The next 3 sections look only at the degree of satisfaction expressed for the domestic and administrative side of the staff's work so that this can be considered in the context of the previous results showing the amount of time that staff spent on these tasks.

Approximately one in six of all the nursing and hostel staff were dissatisfied with their domestic work (see table 39) but this proportion was twice as high amongst the ward sisters although they were less likely to have spent so much time on domestic tasks.

It was not practicable at the main stage of the survey to ask the staff why they were dissatisfied with their domestic work but evidence from the pilot stage suggested that some of the staff did not see this as part of their role as the following example illustrates:—

> "I don't think you should have to do it—domestic side of it. Jobs like cleaning cupboards out—other places have cadets to do them, while you're doing them the kids are left on their own". (Female student nurse, working in a children's ward.)

4.9 The place of domestic work in the staff's role

The results in the preceding sections indicating the time the staff spent on domestic work and the extent of staff dissatisfaction with their domestic work raise several questions: firstly, of whether domestic work by nursing staff forms an important part of the staff's caring role by contributing to an environment like a normal home in which members of the family may do housework while interacting with children; and, if so, whether the staff, and particularly the ward sisters, see their domestic work in this way. Secondly, if it seems that staff spend too much time on domestic tasks, it is worth considering whether more domestic staff should be employed to replace some of the nursing or care staff, and also whether the standards of tidiness and cleanliness are too high in some of the hospitals or hostels so that some time is unnecessarily spent on doing domestic work. Finally the question is raised of whether the residents of higher ability could or should be given more encouragement to help with the domestic work in their own ward or hostel. In this context it is relevant to note that 20% of the staff from the high ability adult wards and adult hostels spent over an hour on teaching or encouraging their residents to do domestic work

Table 39 The extent of satisfaction with domestic work analysed by grade for the day staff

	All wards day nursing staff	All hostels day staff	Ward sisters	Staff nurses	Enrolled nurses	Students/ pupils	Nursing assistants	Officers in charge	Deputy officers in charge	Care assistants
	%	%	%	%	%	%	%	%	%	%
Very satisfied	36	43	22	24	36	35	46	44	38	44
Fairly satisfied	38	36	32	47	36	43	38	35	43	34
A little dissatisfied	11	12	18	12	11	13	6	5	14	13
Very dissatisfied	6	4	16	3	6	4	4	6	3	3
Staff who said this was not applicable to them	9	6	11	14	12	5	6	9	2	6
	100	100	100	100	100	100	100	100	100	100
Base: all day time ward and hostel staff (reweighted)	324	285	213	58	75	101	129	115	59	117

or to read, write or count but a higher proportion, 34%, had spent over an hour on actually doing domestic tasks. This suggests that in these units with higher ability residents the staff could spend less time actually doing domestic work if they spent more time on teaching the residents these skills, which would be of some value to the residents if they ever left the institutions in which they now live.

4.10 The extent of staff satisfaction with their administrative work

As was seen earlier, the officers in charge, deputies, ward sisters and staff nurses were more likely to have spent over an hour on routine administrative work than staff in any of the other grades. The extent of satisfaction with their administrative work is shown for these staff grades and the senior nursing staff in table 40. A quarter of the senior nursing staff and a third of the staff in the other grades were dissatisfied with their administrative work and an example of the reasons for this dissatisfaction can be given from the pilot work:—

"The clerical work, all the form filling-in. At the end of each week you have weekly returns—all say the same thing but in different ways! The difficulty of getting the other staff to understand that they have to be done. They think that when I'm sitting in my office for half an hour doing it, that I'm just having a skive". (Female officer in charge of a children's hostel.)

Table 40 The extent of satisfaction with the staff's administrative work analysed by grade

	Senior nursing staff	Ward sisters	Staff nurses	Officers in charge	Deputy officers in charge
	%	%	%	%	%
Very satisfied	29	19	16	24	33
Fairly satisfied	46	51	49	43	36
A little dissatisfied	16	22	25	22	21
Very dissatisfied	10	8	7	11	9
Staff who said this was not applicable to them	0	0	4	0	2
	100	100	100	100	100
Base: all daytime ward and hostel staff and senior nursing staff responsible for wards (reweighted)	*83*	*217*	*57*	*115*	*59*

These results together with finding that the officers in charge and ward sisters were as or more likely to spend over an hour on routine administrative work as on social tasks, suggest that it would be valuable to investigate further the proportion of staff time spent on routine administrative work, and to find out whether such work could be reduced and simplified and also whether more of it could usefully be carried out by the more junior staff.

5 THE WAY THE WARDS AND HOSTELS WERE RUN

This chapter is concerned with the use of various routine ways of organising and structuring the daily lives of residents in the wards and hostels and with the contacts the residents had with relatives and voluntary workers. The underlying assumption of the analysis is that it is generally desirable to provide an environment for residents which allows them as much independence as possible, which recognises their individuality and which supports links with their families and others from the outside community.

In the last decade increased emphasis has been placed on avoiding unnecessary routines and restrictions within long term residential units partly because of a reaction against the rigid, hierarchical "total institutions" portrayed by Goffmann in his book *Asylums* (1961). Goffmann considered the key characteristic of total institutions to be "the handling of human needs by the bureaucratic organisation of whole blocks of people—whether or not this is a necessary or effective means of social organisation in the circumstances". Two of the main features of total institutions discerned by Goffmann are firstly that "each phase of the member's daily activity is carried on in the immediate company of a large batch of others, all of whom are treated alike and required to do the same thing together"; and secondly that "all phases of the day's activities are tightly scheduled, with one activity leading at a prearranged time into the next, the whole sequence of activities being imposed from above by a system of explicit formal rulings and a body of officials".

King and his colleagues (1971) applied concepts derived from Goffmann and others in analysing the organisation and running of units for mentally handicapped children. They developed a child-management scale which was used to assess the extent to which units were "child-oriented" or "institutionally oriented" and found that children's wards were more "institutionally oriented" than children's hostels. The following quotation illustrates their view of how the more hierarchical organisation and relatively frequent staff and patient turnover in the hospitals were associated with the institutional orientation of the wards:—

"Both staff and children were moved from unit to unit and there were noticeable differences in the roles of different grades of staff. The wards appeared to function as rather tightly controlled units with little responsibility delegated to the sisters or charge nurses, who were regularly supervised by senior members of the nursing administration. Sisters in turn delegated little responsibility. It seemed likely that this system of organisation imposed strict limits on the variation in patterns of care which could be tolerated between units, and also militated against the personalised treatment of the children. If each ward had a similar routine, which was not dependent upon the unique characteristics of the children within it, then it could more easily assimilate the frequent changes of staff. If tasks such as cooking, buying clothes, laundering and mending were performed by centralised agencies outside the units, staff working in the units were less likely to feel an overall responsibility for events. If the organisation of the ward took little account of individual differences among the children, unit staff were less likely to be aware of them either."

K Jones (1975) in a study of hospitals for the mentally handicapped in one Hospital Region also pointed to the emphasis placed on maintaining routines. Of particular relevence to the present survey is her research team's view that staff in the wards with low grade patients tended to rely on routines to a greater extent than staff in other wards. They discussed various factors which seemed to be related to the importance of the routines in low grade wards including the staff's pessimistic view of the patients' capabilities, the staff's adoption of a parental role which emphasised compliance from the patients, and the way the routines prevented or lessened the effect of untoward incidents and made it possible for staff to satisfy their superiors that the ward was properly run.

In the time available for the interviews in this survey we could examine only a few of the routines or restrictions which could have occurred within the units. Our main objectives were to find out whether the kind and number of restrictions were related to the ability level of the patients, whether there seemed to be major difference between the wards and hostels in particular after allowing for differences in the ability levels of the residents, and how any differences found between units related to the staff's views of their roles. The last question is considered in Chapter 8.

5.1 The method of obtaining the information

Information on whether the units were kept locked, whether the residents stayed indoors and on contacts with relatives and voluntary workers was obtained from the ward sisters and officers in charge at the same time as asking about their residents' abilities. This information was therefore available for all the wards and hostels.

The other information on the running of the units was obtained from all the day staff (excluding trainee nurses) who had worked in their unit for 3 months or longer and who therefore should have known whether the various restrictions applied. In some of the units no day staff who had worked in their unit for over 3 months were interviewed so this information was available for only 82 % of the wards (excluding the acute sickness units) and for 97 % of the hostels.[1] In order to relate this information to the sample of wards and hostels, rather than to the number of interviewed staff, where two staff members had been interviewed from the same unit, their answers were each given a weight of a half and a similar reweighting was applied where 3 or more staff members from the same unit had been interviewed.

5.2 The extent of various restrictions and routines within the units

In selecting the restrictions and routines to be included in the survey we concentrated mainly on those which would be applicable to both higher and lower ability units and which were potentially under the control of the ward or hostel staff.

Information was obtained on the following 8 aspects of the running of the units:—

(1) Whether any of the residents used the ward or hostel kitchen.

---

[1]This was a lower proportion of the wards than of the hostels mainly because the sampling procedure resulted in fewer interviews per ward, on average, than per hostel.

(2)   Whether the residents would be allowed to watch a late TV programme at the weekends.

(3)   Whether the residents all got up at the same time at weekends as on weekdays.

(4)   Whether the ward or hostel was kept locked for some of the time on the previous weekday.

(5)   Whether the residents were asked about what they would like for their meals at least once a month.

(6)   Whether the ward or hostel had meetings with the residents to discuss topics such as meals, bedtimes or other rules.

(7)   Whether the residents all had their own individual lockers or cupboards.

(8)   Whether any of the residents stayed indoors, inside the ward or hostel, on the previous weekday (excluding residents who had to stay inside because of a physical illness).

The question on whether meetings of the residents were held to discuss topics such as meals and bedtimes was included, although it appeared to be inapplicable to lower ability units, because it was felt to be important for comparisons between the adult hostels and the high ability wards. Research on hostels in Wandsworth had shown that their residents had definite views on these topics (Wandsworth Project 74). Questions on the way the residents were washed or toiletted, which were used by King et al in their scales of "block treatment" and "rigidity" were excluded because they would have been inapplicable in the higher ability units.

There were only slight differences between the wards and the hostels in some respects, so that, for example, in at least three-quarters of both the wards and hostels the residents were usually allowed to watch a late TV programme at the weekend, and had their own lockers or cupboards. However, there were more marked differences between the wards and the hostels in other ways, for example, the residents all got up at the same time at weekends as on weekdays in a higher proportion of the wards than of the hostels (see table 41).

The aspects on which there were differences between the wards and the hostels suggested that the hostel residents generally lived more independently and with fewer restrictions than the hospital patients. However, except on one routine, there were only slight differences between the high ability wards and the high ability adult hostels. The exceptions was that the residents all got up at the same time at the weekends as on weekdays in nearly half the high ability wards but in only 13% of the hostels. This may be related to the majority of the hospitals having centrally organised kitchens which prepare breakfast at a fixed time.

Within the adult wards there was a relationship between the ability level of the ward and the number of restrictions or routines which operated, in that restrictions were least likely to occur in the high ability wards. However, in most cases there were only slight differences between the average, low ability and non-ambulant wards and these differences were not always consistently

Table 41 The extent of various restrictions or routines within the wards and hostels.

	All wards	All hostels†	Adult hostels high ability	Adult wards high ability	Adult wards average ability	Adult wards low ability	Adult wards non-ambulant—very low ability	Children's hostels	Children's wards
	%	%	%	%	%	%	%	%	%
1 Some of the residents use the ward or hostel kitchen	80	97	98	95	89	63	61	92	63
none of the residents use the kitchen*	20	4	2	5	12	57	39	9	32
2 The residents would usually be allowed to watch a late TV programme at the weekend	77	85	90	83	72	81	86	73	66
the residents would usually not be allowed to watch a late weekend TV programme*	7	11	7	3	7	8	5	23	16
don't know (eg staff did not work evenings or weekends, or worked with very young children)*	16	4	3	14	21	10	10	5	19
3 Some of the residents get up at a different time at weekends than on weekdays	36	75	85	52	36	16	23	39	29
the residents all get up at the same time at weekends as on weekdays*	61	22	13	47	59	81	75	57	68
don't know (as staff did not work weekends)*	3	3	2	2	5	4	2	3	3
4 The ward or hostel was not kept locked on the previous weekday	82	88	97	92	76	71	93	64	77
the ward or hostel was locked for some of the time on the previous weekday*	18	12	3	8	24	29	7	36	23
5 The residents are asked about what they would like for their meals at least once a month	34	46	40	38	27	40	32	56	28
the residents are not asked about their meals (or asked less frequently than once a month)*	66	54	60	62	63	60	68	44	72
6 The ward or hostel has meetings with the residents to discuss topics such as meals, bedtimes or other rules	17	33	41	32	15	5	8	6	3
the ward or hostel does not have this type of residents' meeting*	83	67	59	68	86	95	92	94	97
7 The residents all have their own individual lockers or cupboards	80	99	100	94	80	69	50	96	80
some, but not all of the residents have their own lockers or cupboards*	12	1	0	2	15	23	29	4	6
none of the residents have their own lockers or cupboards*	8	0	0	4	6	8	21	0	14
8 The percentage of all the residents who stayed indoors, inside the ward or hostel on the previous weekday (excluding any who had to stay inside because of a physical illness)	14	4	4	6	18	14	32	4	9
at least one resident stayed indoors on the previous weekday (excluding any who had to stay inside because of a physical illness)*	42	16	19	37	50	38	64	8	23
Base: all wards and hostels† in which interviews were carried out with day staff who had worked for over three months in the unit (reweighted)	248	100	65	77	74	40	24	34	33

*The number of characteristics marked with an asterisk were calculated to form one of the ...

54

related to the ability levels of the wards. This was possibly partly because some of the restrictions, for example, keeping the ward locked, may have been irrelevant in the non-ambulant wards which had patients who were less likely to create serious behaviour problems.

With one exception, the restrictions occurred in a higher proportion of the children's wards than of the children's hostels. The exception was that a slightly higher proportion of the children's hostels than of the children's wards had been kept locked for some of the time on the previous weekday. This restriction may have been more frequently necessary in the children's hostels because their front doors often led directly onto the street, whereas the children's wards were within the hospital grounds. This illustrates the difficulty of determining whether a particular restriction is undesirable within a specific unit in the absence of more detailed information on the circumstances.

5.3 The restrictions scale

A scale was developed in order to find out how many of the restrictions or routines occurred within each unit and to relate this to other aspects of the staff's work. Scores on the scale were calculated by allotting initially a score of 1 for each restriction or routine which occurred[2] and a score of zero otherwise. These scores were then cumulated for each unit to form the total score on a "restrictions scale" with a range from zero to 8. A score of zero indicated a unit in which the residents were relatively free from restrictions and routines whereas a score of 8 indicated a unit which was evidently run in a rigid and institutional manner.

The average number of restrictions or routines in the wards (3.4) was higher than in the hostels (2.1—see table 42). There was a considerable overlap in the scores of the high ability adult hostels and the high ability wards in that, for example, about a quarter of the adult hostels and half of the high ability wards had scores of 3 or more. Although in some circumstances the staff in the adult hostels and high ability wards may be unable to avoid adopting one, or exceptionally two, of the restrictions or routines, it seems unlikely that 3 or more of the restrictions would be necessary in these units. This suggests that there may be scope for allowing residents to live more independently, with fewer restrictions and routines, in both the adult hostels and the high ability wards.

Although the low ability and non-ambulant wards had more restrictions, on average, than the high ability wards, a third of these wards had only 3 or fewer of the restrictions or routines. This implies that staff working with the more severely handicapped patients do not always find it necessary to adopt a rigid, institutional way of running their wards.

The average number of restrictions or routines in the children's hostels (3.0) was lower than in the children's wards (3.9.) However there was some overlap between the two groups in that three quarters of the children's hostels and a third of the children's wards had only 3 or fewer of the restrictions or routines.

---

[2]A score of 1 was also allotted for some of the items when the staff did not know whether a restriction occurred where this indicated a rigid division of responsibility for the care of residents (for example where the day staff said they did not know whether residents would be allowed to watch a late TV programme because it was the night staff's responsibility). This increased the average scores on the restrictions scale by 0·19 for the wards and by 0·07 for the hostels.

Table 42 Scores on a scale* indicating the number of restrictions or routines analysed by the type of ward or hostel

Higher scores indicate a unit in which there were more of the restrictions or routines:	All wards	All hostels	Adult hostels high ability	Adult wards high ability	Adult wards average ability	Adult wards low ability	Adult wards non-ambulant —very low ability	Children's hostels	Children's wards
	%	%	%	%	%	%	%	%	%
0–1	13	35	46	27	10	5	2	8	7
2–3	36	54	49	46	31	36	32	67	26
4–5	42	10	6	26	51	43	43	20	59
6–8 (maximum)	9	2	0	1	9	17	23	5	9
	100	100	100	100	100	100	100	100	100
Average score	3·4	2·1	1·7	2·5	3·6	3·8	4·2	3·0	3·9
Base for percentages: all wards and hostels in which interviews were carried out with staff who had worked for over 3 months in the unit (reweighted)	248	92	65	77	74	40	24	24	33

The scores are equal to the number of the restrictions or routines marked with asterisks in table 41 within the ward or hostel.

56

In making comparisons between the children's units it is necessary to bear in mind that the children's wards contained a higher proportion of severely handicapped children than the children's hostels. In order to take this into account a separate analysis was carried out for the children's wards which were allocated to the average or low ability groups by the cluster analysis. These children's wards, which were more directly comparable with the children's hostels, had an average of 3.4 restrictions or routines, which was only slightly higher than in the children's hostels (although both these groups of units were samples of less than 25). It is therefore possible that one factor which led to the lower number of restrictions or routines in the children's hostels was that their children were less severely handicapped than the children in the hospitals.

King et al (*op cit*) in their study which took place about 10 years ago, also found that the children's wards had more restrictions and were more "institutionally oriented" than the children's hostels. However they reported more marked differences between the two types of unit with no overlap between the scores of the children's wards and hostels on their child management scale. Although direct comparisons cannot be made[3] between the present study and those carried out by King et al, the available evidence[4] suggests that the children's wards now have fewer restrictions and routines than those studied ten years ago, possibly partly because the hospitals have responded to the type of criticisms made by King et al. This type of improvement is consistent with the interim measures recommended in *Better Services for the Mentally Handicapped* (DHSS, 1971). The recommendations included improving the patients clothing, providing cupboards for all patients' personal possessions, improving the staffing ratios and a special training project for both senior and junior staff.

5.4 The relationship between the number of restrictions and the staffing ratios

It has been suggested that units with poor staff ratios find it necessary to adopt more routines than other units in order to reduce the pressures on the staff (Kushlick 1973). In order to assess the influence of staff ratios on the way the wards were run comparisons were made between the wards and hostels which had better and worse staff ratios than the median for their ability group. No differences were found between the wards with "good" and "poor" staff ratios in their average scores on the restrictions scale and similarly there were no differences between the hostels with "good" and "poor" staff ratios. In particular, the number of restrictions in the high ability wards with "good" staff ratios was greater than in the adult hostels which had similar staff ratios.

---

[3]Any comparisons between the results of King et al and the present survey are qualified firstly because our restrictions scale does not cover the running of children's units as comprehensively as King's child management scale, and secondly, because the samples used by King were not nationally representative.

[4]In addition to the results in table 41, further evidence is available on restrictions on visits in table 45 (cf King's item 5) and from the pilot work for the survey which included four additional questions which were similar to items 4, 15, 19 and 22 of King's revised child management scale (covering the use of bedrooms at set times, the use of the residents' own clothing, possessing toys or books and celebrating the residents' birthdays). There were only slight differences between the wards and hostels on all these items and two of them (19 and 22) were not included in the main survey because less than 20% of the wards or hostels were "institutionally oriented" on them. However the results from the pilot work should not be treated as being nationally representative as they were derived from a random sample of 100 nurses in 9 hospitals and 40 hostel staff in 10 hostels which included only 10 children's wards and 4 children's hostels.

These results should not be taken as conclusive evidence that there was no relationship between the staff ratios and the way the units were run since there may have been other differences, for example in arrangements for washing and toileting patients, which were not examined in the survey. However these results suggest that the overall differences found between the wards and hostels in the average number of restrictions were not directly related to the worse staff ratios in the wards.

Other factors which could influence the extent to which restrictions or routines occur within the units are: the priority that the staff place on providing a less institutional atmosphere, the influence the staff have over the way their unit is run, the training the staff have received and the availability of financial resources. The first three of these factors are discussed in later chapters. Financial resources lay outside the scope of the survey, but would be a crucial factor, for example, in providing individual lockers or making a kitchen area safe for patients to use. However it is likely that the availability of resources for this type of project depends partly on the priority the staff give to it and partly on the influence they have over the way their ward or hostel is run.

5.5 The length of time that the staff have worked in their ward or hostel

The length of time that the staff have worked in their ward or hostel is relevant to the preceding discussion on the extent to which the units are run in an institutional way for two reasons. Firstly because it has been suggested that hospital wards tend to adopt routine ways of dealing with residents and restrictions so that frequent changes of staff can be assimilated. Secondly a degree of continuity of staffing, particularly in the more senior positions, is likely to contribute to the kind of stable background which people normally experience in their own homes and families.

Excluding trainee nurses, about two thirds of the staff in both types of unit had worked continuously in their ward or hostel for a year or more whilst 90% of the day nursing staff and 95% of the day hostel staff had done so for at least 3 months. In general, the hostel staff had worked for a longer time on the same unit than the nurses and, in particular, a lower proportion of the ward sisters (24%) than of the officers in charge (41%) had worked in their unit for over 5 years (see table 43).

The results from the survey did not support the hypothesis that the ward sisters or officers in charge who had worked for a longer time in the same unit were in the wards or hostels which had fewer restrictions or routines[5]. However, there may have been other ways, for example emotionally, that the residents benefited from being in units with more stable staffing but these could not be assessed in the survey.

5.6 Wearing uniforms

The wearing of uniforms by staff is often quoted as an indication of a more rigid and institutional approach to caring for the mentally handicapped.

[5]Information on the number of restrictions in the units was not obtained from staff who had worked in their units for less than three months. This does not affect these comparisons because it excluded only a small proportion of the ward sisters (5%) and officers in charge (7%) including some who may not have had enough time to decide (or find out) whether various restrictions would apply.

Table 43 The length of time that the daytime staff have worked in their present ward or hostel

	All nursing day staff* (excluding trainee nurses)	All hostel day staff	Ward sisters	Staff nurses	Enrolled nurses	Nursing assistants	Students/ pupils	Officers in charge	Deputy officers in charge	Care assistants
Less than 3 months	% 10	% 5	% 5	% 11	% 11	% 10	% 80	% 7	% 3	% 5
3 months but less than a year	29	27	25	37	31	28	19	11	26	32
1 year but less than 2 years	22	17	21	22	18	26	1	14	12	20
2 years but less than 5 years	26	31	25	22	22	30	0	28	39	28
5 years or longer	13	20	24	7	19	6	0	41	20	14
	100	100	100	100	100	100	100	100	100	100
Base for percentages: all day time ward and hostel staff	257	284	205	54	74	117	95	115	59	176

*Excluding 5% of the day nurses who were working on three or more wards at the same time.

Table 44 The wearing of uniforms or overalls analysed by the type of unit

	All nursing day staff	All hostel day staff	Adult hostels high ability	Adult wards high ability	Adult wards average ability	Adult wards low ability	Adult wards non-ambulant —very low ability	Children's hostels	Children's wards
	%	%	%	%	%	%	%	%	%
Staff were obliged to wear uniforms by their hospital or hostel	51	1	0	45	51	59	66	3	48
Staff wore uniforms voluntarily	12	0	0	11	11	11	14	0	8
Staff were obliged to wear overalls by their hospital or hostel	9	16	17	9	13	6	14	7	0
Staff wore overalls voluntarily	7	25	25	8	10	6	4	23	3
Staff did not wear uniforms or overalls	21	58	58	28	15	20	2	67	40
	100	100	100	100	100	100	100	100	100
Base: all daytime ward or hostel staff who had worked in their unit for at least 3 months (reweighted)	232	271	166	66	65	33	22	73	29

About 60% of the daytime nurses wore uniforms, usually because they were obliged to do so by their hospital administration, and a further 16% of the nurses wore overalls (see table 44). By contrast hardly any of the hostel staff wore a uniform but 41% of them wore overalls, mainly voluntarily. The proportion of the nurses who wore uniforms was highest in the non-ambulant group of adult wards and lowest in the high ability adult wards and the children's wards.

Within the hospitals an association was found between wearing a uniform and working in wards which had more restrictions or routines. The nurses who were obliged to wear uniforms were working on wards which had a higher average number of restrictions (3.9) than the nurses who only wore them voluntarily (3.6) or who did not wear them (2.8). This relationship occurred within wards of each ability group[6] so that it could not be accounted for by the relationship between the wearing of uniforms and the ability level of the wards. The hostel staff who wore a uniform or overalls also tended to be in units which had a slightly higher average number of restrictions but the differences were less marked than in the hospitals.

Evidently the use of uniforms does not itself cause the restrictions and it is likely that there is a common factor or factors which are linked both to wearing uniforms and to adopting a more institutional approach to the care of the mentally handicapped. One possible explanation is that the ward sisters who are obliged to wear uniforms are generally constrained by a more rigid and hierarchical style of management which discourages the minimisation of restrictions and routines within their units. A second possible explanation is that the nurses who wear uniforms are more likely to see their job as being closely related to other types of nursing and so place relatively less emphasis on the social caring side of their role.

5.7 The relationship between the extent of restrictions in the units and the time that the staff spend on social tasks

In general no relationship was found between the time staff spent on social tasks (one hour or less versus more than one hour) and the number of restrictions operating in their unit except in one sub-group. This sub-group comprised a tenth of the day nursing staff who were in wards which had a score from 6 to 8 on the restrictions scale, that is the wards in which all or almost all of the restrictions or routines operated. Only a quarter of these nurses had spent over an hour on one of the four social tasks described in chapter 4 compared with 44% of all the daytime nursing staff. Although most of these wards were in the low ability and non-ambulant groups this was not the reason for the difference as a higher proportion, 40%, of the nurses in the other wards in these ability groups had spent over an hour on one of the social tasks.

This suggests that there is a small group of wards which are run on traditional institutional lines in which concern for the patients as individuals is at a minimum. As these wards were mainly in the low ability or non-ambulant groups they seemed to have several of the characteristics of the low grade wards described by Jones (1975) in which the staff relied heavily on routines

---

[6]After combining the low ability and non-ambulant groups because of the small numbers involved.

Table 45 Arrangements for and contacts with relatives

	All wards	All hostels	Adult hostels high ability	Adult wards high ability	Adult wards average ability	Adult wards low ability	Adult wards non-ambulant —very low ability	Children's hostels	Children's wards
	%	%	%	%	%	%	%	%	%
(a) Relatives should only come on fixed visiting days or times (but exceptions are made)	4	2	1	1	6	4	7	2	3
Relatives can come when they like if they ring first	23	12	8	27	23	12	33	27	10
Relatives can come at any time in the day or evening	74	86	91	72	72	84	60	70	86
	100	100	100	100	100	100	100	100	100
(b) None of the residents were visited by relatives in the previous week	12	15	16	18	10	10	14	12	6
Percentage of all the residents who were seen by relatives in the previous week	17	18	14	17	15	18	17	35	25
(c) Some relatives take part in activities with the residents (as well as taking out their own relative)	22	28	28	29	17	10	32	25	26
None of the relatives take part in activities with the residents	78	72	72	71	83	90	68	75	74
	100	100	100	100	100	100	100	100	100
Base for percentages: (a) and (c) all wards and hostels in which interviews were carried out with staff who had worked for over three months in the unit (reweighted)	248	100	65	77	74	40	24	24	33

62

and restrictions. However, it is necessary to point out that less than a quarter of the low ability or non-ambulant wards were in this group, and that we had no information on whether these wards had some of the other characteristics described by Jones (for example minimal task performance by the staff).

5.8 Arrangements for and contacts with relatives and voluntary workers

The DHSS recommends that residents should have frequent contacts with relatives and other people from outside their hospital or hostel (see *Better Services for the Mentally Handicapped*, 1971). Information was therefore obtained on the residents' contacts with relatives and voluntary workers.

Relatives. In general the arrangements for, and the frequency of contacts with relatives followed a similar pattern in the hospitals and hostels (see table 45). In almost all the wards and hostels relatives were able to visit at any time throughout the week, although in some units they were expected to telephone before they came. An average of about 17% of the hostel and hospital residents had been seen by relatives in the previous week and in a quarter of the wards and hostels the relatives took part in activities with the residents when they came to visit.

It was surprising to find that the same proportion of residents had been seen by relatives in the hostels as in the hospitals, because a potential advantage of the hostels is their accessibility. There would therefore appear to be greater scope for increasing the contact with relatives in the hostels than in the hospitals. However, these results could only be fully interpreted if we also knew the proportion of the residents who had relatives and whether the hostel residents had been placed in the nearest hostel to their relatives.

Voluntary workers. The survey examined contacts with voluntary workers who talked to the residents or assisted in activities with them but did not cover the role of volunteers in fund raising or other work.

Contacts with voluntary workers and the staff's views on the desirability of volunteers helping with the residents were similar in the wards and hostels. Within the previous fortnight, voluntary workers had spent half an hour or longer with at least one resident in about half of the wards and hostels (see table 46). Over three quarters of the staff in both types of unit said they would encourage voluntary workers, including 60% who said they would give them some training or advice on the sort of things they could do with the residents.

Twenty-four per cent. of the nurses and 16% of the hostel staff said they would not encourage voluntary workers to take part in activities with the residents but preferred this to be left to the nursing or care staff. Within the hospitals this view was not confined to the ward nursing staff as 15% of the senior nursing staff said they would not encourage voluntary workers. This view may have been related to local difficulties in finding suitable volunteers but it is possible that some of the nursing and hostel staff would benefit from advice on ways of obtaining and using suitable voluntary workers.

Table 46 The staff's views on encouraging voluntary workers and the contact that the residents have with them

	All wards	All hostels	Adult hostels high ability	Adult wards high ability	Adult wards average ability	Adult wards low ability	Adult wards non-ambulant —very low ability	Children's hostels	Children's wards
	%	%	%	%	%	%	%	%	%
(a) Voluntary workers would be encouraged to take part in activities with the residents and give some training or advice	63	59	53	63	57	72	75	75	59
Voluntary workers would be encouraged but not given any training or advice	15	23	29	15	15	11	13	10	20
Voluntary workers would not be encouraged to take part in activities with the residents	22	18	18	22	28	17	12	15	21
	100	100	100	100	100	100	100	100	100
(b) At least one voluntary worker spent half an hour or longer with the residents in the previous fortnight	47	54	57	42	47	40	57	48	63
No voluntary workers spent half an hour or longer with the residents in the previous fortnight	53	46	43	58	53	60	43	52	37
	100	100	100	100	100	100	100	100	100
Base for percentages: all wards and hostels in which interviews were carried out with staff who had worked for over three months in the unit (reweighted)	248	100	65	177	74	40	24	24	33

6. CONTACT WITH STAFF IN OTHER PROFESSIONS AND INFLUENCE OVER DECISIONS ON INDIVIDUAL RESIDENTS

This chapter is concerned with the extent to which the staff work as part of a professional team and their involvement in routine discussions and key decisions affecting the lives of their residents. This is first approached by considering how recently staff discussed a resident's progress with members of various other professions. Clearly the staff could not be considered to be working as part of a professional team if, in fact, they rarely have any contact with other professions. The second part of the chapter provides some information on the relationship between the role of the nursing or care staff and that of other professions by examining the degree of influence the staff felt they had over decisions about individual residents, for example on admitting or transferring residents out of the units. Chapter 10 looks at the staff's opinions on the extent of contact they have with staff in other professions, and at their satisfaction or otherwise with the amount of influence they have over decisions about residents.

6.1 The residents' occupation during the day

The residents' occupation was touched upon previously in discussing the staff ratios and the staff's contact with residents during the day. It is considered here primarily because it is relevant to the later discussion of the staff's contact with staff from the occupational centres and school teachers.

The adult hostel residents were more likely than the adult hospital patients to have some sort of occupation during the day which was distinct from activities supervised by the hostel or ward staff (see table 47). Attending an occupational or recreational centre was related to the ability level of the patients and the proportion who attended was highest in the high ability wards (78%) and lowest in the non-ambulant wards (25%). The proportion of residents who "regularly" attended a centre was the same in the adult hostels as in the high ability wards[1] but in addition to this 13% of the hostel residents were in paid work outside the hostel, as compared with only 3% of the patients from the high ability wards.

In the children's wards 96% of the children aged from 5–15 regularly attended school or were seen by a teacher and in the children's hostels all apart from one child in this age range regularly attended school. Most of the children who did not go to school were said to have either a severe physical handicap (or illness), or to create too many behaviour problems for the schools.

These results can be compared with those obtained by Bone et al (1972) from a questionnaire sent to all sub-normality hospitals in England and Wales in 1965. They found that 39% of the adult patients attended an occupational centre and 48% of the children aged under 16 attended a school. These proportions are both lower than the comparable figures in this survey (60% and 87%) indicating that within the past 10 years the proportion of hospital patients who attend an occupational centre or school has increased. This is also confirmed by the DHSS statistics relating to the patients' occupation on a specific

---

[1]However a much lower proportion of the hostel residents, than of the patients from the high ability wards, had stayed in the care of the hostel or ward staff throughout the day (table 30) suggesting that the hostel residents may attend the centres more frequently than the hospital patients.

Table 47 The residents' attendance at schools, occupational centres and outside employment

	All wards†	All hostels†	Adult hostels high ability	Adult wards high ability	Adult wards average ability	Adult wards low ability	Adult wards non-ambulant —very low ability	Children's hostels	Children's wards
The percentage of the residents who regularly*	%	%	%	%	%	%	%	%	%
go to school or are seen by a teacher (for children aged 5–15)	9	16	0	2	2	7	6	86	75
go to any type of occupational, recreational or training centre, or sheltered workshop**	55	66	80	78	59	35	25	5	12
do any paid work outside the hospital or hostel	1	10	13	3	1	0	0	0	1
Base for percentages: total number of residents (reweighted)	8,441	1,260	1,416	2,983	2,699	1,347	742	325	673

*Comparing these proportions with those in table 30 shows that generally the proportion of the residents who "regularly" attended a school or centre is higher than the proportion who had attended a school or centre on the previous weekday. This was presumably because some of the patients and residents attended the centres regularly but not on a daily basis.
†Excluding acute sickness wards, and hostels with 3 or more residents who were not mentally handicapped.
**This category includes a few residents aged over 15 who were still attending school.

day in that in 1969 28% of the patients (of all ages) were in some form of occupation[2] compared with 55% in 1976. The increased proportions of patients who attend occupational centres or schools is one factor which has contributed to the improvement over the past 10 years in the average staff ratios in the wards (see chapter 3).

6.2 Contact with staff from the occupational centres and with teachers

The questions on contacts with staff in other professions were asked only of the daytime staff who had worked in their unit for at least 3 months (excluding trainee nurses).

Most, but not all, of the ward sisters and officers in charge seemed to have frequent discussions with staff from the occupational centres and with school teachers. In the units which had residents who attended occupational centres half of the ward sisters and three-quarters of the officers in charge had discussed the progress of at least one of their residents with a member of staff from the centre within the previous 4 weeks (see table 48). About three-quarters of the ward sisters and officers in charge, who had children who went to school, had discussed the progress of at least one of their children with a teacher within the previous 4 weeks. However a quarter of the ward sisters with patients who

Table 48 The time since the nursing or care staff last discussed the progress of any of their residents with staff from the occupational centres or with teachers.

The time since the nursing or care staff last discussed a resident's progress with:	Ward nursing staff on day shifts	Hostel staff on day shifts	Ward sisters	Officers in charge
	%	%	%	%
Staff from occupational or recreational centres				
Less than 4 weeks	33	34	52	77
At least 4 weeks but less than 6 months	17	15	22	18
6 months or longer	9	2	9	3
Never	41	49	17	1
	100	100	100	100
Base for percentages: day staff who have worked for at least 3 months in their ward or hostel and have residents who attend a centre (reweighted)	*205*	*230*	*175*	*93*
Teachers from their residents' schools	%	%	%	%
Less than 4 weeks	50	40	78	73
At least 4 weeks but less than 6 months	8	26	7	22
6 months or longer	7	1	6	0
Never	35	33	9	5
	100	100	100	100
Base for percentages: day staff who have worked for at least 3 months in their ward or hostel and have children who go to school (reweighted)	*83*	*110*	*68*	*41*

[2]Excluding patients who assisted with domestic work or in the Hospital Service Departments.

attended occupational centres had not discussed the progress of any of their residents with staff from the centres for at least 6 months compared with 4% of officers in charge; and 15% of the ward sisters with school children had not had this type of discussion with a teacher for at least 6 months compared with 5% of officers in charge.

The enrolled nurses, nursing assistants and care assistants had much less contact, than the more senior ward or hostel staff, with staff from the occupational centres or school teachers. About half or more of the staff in these grades had not discussed the progress of any of their residents with staff from the occupational centres or with school teachers for at least 6 months. In most of these cases the staff had never been involved in this type of discussion.

Within the previous two years only a third of the nursing and hostel staff had spent two hours or longer at one of the occupational centres with their residents either working with the staff or just observing the work. This implies that most of the staff's information on the activities of the centres was obtained from their residents or from discussions with the staff.

The optimal amount of contact between nursing and hostel staff on the one hand and those concerned with the education and occupation of residents on the other, has not been determined but it is generally assumed that fairly frequent contact is desirable for the residents. This would imply that some of the ward sisters should have more contact with staff from the occupational centres and with school teachers than at present, and also that it may be useful for the more junior ward or hostel staff to be involved more frequently in this type of discussion.

6.3 Contact with staff in other professions

Table 49 shows the overall number of staff in various professions per 100 resident hospital patients in England, 1976, from the DHSS statistics on facilities for the mentally handicapped. It is interesting to note that there were approximately ten times as many nurses as staff in all the other professions combined. As there were relatively few physiotherapists, speech therapists or chiropodists, contact with these professions was not included in the survey questions.

Table 49   Average number of staff in various professions per 100 resident patients in English hospitals for the mentally handicapped in 1976 (source DHSS 1976)

Staff per 100 resident patients	England 1976
Registered and enrolled nurses	21·5
Other nurses	27·02
Consultants in psychiatry*	0·34
Other hospital medical staff†	0·52
Rehabilitative therapists (occupational and industrial therapists)	2·55
Remedial therapists (physio, speech, chiropodists etc)	0·48
Social workers	0·31
Psychologists	0·25

*These include consultants in:—mental illness, mental illness children and adolescents and mental handicap, employed in mental handicap hospitals and units.
†Comparable figures are not available for GPs working in hospitals for the mentally handicapped on a sessional basis.

In comparison with officers in charge, the ward sisters generally had more contact with doctors and consultants but less contact with social workers (see table 50). Within the previous 4 weeks, 90% of the ward sisters had discussed a patient's progress with a junior member of the medical (psychiatric) staff, which was higher than the proportion who had held this type of discussion with a member of any of the other professions. This was to be expected as almost all of the wards were visited at least once a week by a ward doctor (or a GP) including 60% which were visited at least 5 times a week. In some cases the officers in charge only contacted a GP when a resident was ill so that 40% of them had not discussed a resident's progress with a GP for at least 4 weeks. Almost half of the officers in charge had not discussed a resident's progress with a consultant for at least 6 months or longer, as compared with less than a tenth of the ward sisters.

Although most of the ward sisters seemed to regularly discuss their residents' progress with the hospital medical staff, research in Wessex has found that the average number of recorded contacts between the medical staff and patients is relatively low (6·7 contacts per patient per year including contacts with GPs—see Glossop et al (1977)). This apparent discrepancy may stem from the outcome of these discussions rarely being recorded which the Wessex team feel is unlikely to result in any recommendations being consistently implemented, particularly if they involve more than one member of staff.

Eighty-one per cent. of the officers in charge had talked about one of their residents with a social worker in the previous 4 weeks, whereas a third of the ward sisters had not talked to a social worker for at least 6 months. The hostel staff probably had more contact than the nurses with social workers because the hostels were run by the local authority social services departments. Consequently social workers would usually be involved in deciding to admit or discharge the hostel residents whereas in the hospital this could be arranged by the consultants and GPs. However, the ward sisters who had not talked to a social worker about their patients for at least 6 months might have been able to develop closer links with their patients' families and with the community if they had had more contact with social workers.

The nursing and hostel staff seemed to have less contact with psychologists than with any of the other professions covered in the survey. This is presumably related to the comparative rarity of psychologists in the hospitals and in local authority employment. It is possible that the officers in charge would benefit from having more frequent contact with consultants or with psychologists because, as was seen in chapter 3, 12% of their residents had a serious behaviour problem (for example being aggressive, destructive or overactive). Although we could not examine the quality of the interaction between professional groups this section does show that the nursing and hostel staff are generally not working in isolation from other professional staff. Most of the wards were visited by medical or psychiatric staff at least once a week and 80% of the officers in charge had talked to a social worker about one of their residents within the previous 4 weeks. However the results do raise the questions firstly, of whether it would be valuable for the nurses to have more contact with social workers and secondly, of whether some of the officers in charge would be assisted by having more contact with consultant psychiatrists or with psychologists.

69

Table 50   The time since the nursing or care staff last discussed the progress of any of their residents with a member of other specified professions

The time since the nursing or care staff last discussed a resident's progress with:—	Trained nurses— ward nurses on day shifts	Officers in charge and deputies*	Ward sisters	Officers in charge
Consultant psychiatrists for the mentally handicapped	%	%	%	%
Less than 4 weeks	52	22	66	30
At least 4 weeks but less than 6 months	20	26	25	23
6 months or longer	11	20	6	24
Never	17	32	3	23
	100	100	100	100
Other hospital medical staff or GPs				
Less than 4 weeks	79	50	90	59
At least 4 weeks but less than 6 months	14	29	8	27
6 months or longer	2	8	2	5
Never	5	13	1	9
	100	100	100	100
Social workers				
Less than 4 weeks	38	74	47	81
At least 4 weeks but less than 6 months	20	19	19	14
6 months or longer	17	4	17	4
Never	25	3	16	1
	100	100	100	100
Psychologists				
Less than 4 weeks	17	11	23	17
At least 4 weeks but less than 6 months	21	14	22	16
6 months or longer	22	19	25	19
Never	40	56	30	49
	100	100	100	100
Base for percentages: day staff who have worked for at least 3 months in their ward or hostel (reweighted)	*155*	*102**	*195*	*107*

Combined figures are presented for the officers in charge and deputies as these hostel grades are most closely equivalent to the trained nurses. The base figures for the officers in charge and deputies combined is slightly smaller than the base figure for the officers in charge because of the reweighting factors used to combine grades.

6.4   Participation in decisions affecting the care of the residents

This section examines the extent to which the staff take part in discussions about their residents and in making decisions which affect their residents' care. The main objective was to find out whether the nursing and care staff were involved in making decisions as part of a mixed professional team, or whether the nursing or care staff, or other professions, made these decisions by themselves.

Case conferences   The DHSS has recommended that regular discussions should be held at ward level between doctors, nurses and other therapeutic staff (*Better Services for the Mentally Handicapped* paragraph 228, 1971). It was therefore surprising to find that a third of the trained nurses and a sixth of the officers in charge and deputies said that no case conferences or discussions on individual residents were held with staff from other professions (see table 51). It is possible that some of the nurses did not know that case conferences were in fact held because they were not invited to attend, as only 16% of the nursing officers responsible for wards said that no case conferences were held.

Table 51 Attendance at and participation in case conferences or discussions with members of other professions on individual residents

	Nursing officers responsible for wards	Ward sisters	Staff nurses	Enrolled nurses	Officers in charge	Deputies
	%	%	%	%	%	%
Last attended a case conference (or discussion):						
Less than 3 months ago*	68	40	42	22	55	52
3 months ago or longer	10	19	17	30	26	20
Has never attended a case conference (or did not know whether they were held)	6	4	12	20	2	10
Case conferences were not held on their residents	16	37	29	28	17	18
	100	100	100	100	100	100
Participation in case conferences (or discussions)						
Staff in their grades usually contribute to the discussion at case conferences*	Not asked	46	42	33	73	55
Most of the talking at the case conferences is done by more senior staff or staff in other professions	Not asked	6	2	6	8	11
Case conferences are not held, or they do not usually attend the case conferences	28	47	56	61	19	34
		100	100	100	100	100
Base for percentages: day staff who have worked in their ward or hostel for at least 3 months (reweighted)	*50*	*195*	*48*	*66*	*107*	*56*

*The cumulated number of the two asterisked codes formed part of the score on the scale of participation in decisions (see table 54). As nursing officers were not asked about participating in the discussion at case conferences it was assumed, for this purpose, that nursing officers who usually attended case conferences also contributed to the discussions.

The registered nurses, it seemed, attended case conferences more frequently than the enrolled nurses, but not as frequently as the nursing officers or officers in charge. Most of the nursing and care staff who regularly attended case conferences said they contributed to the discussion but about 12% of those who attended said that most of the talking was done by more senior staff in other professions.

Meetings of the ward or hostel staff We asked whether meetings of the ward or hostel staff were held to discuss individual residents as it was felt that this would give an indication of whether the more junior staff had an opportunity to participate in deciding on the appropriate care for their residents. About two thirds of the junior staff, ie below the ward sister or officer in charge grades, said that this type of formal or informal meeting was held in their unit. Most of these junior staff said that staff in their grades regularly attended and contributed to the discussions (see table 52). A higher proportion of the ward sisters

71

Table 52 Attendance at and participation in meetings† of the ward or hostel staff held to discuss individual residents

	Nursing officers responsible for wards	Ward sisters	Officers in charge	Other nurses	Other hostel staff
Has attended this type of formal or informal meeting:	%	%	%	%	%
Less than 3 months ago*	75	81	71	56	55
3 months ago or longer	6	2	9	11	7
Their ward or hostel does not hold this type of meeting (or they have never attended this type of meeting)	19	17	20	33	38
	100	100	100	100	100
Participation in these meetings:					
Staff in their grades usually contribute to the discussion at these meetings	Not asked			58	53
Most of the talking at these meetings is done by the more senior staff	Not asked			8	9
Their ward or hostel does not hold this type of meeting (or they do not usually attend the meetings)	33	17	25	34	38
				100	100
Base for percentage: all day staff who have worked in their ward or hostel for at least 3 months (reweighted)	*50*	*195*	*107*	*183*	*225*

†*This referred to formal or informal meetings of the ward nursing staff or hostel care staff which lasted for at least a quarter of an hour.*
This is one of the items used to form scores on the scale of participation in decisions (see table 54).

and officers in charge than of the more junior staff said that they held this type of meeting which suggests that some meetings may have involved only the more senior staff.

The influence of senior ward and hostel staff over decisions affecting individual residents The officers in charge, nursing officers and ward sisters were asked whether they took part in making the final decision or whether their views were fully taken into account in making the following five types of decisions:—

(1) Whether a new resident should be admitted to their unit.

(2) Whether a resident should be transferred out of their unit.

(3) Whether a resident should attend a training centre or occupational therapy unit.

(4) Whether a resident should attend a school.

(5) Whether a resident should be allowed to go home with relatives for the weekend.

The officers in charge generally had more influence over each of these decisions than the nursing officers or ward sisters, and the nursing officers more than the ward sisters (see table 53). At least two thirds of the officers in charge took part in making each decision, including 72% who normally made the final decisions themselves, on allowing a resident to go home for the weekend. By contrast less than half of the ward sisters took part in making decisions (1)–(4) and only 28% normally made the final decision on letting a patient go home for the weekend.

The ward sisters had less influence over admitting a new patient or transferring a patient out of their ward than over any of the other decisions. Slightly over half of the ward sisters said their views were not fully taken into account or they had no influence over admitting a new patient and 41% had little or no influence over transferring a patient out of their ward. The nursing officers had slightly more influence over these decisions than the ward sisters but even so about two fifths of them said their views were not fully taken into account in deciding to admit a patient to their wards and almost a third said the same about the decision on whether to transfer a patient out of their wards.

About 80% of the ward sisters and nursing officers who did not take part in deciding whether a patient should be admitted to or transferred from their wards said that the final decision was taken by a consultant.

According to the interviewed nurses the consultants also took part in making about half of the other types of decisions which were not made by the ward sisters or nursing officers, with the remainder being taken by the more junior medical (psychiatric) staff, senior nursing officers or staff from the schools or occupational centres. Most of the decisions on the hostel residents, which had not been made by the officers in charge, had been taken by residential homes advisors, social workers or more senior social services staff.

6.5 "Participation in decisions" scale

In order to summarise the results from the previous section and relate them to other aspects of the staff's role a scale was formed which indicated the extent to which the ward sisters, nursing officers and officers in charge took part in making decisions or in discussions on their residents. The score on the scale was equal to the number of the decisions (with a maximum of four[3]) in which the staff participated or made by themselves, plus an additional score of one for each asterisked item in tables 51 and 52 indicating attending a case conference or a staff discussion within the previous three months, or contributing to the discussion at case conferences. Staff with the maximum score of seven normally took part in making each of the decisions affecting individual residents and had attended a case conference and staff discussion within the previous three months, whereas staff with the minimum score of zero were not involved in making any of the decisions, had not attended a case conference or staff discussion for at least three months and did not contribute to the discussion at case conferences.

The officers in charge had the highest average scores on the scale (4.9), followed by the nursing officers (4.2) and the ward sisters (3.3) (see table 54).

[3] As less than half the staff worked in units which had children who went to school, the staff's influence over deciding whether a resident should go to school was only scored, in forming the scale, for the staff who had no contact with occupational centres.

Table 53 The amount of influence that the senior staff had over various decisions affecting the care of the residents in their ward(s) or hostel for:
(a) Ward sisters (w.s.)
(b) Nursing officers responsible for wards (n.o.)
(c) Officers in charge (o.c.)

Amount of influence over decisions on:—		Normally make the final decision them-selves†	Participate in making the decision as part of a team†	Their views are fully taken into account but they do not take part in making the decision	Their views are not fully taken into account or they have no influence over this decision	Total
		%	%	%	%	%
(1) Whether a new resident should be admitted to their ward or hostel	(a) w.s.	2	21	23	55	100
	(b) n.o.	4	42	13	42	100
	(c) o.c.	30	44	8	19	100
(2) Whether a resident should be transferred out of their ward or hostel	(a) w.s.	4	26	30	41	100
	(b) n.o.	8	40	22	30	100
	(c) o.c.	9	58	17	16	100
(3) Whether a resident should attend a training centre or occupational therapy unit	(a) w.s.	12	35	25	28	100
	(b) n.o.	18	53	11	29	100
	(c) o.c.	24	50	11	15	100
(4) Whether a resident should attend a school	(a) w.s.	9	29	26	36	100
	(b) n.o.	0	50	15	35	100
	(c) o.c.	38	41	0	21	100
(5) Whether a resident should be allowed to go home with relatives for the weekend	(a) w.s.	28	37	19	15	100
	(b) n.o.	29	29	19	23	100
	(c) o.c.	72	27	1	0	100

Base for percentages: daytime ward sisters and officers in charge who have worked in their ward or hostel for at least 3 months, and nursing officers responsible for wards (reweighted)	*for (1)–(2) and (5)* *(a) 195* *(b) 50* *(c) 107*	*for (3)* *(a) 170* *staff with* *residents* *attending* *these* *centres* *(b) 45* *(c) 82*	*for (4)* *(a) 66* *staff with* *children* *attending* *school* *(b) 20* *(c) 29*

*Excluding a few staff who said that decisions (3), (4) or (5) did not apply in their units.

†The number of the decisions that the staff normally made or participated in making formed part of the score on the scale of participation in decisions (see table 54). As only a few of the staff had contact with both occupational centres and schools, the staff's influence over decision (4) was scored, only for staff who said that decision (3) was not applicable to their residents.

Only 2% of the officers in charge, compared with 19% of the ward sisters and 12% of the nursing officers had scores of zero or one indicating that these hospital staff had relatively little involvement in making decisions on their patients or in discussions with staff from other professions.

In general, the scores of the ward sisters on the participation in decisions scales were not related to the ability level of their wards.

Table 54 The scores of the ward sisters and officers in charge on a scale indicating the extent to which they participate in making decisions affecting the care of their residents

Scores on participation in decisions scale* High scores indicate that the staff are more likely to take part in decisions or discussions affecting the care of their residents	Ward sisters	Nursing Officers	Officers in charge
	%	%	%
0–1	19	12	2
2–3	38	28	20
4–5	31	26	38
6–7	12	35	40
	100	100	100
Average score	3·3	4·2	4·9
Base for percentages: daytime ward sisters and officers in charge who had worked in their ward or hostel for at least 3 months, and nursing officers responsible for wards (reweighted)	*196*	*50*	*107*

*The scores on this scale are equal to the number of decisions which the staff make themselves or participate in making as part of a team (see table 53); plus the number of asterisked items in tables 51 and 52 indicating attending a case conference or staff discussion in the previous 3 months and usually contributing to the discussion at case conferences.

The relationship between the extent to which the staff participate in making decisions and the running of the units King et al (1971) have suggested that a lack of overall responsibility for their patients was one factor which led nurses in children's wards compared with staff in children's hostels to adopt an institutional approach to the care of the children. More recently a study on three American institutes for mentally handicapped adults by Raynes et al (1977) found that the provision of care which stimulated the residents was positively related to the extent to which the unit heads (and other staff) were involved in making decisions on various aspects of their work. Taking part in making decisions on individual residents is one way that the staff can have more overall responsibility and it is therefore useful to look at the way this related to the number of restrictions within the units covered in the present survey.

For the ward sisters there was a positive correlation between taking part in making more decisions and working in a ward which had fewer restrictions (see table 55). The ward sisters with scores of six or seven on the participation in decisions scale ie who had the most influence over the decisions were in wards with an average of 2·2 restrictions whereas the ward sisters with scores of 0–1 were in wards with an average of 3·7 restrictions. It was seen earlier that there was a relationship between the ability level of the wards and the number of restrictions in the wards which might have led to this correlation. However further analysis showed that the association between taking part in making more decisions and working in a ward with fewer restrictions could not be attributed to differences in the abilities of the patients.

It is worth pointing out that ward sisters having relatively little influence over decisions on their patients would be consistent with there being a more rigid and hierarchical style of management within their hospitals. These ward

75

sisters may find that they are generally not encouraged to minimise the extent of restrictions on their patients which would contribute to the association between having relatively little influence over decisions and adopting more restrictions in running the wards.

The average number of restrictions in the hostels did not vary with the extent to which the officers in charge were involved in decision making.

Table 55 The relationship between the extent to which the ward sisters participate in making decisions on their patients and the extent of restrictions on their wards

Scores on number of restrictions scale	All day time ward sisters*	Ward sisters—scores on participation in decisions scale			
		0–1	2–3	4–5	6–7
	%	%	%	%	%
0–2	30	14	18	39	68
3–4	48	62	58	36	18
5–8	23	24	24	24	14
	100	100	100	100	100
Average number of restrictions	3·3	3·7	3·6	3·1	2·2
Base: daytime ward sisters* who had worked in their ward for at least 3 months (reweighted)	196	37	74	61	24

*Excluding 6 ward sisters who were not working in the ward to which they were allocated at the time of sampling.

6.6 Discussion on the extent to which the staff take part in making decisions on individual residents

The previous sections of this chapter raise the question of whether the nursing and hostel staff, and particularly the ward sisters and nursing officers should, in the interests of their residents, have more influence over decisions affecting individual residents. Although in some cases it may be inappropriate for the ward or hostel staff to make the final decision, for example on whether a resident should be transferred to a different unit, it should usually be possible for them to contribute to such decisions. It was seen in chapter 5 that almost three-quarters of the ward sisters had worked in their ward for a year or longer and so would have considerable experience of their patients' abilities. It was therefore surprising to find that the ward sisters and nursing officers frequently felt that their views were not taken fully into account in making important decisions on individual patients.

This survey is particularly concerned with the social care provided by the staff, by which we mean the extent to which the staff take into account their residents' individuality, and enable the residents to achieve their full potential to live as independently as possible. The fact that the ward sisters and nursing officers were often not involved in decisions on admitting or transferring their patients, or in deciding whether a patient should attend a training centre or go to school, could reduce the quality of the social care provided for the patients in three main ways. Firstly there is the possibility that these staff will perceive their social role as being of minor importance if they are not expected to contribute their views on these major questions affecting the lives of their patients. These staff may then devote most of their interest and energy to other aspects of their work (for example providing basic care for the patients, or maintaining routines which prevent any trouble in the wards), leaving the responsibility for the residents' social development to staff in other professions. There is some support for this speculation from the association between having relatively little influence over these decisions and adopting more restrictions in running the wards. Also it will be seen in Chapter 8 that whereas 82% of all the daytime ward sisters felt that the most important aim of their ward was connected with providing social care for the patients, this proportion was highest (96%) amongst the ward sisters who had scores of 6–7 on the participation in decisions scale and lowest (72%) amongst the ward sisters who had scores of 0–1 on the participation scale.

Secondly, it is possible that the nurses who do not take part in case conferences or discussions will be less effective in attempting to develop their residents to their full potential. This is partly because they may have less reason and fewer opportunities to cultivate an insight into the problems of individual residents (for example, connected with their home situation, or with the implication of any physical handicaps) and partly because they may lack the opportunity to profit from the views of other professions.

Thirdly there is the danger that the staffs' morale will be depressed by a lack of influence over decisions affecting individual patients, particularly amongst the staff who place the most importance on the social caring side of their work. This is discussed more fully in chapter 10 which shows that the vast majority of the nurses with the lowest scores on the participation in decisions scale were dissatisfied with the amount of influence they had over decisions on admitting or transferring patients. If such specific dissatisfactions lead to low morale, this in turn could reduce the staff's concern with the effectiveness of their social role and possibly result in a higher staff turnover.

Although the above points have been primarily discussed in connection with the ward sisters and nursing officers, they may also apply to the smaller proportion of the officers in charge who have relatively little influence over these decisions or who do not attend case conferences on their residents.

7. THE STAFF'S GENERAL ATTITUDES TOWARDS MENTALLY HANDICAPPED PEOPLE

It is often assumed that the staff's general views on the possibility of developing the capacities of mentally handicapped people affects the emphasis they place on the social caring side of their role. An example of this type of assumption is the suggestion by Jones (1975) that nurses in wards with the most severely handicapped patients have no interest in teaching their patients because they believe that the severely mentally handicapped are effectively without a mind or brain.

The two main objectives of this chapter are : firstly to compare the staff's views on the potential of the mentally handicapped with those implicit in the Government's White Paper *Better Services for the Mentally Handicapped* (1971), and secondly to discover whether their views are reflected in the way they carry out their work. The relationships between the staff's views and their type of formal training will be considered in a later chapter.

7.1 Method of obtaining information on the staff's attitudes

The main attitudes of interest were on the scope for developing the individual potential of mentally handicapped people and on the value of community care and provision for the mentally handicapped. In addition to these topics the staff's views on sterilisation and sexual relationships of the mentally handicapped were covered because pilot work for the survey and other research had indicated that there were potential difficulties for the staff in this area.

The staff were asked to consider 12 statements on these topics and to tick a box to show whether they agreed or disagreed, strongly or slightly, with each. Staff who were unable to tick a box because they said they did not know how they felt about a statement were included with those who said they neither agreed nor disagreed.

Several of the statements on the scope for developing the potential of the mentally handicapped were derived from items used by Jones (1975) in assessing nurses' attitudes on a "treatment orientation scale".

The complete list of the statements was:
  (a) On the value of developing the individual potential of mentally handicapped people:—

> Low grade patients can make considerable progress with a carefully designed training programme.
> We cannot expect to understand the odd behaviour of patients/residents.
> A carefully designed training programme for a patient is more important than kindness.
> Adult patients/residents should be treated like young children.
> Mentally handicapped patients/residents appreciate attractive surroundings.

  (b) On the value of community care and provision for the mentally handicapped:—

> Hardly any mentally handicapped adults who are at present in hospitals are capable of living in local authority hostels.
> Hardly any severely mentally handicapped children could be properly looked after at home by their parents.

78

Residential homes or hospitals for the mentally handicapped should be sited as close as possible to the community they serve.

More mentally handicapped adults could benefit from being in paid employment (apart from in a hospital job or a sheltered workshop).

Mentally handicapped patients who have been discharged from hospitals are often not properly cared for in hostels.

(c) On sterilisation and sexual relationships of the mentally handicapped:—

More mentally handicapped patients/residents should be sterilised.

Mentally handicapped adults should be discouraged from developing sexual relationships.

It can be seen that all the statements are of a general nature and were not intended to relate specifically to the group of residents cared for by the informant. The next chapter examines what the staff felt they were aiming to achieve for the residents in their own ward or hostel.

7.2 Attitudes towards the value of developing the individual potential of mentally handicapped patients or residents

One of the central principles of *Better Services for the Mentally Handicapped* was that each mentally handicapped person needs appropriate stimulation, training, education and occupation in order to develop to his maximum capacity and to exercise the skills he acquires, however limited they may be.

A clear majority of both the nurses and hostel staff indicated that they appreciated the value of developing the individual potential of mentally handicapped people in four of the five ways exemplified by the statements on this topic (see table 56). The exception was that only a third of both staff groups agreed that a carefully designed training programme was more important than kindness. However, the interpretation of responses to this statement is uncertain because some of the staff may have been contrasting not having a training programme with being unkind and so answered that kindness was more important. Generally only a small minority of the staff expressed pessimistic views on the other four statements but a quarter of the nurses and of the hostel staff felt that they could not expect to understand the odd behaviour of patients or residents.

Four of these statements were included in a similar, though not always identical, form in the research carried out by Jones in 1972. In each case the responses given by the nurses in the present survey indicated a more optimistic attitude towards the value of training than those reported by Jones: on average the proportion of the nurses who gave an "optimistic" response was greater by 22% in the present survey. However, we cannot tell whether these differences reflect an improvement in the nurses' attitudes since 1972 or are related to the changes in the wording of the statements or to the fact that the 1972 results were obtained in one Region and may have not been nationally representative.

7.3 Scope for individual development scale

(a) **Derivation.** In order to relate the staff's attitudes to other aspects of their work they were assigned scores on a scale which summarised their views on the possibility of developing the individual potential of mentally handicapped

Table 56 Staff's attitudes on the scope for developing the individual potential of mentally handicapped patients or residents

	Daytime ward nurses			Daytime hostel staff		
	Agree slightly or strongly	Neither agree nor disagree	Disagree slightly or strongly	Agree slightly or strongly	Neither agree nor disagree	Disagree slightly or strongly
	%	%	%	%	%	%
Low grade patients can make considerable progress with a carefully designed training programme	84*	5	11	89	7	5
We cannot expect to understand the odd behaviour of patients/residents	26	9	65	23	7	70
A carefully designed training programme for a patient is more important than kindness	33	13	55	34	11	56
Adult patients/residents should be treated like young children	15	10	75	6	3	91
Mentally handicapped patients/residents appreciate attractive surroundings	93	4	3	88	7	5
Base for percentages: all ward nursing and hostel staff on day shifts (reweighted)	324			285		

*The bold figures show the "optimistic" responses used in forming the scope for individual development scale (see page 79).

people. The scores were calculated by allotting a score from one to five on each of the statements depending on whether the respondent had given a strongly optimistic response (scoring five), slightly optimistic (scoring four), neither (scoring three), slightly pessimistic (scoring two) or strongly pessimistic response (scoring one). For three of the statements optimistic answers involved agreeing with the statement while for the other two optimistic answers involved disagreeing (as shown in table 56). These scores were then added to form a staff member's score on the scope for individual development scale on which the maximum score of 25 is taken to represent a strong belief in the value and possibility of individual development and the minimum score of five represents the opposite.

(b) Relationship with the staff's grade and type of unit. There was only a slight difference between the average scores of the daytime nurses (19·3) and the hostel staff (20·2) on the scope for development scale (see table 57). Although this difference was significant in a statistical sense it could have come about, for example, simply through most of the hostel staff giving a "strongly" optimistic response to one of the statements to which the nurses had only given a "slightly" optimistic response. The results in table 56 show that there were only minor differences between the two staff groups in the proportions agreeing with each statement.

Table 57   The staff's scores on the scope for individual development scale

High scores indicate a strong belief in the scope for individual development	All ward nursing staff on day shifts	All hostel staff on day shifts
	%	%
23–25	12	19
20–22	39	47
17–19	33	27
5–16	16	8
	100	100
Average score	19·3	20·2
Standard deviation	2·9	2·8
Base for percentages: all ward nursing staff and hostel staff (reweighted)	324	285

The differences in the average scores between the staff grades were very small but, in both the hospitals and hostels, it was the more senior staff and the trainee nurses, who had the more optimistic views (see table 58). On the other hand, staff in the more junior grades (the enrolled nurses and nursing and care assistants) expressed more pessimistic views. Jones (1972) and Moores et al (1976) using comparable attitude scales also found that enrolled nurses and nursing assistants had more pessimistic attitudes than the other nurses. As the majority of the ward and hostel staff were in one of these junior grades it follows that any action taken to raise the staff's expectations of the potential capacities of the mentally handicapped should cover these grades as well as trainees and the more senior staff.

Table 58 Average scores on the scope for individual development scale analysed by grades and type of unit

	Senior nursing staff	Ward sisters	Staff nurses	Enrolled nurses	Nursing assistants	Student nurses	Pupil nurses	Officers in charge	Deputies	Care assistants
Average scores on the scope for individual development scale	21·0	19·9	19·9	19·1	18·7	20·3	19·6	21·1	20·6	19·8
Base: ward and hostel day staff and senior nursing staff (reweighted)	113	213	58	75	129	53	48	115	59	177

Type of unit

	DAY STAFF IN						
	Adult hostels high ability	Adult wards high ability	Adult wards average ability	Adult wards low ability	Adult wards non-ambulant —very low ability	Children's hostels	Children's wards
Average scores on the scope for individual development scale	20·4	19·5	19·1	19·1	19·3	20·0	19·8
Base: ward and hostel day staff (reweighted)	174	71	77	42	33	76	41

82

The extent to which the nurses believed in the possibility of developing the potential of the mentally handicapped was not related to the ability level of the patients in their wards (see table 58). There is therefore no evidence from the survey to suggest that the patients in the higher ability wards had acquired more of the basic skills (such as being able to wash and dress themselves) because their nurses had a stronger general belief than nurses in lower ability wards in the scope for individual development. However, it may be that differences between staff working with different ability levels would have appeared had the statements been related to the residents in the staff's own units rather than to mentally handicapped patients or residents in general.

Only slight differences were found between the general attitudes of staff in units with relatively good staff ratios and staff in units with relatively poor staff ratios.

7.4 The relationship between the staff's attitudes towards the scope for individual development and the work they carried out

Within both the wards and hostels the staff's general views on the scope for developing the individual potential of mentally handicapped people were consistent to some extent with the work they carried out in their units although the differences found between groups were small. The staff who most strongly believed in the possibilities for individual development were rather more likely than others to have spent over an hour on one of the social tasks such as teaching or playing with their residents (see table 59 (a) and (b)). When assisting with basic care a higher proportion of the staff with the more optimistic attitudes, than of the other staff, were mainly encouraging their residents rather than actually doing these tasks for them. Similarly the staff with the more optimistic attitudes towards individual development tended to be in units in which there were fewer restrictions on the residents. Conversely the nurses who were in the small group of wards in which most or all of the restrictions were applied were the most pessimistic about the scope for developing the potential abilities of mentally handicapped people.

This section shows that there is some evidence that staff with the more optimistic attitudes towards individual development tended to work in ways which were more likely to develop their residents to their full potential. However the relationships between the staff's attitudes and their work were fairly tenuous and their implications unclear. In the first place the relationships may be limited partly because there are constraints (eg shortages of recreational facilities) which prevent the staff from working in ways which are consistent with their views. Secondly, the relationships which were found may mean that the staff's attitudes influence their work or conversely that the way they work affects their attitudes. For example a unit with a custodial approach which produces no progress in residents may generate a pessimistic view of the potentialities of the mentally handicapped which engulfs new staff, after they arrive, irrespective of any formal training they have received.

7.5 Attitudes towards community provision for the mentally handicapped

Better Services for the Mentally Handicapped recommended that mentally handicapped people should not be segregated unnecessarily from the general

Table 59 (a) Relationships between the nurses' scores on the scope for individual development scale and their work. Higher scores on this scale indicate a stronger belief in the possibility of developing the individual potential of mentally handicapped people

For daytime ward nursing staff	Nurses—scores on scope for individual development scale			
	High 23–25	20–22	17–19	Low 5–16
(i) Proportion of the nurses with the stated scores who spent over an hour on one of the social tasks	% 47	% 47	% 44	% 31
Base: all daytime ward nursing staff (reweighted)	*39*	*121*	*105*	*49*
(ii) Proportion of the nurses with the stated scores who assisted with feeding, washing or dressing and spent most of this time:—	%	%	%	%
encouraging their patients to do these tasks for themselves	46	35	29	29
actually feeding, washing or dressing the patients	54	65	71	71
	100	100	100	100
Base: daytime ward nurses who had assisted with these tasks* on their previous day at work (reweighted)	*27*	*67*	*67*	*34*
(iii) Average number of restrictions in the wards of these nurses	3·1	3·6	3·5	4·3
Base: daytime ward nurses (excluding trainees) who had worked in a sampled ward for at least 3 months (reweighted)	*24*	*81*	*69*	*37*

*Excluding nurses who mainly assisted by supervising while their patients fed, washed and dressed themselves, or who were unable to say how they spent most of their time.

life of the public, and that subnormality hospitals should be responsible only for patients who required specialist medical treatment or constant nursing care. It recognised that, because of the shortage of residential facilities in the community, the hospitals contained many patients who when first admitted needed residential rather than nursing care, and recommended that local authority residential services should be expanded so as to enable many of these patients to be discharged. A recent report by the National Development Group,[1] which considered these principles with reference to children, stated that improved domiciliary support would make it possible for most mentally handicapped children to be properly looked after by their families and so reduce the number of children who were admitted to subnormality hospitals. It is estimated that at present about 80% of severely mentally handicapped children live with their families.

[1]Mentally Handicapped Children: A Plan for Action (1977).

Table 59 (b) Relationships between the scores of the hostel staff on the scope for individual development scale and their work. Higher scores on this scale indicate a stronger belief in the possibility of developing the individual potential of mentally handicapped people.

For daytime hostel staff	Hostel staff—scores on scope for individual development scale			
	High 23–25	20–22	17–19	Low 5–16
	%	%	%	%
(i) Proportion of the staff with the stated scores who spent over an hour on one of the social tasks	51	45	41	33
Base: all daytime hostel staff (reweighted)	*52*	*130*	*78*	*25*
(ii) Proportion of the staff with the stated scores who assisted with feeding, washing or dressing* and spent most of this time:—		%		%
encouraging their residents to do these tasks for themselves		72†		64†
actually feeding, washing or dressing the residents		28		36
Base: daytime hostel staff who had assisted with these tasks on their previous day at work (reweighted)*		*60*		*38*
(iii) Average number of restrictions in their hostels	2·1	2·3	2·3	2·8
Base: daytime hostel staff who had worked in their hostels for at least 3 months (reweighted)	*44*	*111*	*64*	*20*

Excluding staff who mainly assisted by supervising while their residents fed, washed and dressed themselves, or who were unable to say how they spent most of the time.
†*These scores have been combined because of the small numbers of staff in the high and low groups who had assisted with these tasks.*

In contrast to the positive emphasis on community care in the White Paper the nurses expressed only qualified support for community provision and integration of the mentally handicapped (see table 60). The hostel staff, however, were generally in favour of community care. Slightly over a third of the nurses compared with 13% of hostel staff felt that hardly any adult hospital patients were capable of living in local authority hostels and about 40% of the nurses but only a quarter of the hostel staff thought that hardly any severely mentally handicapped children could be properly looked after by their parents. The nurses were particularly sceptical about the quality of care provided for discharged patients living in hostels although this view may not have been unreasonable because of recent adverse publicity about some privately run hostels.[2]

[2]The survey took place within six months of a television programme about the care provided for discharged patients in some privately run hostels.

Table 60 Staff's attitudes towards caring for and integrating the mentally handicapped within the community

	Daytime ward nurses			Daytime hostel staff		
	Agree slightly or strongly	Neither agree nor disagree	Disagree slightly or strongly	Agree slightly or strongly	Neither agree nor disagree	Disagree slightly or strongly
	%	%	%	%	%	%
Hardly any mentally handicapped adults who are at present in hospitals are capable of living in local authority hostels	36	8	55*	13	9	78
Hardly any severely mentally handicapped children could be properly looked after at home by their parents	43	9	48	26	11	62
Residential homes or hospitals for the mentally handicapped should be sited as close as possible to the community they serve	86	7	7	94	4	3
More mentally handicapped adults could benefit from being in paid employment (apart from a hospital job or a sheltered workshop)	80	9	11	90	5	5
Mentally handicapped patients who have been discharged from hospitals are often not properly cared for in hostels	37	37	26	18	11	71
Base for percentages: all ward nursing and hostel staff on day shifts (reweighted)		324			285	

*The bold figures show the "positive" responses used in forming the community orientation scale (see page 87).

7.6 Community orientation scale

(a) **Derivation** A scale was formed to summarise the staff's orientation towards caring for and integrating the mentally handicapped within the community. The staff were assigned scores derived from their responses to the five statements shown in table 60 using the same method as for the scope for individual development scale. The maximum score of 25 is taken to mean unqualified support for community integration whereas the minimum score of 5 indicates complete disapproval.

(b) **Relationship with the staff's grades and type of unit** The daytime nurses had a lower average score (17·9) on the community orientation scale than the hostel staff (21·1) and this difference was more marked than the differences between these staff on the scope for individual development scale (table 61). In general the more senior staff and trainee nurses had higher average scores than others, indicating that they had a more positive attitude towards the possibility of community care (see table 62).

Table 61 The staff's scores on the community orientation scale

Higher scores indicate having a more positive attitude towards caring for and integrating the mentally handicapped within the community	All ward nursing staff on day shifts	All hostel staff on day shifts
23–25	8	33
20–22	25	40
17–19	34	18
5–16	33	8
	100	100
Average score	17·9	21·1
Standard derivation	3·4	2·9
Base for percentages all ward nursing staff and hostel staff (reweighted)	*324*	*285*

The nurses' scores on the community orientation scale scarcely varied with the ability level of their wards (see table 62). This suggests that the nurses' comparative lack of enthusiasm for community care may stem from their hospital backgrounds rather than from an objective appraisal of whether community facilities could be suitable for their patients.

The staff's orientation towards community provision was positively related to their attitude towards the scope for developing the individual potential of mentally handicapped people so that, in general, staff who agreed that more mentally handicapped people could be integrated within the community were also more optimistic about the capacity of mentally handicapped people to develop with suitable training.

7.7 The relationship between the staff's orientation towards community care and the work they carried out

No consistent relationships were found between the nurses' orientation towards community provision for the mentally handicapped and the type of

Table 62 Average scores on the community orientation scale analysed by grades and type of unit

	Senior nursing staff	Ward sisters	Staff nurses	Enrolled nurses	Nursing assistants	Student nurses	Pupil nurses	Officers in charge	Deputies	Care assistants
Average scores on community orientation scale	19·6	18·3	18·9	17·7	17·3	18·7	18·4	21·5	21·9	20·7
Base: ward and hostel day staff and senior nursing staff (reweighted)	113	213	58	75	129	53	48	115	59	177
Type of unit	DAY STAFF IN Adult hostels high ability	Adult wards high ability	Adult wards average ability	Adult wards low ability	Adult wards non-ambulant —very low ability	Children's hostels	Children's wards			
Average scores on community orientation scale	21·4	17·7	17·4	17·7	17·7	20·8	18·3			
Base: ward and hostel day staff	174	71	77	42	33	76	41			

care they provided for their patients. This suggests that the nurses' general attitude towards integrating the mentally handicapped within the community does not directly affect their present work and is not affected by it. The suggestion is tentative because it is based on an analysis which is restricted to only a few facets of the staff's work.

However the views of the hostel staff on the value of community provision for the mentally handicapped were related to their work in a similar way to their views on the value of individual development. In general the hostel staff who had a more positive orientation towards integrating the mentally handi-capped within the community were in hostels in which fewer restrictions were applied and were more likely to have spent over an hour on one of the social tasks (see table 63). Thus the hostel staff who were more strongly in favour of community integration tended to carry out their work in ways which were more likely to enable it to take place.

Table 63 The relationship between the hostel staff's orientation towards commu-nity provision for the mentally handicapped, the time they spent on social tasks and the extent of restrictions in their units.

| | Scores on orientation towards community provision scale | | | |
	High 23–25	20–22	17–19	Low 5–16
Proportion of the staff who spent over an hour on one of the social tasks	47%	45%	43%	26%
Base: all daytime hostel staff (reweighted)	*95*	*116*	*52*	*23*
Average number of restrictions in their hostel	2·1	2·3	2·4	2·8
Base: daytime hostel staff who had worked in their hostel for at least 3 months (reweighted)	*86*	*94*	*43*	*17*

7.8 Attitudes towards sterilisation and sexual relationships

Over the past 20 years reports from several countries have shown that with suitable support many mentally handicapped people are able to marry and live together successfully (A and M Craft, 1976). There are varied opinions on the question of sterilisation: several authors warn of the adverse psychological effects of sterilisation and recommend other forms of birth control (eg Andron, 1973) whereas others recommend voluntary sterilisation for mentally handi-capped people who are likely to live in the community, mainly because of the stress and difficulties which may result when a mentally handicapped mother brings up a child (Pallister et al (1973)). However, there is generally agreement that advice on sexual behaviour and marriage counselling are essential for mentally handicapped people, and for their parents and the staff who care for them (M Craft, 1976, Perkins, 1976 and Community Care, July 1976).

The staff's attitudes towards the questions of sterilisation and of whether to discourage or encourage sexual relationships amongst the mentally handi-capped suggested that this was an area which sometimes presents them with

89

Table 64 The staff's attitudes towards sterilisation and sexual relationships of the mentally handicapped

	Daytime ward nurses			Daytime hostel staff		
	Agree slightly or strongly	Neither agree nor disagree	Disagree slightly or strongly	Agree slightly or strongly	Neither agree nor disagree	Disagree slightly or strongly
	%	%	%	%	%	%
More mentally handicapped patients/residents should be sterilised	40	24	36	45	25	29
Mentally handicapped adults should be discouraged from developing sexual relationships	27	20	53	19	22	59
Base for percentages: all ward nursing and hostel staff on day shifts (reweighted)	324			285		

90

difficulties. About two-fifths of both groups of staff felt that more mentally handicapped patients or residents should be sterilised (see table 64). A quarter of the nurses and a fifth of the hostel staff thought that adult residents should be discouraged from developing sexual relationships. When faced with such discouragement mentally handicapped people are likely to find it difficult to reach the point of marriage.

In considering this issue it is interesting to note that about a third of the wards contained only male patients, a third contained only females and a third were mixed, whereas almost all of the hostels were mixed. The nurses in the female wards and in the mixed wards were slightly more prone to worry about sexual relationships amongst the mentally handicapped than nurses in the male wards.

The following examples given by staff interviewed during the pilot work for the survey illustrate some of the difficulties that the staff said they faced in this area:—

"If a female resident wishes to go up to her room and a male decides to go as well, with only one care assistant, and me in my office otherwise engaged, there's nothing to stop that boy assaulting that girl—not without provocation from the female, she will entice him. You must always be on the alert, you can't leave them indefinitely". (A female officer in charge of a hostel for adults.)

"One of the boys who is in a wheelchair will get to one of the younger boys and fondle him, but we are on our toes to watch these and one or two of the girls who will pet up to the younger ones". (A female nursing assistant in a mixed adult ward.)

"One of the girls has sexual problems, she only has to see a man and she tends to strip off". (A female nursing assistant in an adolescent ward.)

It may be, as these examples suggest, that the staff's general worries about sexual relationships of the mentally handicapped are linked to specific difficulties within their own units. These problems may have become more pressing as a result of the reduction of restrictions on residents and the encouragement of independence. This would imply that in the future it may become even more important to ensure that nurses and care staff are given an adequate training on sexual behaviour and ways of counselling the mentally handicapped.

8 THE STAFF'S VIEWS OF THEIR PRESENT AIMS

The main objective of this chapter is to examine the extent to which the staff felt they were aiming to enable their residents to live more independently and to develop their potential as individuals in contrast to providing them with basic care. Interest in the staff's aims stems from the assumption that what the staff strive to achieve will influence the way they carry out their work. For example, it might be expected that staff who are primarily aiming to enable their residents to live independently will place fewer restrictions on their residents and devote more time to teaching them than staff whose main objective is to ensure that their residents are properly washed, fed and given appropriate medical attention. A second purpose of this chapter is, therefore, to find out whether there is a relationship between the aims of the staff and the type of care they provide.

8.1 Method of measurement used

The staff were asked to select from a set of 10 cards those which described the most important, and second and third most important aims of their ward or hostel.[1] Six of these cards described aims which related to the social side of the staff's work, including three which directly concerned enabling the residents to live more independently within society. Most of the results in this chapter relate to the staff's most important aim, but similar conclusions were drawn from a fuller analysis which examined the second and third most important aims.

8.2 The relationship between the staff's aims and their type of unit

Almost half of the daytime ward nurses and three-quarters of the hostel staff felt that the most important aim of their unit was directly concerned with enabling their residents to live more independently in society or teaching them to feed, wash, or dress themselves. This excludes 30% of the nurses and 20% of the hostel staff who were aiming to provide a homelike atmosphere which also may have involved giving the residents more independence. Almost all of the remaining staff felt that their most important aim involved providing basic care for their residents, for example, by ensuring that they were fed, washed and clothed, or given proper medical attention.

The staff's views of their aims were analysed by the ability level of their wards to see whether any of the differences in their residents' present abilities might be associated with differences in the staff's aims.

Compared with the nurses in the high ability wards, the staff in the adult hostels placed slightly more emphasis on aims which were directly related to enabling their residents to live more independently within society. This may partly explain why, compared with the patients in the high ability wards, a higher proportion of the residents in the adult hostels were allowed out of the hostel grounds on their own (table 25).

---

[1] 5% of the daytime ward nurses and 9% of the hostel staff worked with only a group of the residents within their ward or hostel and so referred to the aims for their group. The other staff referred to the aims for all the residents in their ward or hostel.

	All daytime ward nurses	All day hostel staff	STAFF IN						
			Adult hostels high ability	Adult wards high ability	Adult wards average ability	Adult wards low ability	Adult wards non-ambulant very low ability	Children's hostels	Children's wards
	%	%	%	%	%	%	%	%	%
Aims directly related to enabling their residents to live more independently in society									
To enable some of the residents to live out of the hospital or hostel within the next few years	11	26	29	22	9	2	8	19	10
To enable the residents to live more independently in society (eg preparing them to go to work or teaching them to understand money)	10	23	25	17	8	2	4	17	3
To enable the residents to develop emotionally and psychologically and help them to make more choices for themselves	9	20	22	11	14	3	4	18	7
	30	69	76	50	31	7	16	54	20
To teach the residents how to feed, wash, toilet and dress themselves	19	4	3	9	16	30	21	7	28
To provide a homelike atmosphere (eg by trying to minimise routines)	30	20	18	24	34	39	36	27	31
To provide emotional support for the residents' parents	1	1	0	0	2	0	0	3	4
Aims related to providing suitable basic care or medical attention									
To provide basic care for the residents (ensuring that they are washed, fed, clothed)	11	2	2	10	10	17	15	4	8
To provide the residents with proper medical attention	5	1	1	3	0	5	11	0	8
To provide a more sheltered atmosphere for the residents	2	0	0	1	2	2	2	0	1
To prevent the residents from becoming aggressive or destructive	3	2	0	4	6	0	0	5	0
	21	5	3	18	18	24	28	9	17
Total percentages	100	100	100	100	100	100	100	100	100
Base: all daytime ward nurses and care staff	*324*	*285*	*174*	*71*	*77*	*42*	*33*	*76*	*41*

*5% of the daytime nurses and 9% of the hostel staff worked with only a group of the residents within their ward or hostel and so referred to the aims for their group. The other staff referred to the aims for all the residents in their ward or hostel.

The aims of the staff in the adult wards varied according to the type of ward so that a higher proportion of the nurses in the high ability wards than of the other nurses felt their most important aim was directly related to enabling their patients to live more independently in society. About half of the nurses in the average and lower ability wards said that teaching their patients how to feed and wash themselves was one of their 3 most important aims as compared with less than a quarter of the nurses in the high ability wards. This appears to be appropriate to their patients' present abilities because, as was seen previously, at least two-thirds of the patients in the average and lower ability wards were unable to wash and dress themselves compared with only 15% of the patients in the high ability wards (table 25). A slightly higher proportion of the nurses in the lower ability adult wards than of the other nurses felt that their main aim involved either providing (rather than teaching) basic care, or giving medical attention to their patients.

A higher proportion of the staff in the children's hostels than in the children's wards placed importance on enabling the children to live independently in society. On the other hand almost two-thirds of the nurses in the children's wards compared with slightly less than half of the staff in the children's hostels said that teaching the children to feed, wash and dress themselves was one of their 3 most important aims. Since only a fifth of the children in the wards could do these things for themselves, compared with half of the hostel children, the difference in objectives between these two staff groups reflects the different situations which faced them.

There were only slight differences between the most important aims of staff in units with relatively good staff ratios and staff in units with relatively poor staff ratios.

8.3 The relationship between the staff's aims and their grade

Within the hospitals there was a marked difference between the senior nursing staff and the ward nursing staff in their view of the aims of their wards, but relatively minor differences between the various nursing grades up to and including ward sisters (see table 66). Compared with the ward nurses a higher proportion of the senior nursing staff felt that the most important aim of their wards was directly related to enabling the patients to live more independently in society and a lower proportion felt that their most important aim involved providing basic care. Because the senior nursing staff were referring to the aims of the group of wards for which they were responsible it is not possible to examine the extent to which their views on the aims of a specific ward differed from the views of the nurses working on that ward. Consequently firm conclusions cannot be drawn from these results but they do suggest firstly that the senior nursing staff may have an over-optimistic view of what the ward nurses are aiming to achieve, particularly within the average and lower ability wards. Secondly, it appears that only a minority of the ward nurses who thought that the most important aim of their ward was connected with providing suitable basic care would be supported in this view by the more senior nursing staff.

Within the hostels the staff in the grades included in the survey generally held similar views on the most important aim of their hostel (see table 66).

Table 66 The staff's view of their most important aim analysed by grade

Nursing staff	Senior nursing staff	Ward sisters	Staff nurses	Enrolled nurses	Nursing assistants	Students/ pupils
	%	%	%	%	%	%
Aims directly related to enabling their residents to live more independently in society	62	35	30	25	26	36
To teach the residents to feed, wash, toilet and dress themselves	9	12	12	16	25	18
To provide a more homelike atmosphere	24	34	39	41	24	24
To provide emotional support for the residents' parents	0	1	0	0	2	3
Aims related to providing suitable basic care or medical attention	5	18	19	17	24	18
	100	100	100	100	100	100
Base for percentages: all daytime ward nurses and senior nursing staff (reweighted)	*113*	*213*	*58*	*75*	*129*	*101*

Hostel staff	Officers in charge	Deputies	Care assistants
	%	%	%
Aims directly related to enabling their residents to live more independently in society	72	73	67
To teach the residents to feed, wash, toilet and dress themselves	2	3	5
To provide a more homelike atmosphere	24	22	19
To provide emotional support for the residents' parents	0	0	1
Aims related to providing suitable basic care or medical attention	2	2	8
	100	100	100
Base for percentages: all daytime hostel staff (reweighted)	*115*	*59*	*177*

8.4 The relationship between the staff's work and the aims of their unit

This section examines the extent to which the staff's views of their aims were related to the type of care they provided for their residents.

The proportion of the nurses who had spent over an hour on at least one of

Table 67 Relationships between the nurses' most important aim and their work

	Daytime ward nurses whose most important aim was:			
	Directly related to enabling the patients to live more independently in society	Teaching their residents to feed, wash, toilet and dress themselves	Providing a homelike atmosphere	Providing suitable basic care or medical attention
	%	%	%	%
1 The proportion of these nurses who on their previous day at work:—				
spent over 15 minutes* on teaching their patients to do domestic tasks, or reading, writing or counting	38	15	30	25
spent over 15 minutes* on encouraging their patients to organise their own activities	36	22	29	17
spent over an hour on at least one of the four social tasks (playing, going on outings, teaching or encouraging the patients' own activities)	45	41	41	45
Base: all daytime nurses (reweighted)	93	60	97	65
2 The proportion of the nurses who assisted with feeding, washing or dressing the patients and spent most of this time:—				
encouraging their patients to do these tasks for themselves	48	33	34	21
actually feeding, washing or dressing the patients	52	67	66	79
Base: daytime nurses who had assisted with these tasks† on their previous day at work (reweighted)	44	42	64	46
3 The average number of the restrictions or routines which were applied in their wards	3·0	3·7	3·9	3·9
Base: daytime nurses who had worked on the sampled wards for at least 3 months (reweighted)	59	35	73	44

*These two tasks were included here because they are most closely related to enabling higher ability residents to live more independently in society. Since only a small proportion of the nurses had spent over an hour on either of these tasks the criterion of spending over 15 minutes on them was adopted.
†Excluding any nurses who mainly assisted by supervising while the patients fed, washed and dressed themselves, or who were unable to say how they had spent most of the time.

the four social tasks did not vary appreciably according to the staff's most important aim. However, when attention is confined to the parts of the staff's social role which are most clearly relevant to enabling their patients to live more independently in society, there were indications that, in comparison with the other nurses, those who said that this was their most important aim did

96

devote more attention to encouraging their patients to be independent (see table 67). These relationships could be partly attributed to differences between the aims and the work of the nurses in the high ability wards and the other nurses. However, most of the relationships were still found in a more attenuated form in the average and lower ability wards. There were generally only minor differences between the work carried out by the nurses who said that their most important aim involved providing a homelike atmosphere or teaching their patients to feed, wash and dress themselves and the nurses whose most important aim was to provide suitable basic care or medical attention.

Within the high ability adult wards and adult hostels there seemed to be only slight differences between the work carried out by staff who said their most important aim was directly related to encouraging their residents to live more independently and by staff whose most important aim was to provide a home-like atmosphere or to teach their residents to feed, wash and dress themselves. Very few staff in the high ability units felt that the most important aim of their unit was the provision of suitable basic care or medical attention and their work could therefore not be separately analysed.

8.5 Discussion on the relationship between the staff's aims and their work

Although some overall relationships were found between the staff's aims and the type of care they provided, these relationships were generally not as clear-cut as might have been expected. In particular, no consistent differences were found between the work carried out by the nurses whose most important aim was teaching basic care or providing a homelike atmosphere and those whose main objective was providing basic care or medical attention.

These results imply that the staff's views of the aims of their units are an unreliable guide to the type of care provided for their residents. This may be partly because some of the staff carry out their work on a day to day basis without considering their overall objectives. Asking these staff to identify the most important aim of their unit may have led them to make a rather arbitrary choice. There is also the possibility that some of the staff may have referred to aims which they would ideally like their units to pursue although they could not be carried out with their existing resources.

8.6 The relationship between the staff's aims and other aspects of their work

This section describes two factors which seemed to affect whether or not the ward sisters or officers in charge saw their most important aim as being related to the social caring side of their work: their influence over decisions on individual residents and (for the ward sisters only) wearing uniforms. These relationships are considered here because any action taken to improve the formal training that staff are given on the aims of their units may be of greater value if the possible effects of these other factors are also taken into account.

The extent to which the ward sisters and officers in charge took part in making decisions on individual residents Amongst both the ward sisters and the officers in charge, the staff who were most likely to attend case conferences and take part in making decisions on individual residents were also most likely to feel that the principle aim of their unit was to encourage their residents to live more independently in society (see table 68). Only 4% of the ward sisters with

Table 68 The relationship between the extent to which the ward sisters and officers in charge participated in making decisions on individual residents and their view of the most important aim of their ward or hostel

	Daytime ward sisters—scores on participation in decisions scale*			
	0–1	2–3	4–5	6–7
Most important aim of their ward was:	%	%	%	%
Directly related to enabling their residents to live more independently in society	31	26	39	54
Other social aims (teaching basic care, providing a homelike atmosphere or supporting parents)	42	57	44	42
To provide suitable basic care or medical attention	28	18	16	4
Base: daytime ward sisters who had worked in their ward for at least 3 months (reweighted)	*37*	*74*	*61*	*24*

	Officers in charge—scores on participation in decisions scale*		
	0–3	4–5	6–7
	%	%	%
Most important aim of their hostel was:			
Directly related to enabling their residents to live more independently	57	64	86
Other social aims (teaching basic care, providing a homelike atmosphere or supporting parents)	39	33	14
To provide suitable basic care or medical attention	4	3	0
Base: officers in charge who had worked in their hostel for at least 3 months (reweighted)	*23*	*39*	*42*

Staff with higher scores on the participation in decisions scale took part in making more decisions on individual residents and were more likely to have recently attended case conferences and staff discussions (see chapter 6).

the highest scores on the participation in decisions scale felt that their most important aim was connected with providing basic care or medical attention as compared with 28 % of the the ward sisters with the lowest scores.

It is relevant to note here that the ward sisters who were regularly involved in making these decisions were more likely than others to be optimistic about the scope for developing the abilities of the mentally handicapped and community integration (see table 69). Together these results support the suggestion in chapter 6 that the ward sisters who do not take part in case conferences or in making these decisions were more likely than others to be optimistic about patients may come to attach less importance to their social role.

Wearing uniforms A higher proportion (22 %) of the ward sisters who wore uniforms than of the other ward sisters (2 %) said that the most important aim of their unit was related to providing suitable basic care or medical attention for their patients. This is consistent with the suggestion in chapter 5 that the nurses who wore uniforms may see their work as being more closely related to other types of nursing, in which providing basic care and medical attention are of primary importance.

Table 69   The relationship between the extent to which the ward sisters take part in making decisions on individual patients and their general attitudes towards the mentally handicapped

	Ward sisters—scores on participation in decisions scale*			
	0–1	2–3	4–5	6–7
Average score on:				
scope for individual development scale	19·0	19·6	20·3	20·9
orientation towards community care scale	17·2	18·3	18·7	19·3
Base for percentages: daytime ward sisters (reweighted)	*37*	*74*	*61*	*24*

*Staff with higher scores on the participation in decisions scale took part in making more decisions on individual residents and were more likely to have recently attended case conferences and staff discussions (see chapter 6).

9. THE STAFF'S VIEWS ON THEIR WORK AT PRESENT AND IN THE FUTURE

The major purpose of the survey was to provide information relevant to the Jay Committee's interest in the value of developing the social caring aspects of the staff's work as recommended by the Briggs Committee. The staff's reactions to possible changes of this kind were recognised to be important but pilot work had indicated that only a few of the staff had a clear idea of the proposals made by the Briggs Committee. We therefore approached this question in a more indirect way at the mainstage by setting out to find the extent to which the staff were attached to their clinical nursing role on the one hand and the extent to which they valued the social caring side of their work on the other. This was carried out firstly by eliciting staff's views on their present work and the way it should develop in the future, which is the subject of this chapter, and secondly by considering their views on their careers and training which are covered in chapters 11 and 12.

9.1 The staff's views on their present work—the parts which they liked the best

All the staff, except for the nursing officers, were asked to select from a set of eight cards those which described the parts of their work which they liked the best. Three of these cards referred to aspects of their social caring role (ie encouraging their residents to make more decisions for themselves, teaching or training their residents and playing or taking part in activities with the residents). The other cards referred to providing basic care, looking after residents who were ill or needed medical attention and various miscellaneous professional tasks.

Almost half of the day-time ward nurses and three-quarters of the hostel staff liked some aspect of the social caring side of their work the best.

The proportion of the nurses who liked part of their social caring role the best was slightly higher amongst nurses in the high ability and children's wards than amongst those in the average or lower ability wards but was even higher amongst the hostel staff (see table 70).

In many ways the relationship between the part of the work staff liked the best and their type of unit reflected the differences in the aims of their units shown in the previous chapter. Compared with nurses in the high ability wards, more of the staff in the adult hostels selected encouraging their residents to make more decisions for themselves as the part of their work that they liked the best and it was seen previously that they were more likely to be mainly aiming to enable their residents to live independently in society. Conversely, nurses in the non-ambulant wards were the least likely to like part of their social caring role the best and were the nurses who were the most likely to feel that they were mainly aiming to provide suitable basic care or medical attention.

There was one important respect in which the part of the work the staff liked the best did not seem to be consistent with the main objectives of their units. Appreciable proportions of the nurses liked the clinical nursing side of their work the best (22%) or second best (16%) whereas only 5% of them felt that providing their patients with proper medical attention was the most important aim of their ward. The proportion of nurses who liked clinical

100

Table 70 The part of their work that the staff liked the best analysed by their type of unit.

	All daytime ward nurses	All daytime hostel staff	STAFF IN						Children's hostels	Children's wards
			Adult hostels high ability	Adult wards high ability	Adult wards average ability	Adult wards low ability	Adult wards non-ambulant —very low ability			
	%	%	%	%	%	%	%		%	%
Part of their social caring role: encouraging their residents to make more decisions for themselves	5	21	27	9	3	0	0		11	3
training or teaching the residents to do things for themselves (eg feeding, dressing or domestic tasks)	28	31	29	26	22	33	18		42	34
playing or taking part in activities with the residents	14	20	15	12	14	8	12		27	20
	47	72	71	47	39	41	30		80	57
Providing more comfort or basic care for their residents	28	17	19	24	38	33	38		11	18
Looking after residents when they are ill or need some medical attention	22	6	7	26	21	21	26		2	21
Other professional tasks (training other nurses or care staff, advising relatives or taking part in discussions with other professional staff)	3	4	3	2	2	5	6		7	4
	100	100	100	100	100	100	100		100	100
Base: all daytime ward nurses and hostel staff (reweighted)	324	285	174	71	77	42	33		76	41

101

Table 71 The part of their work that the nurses liked the best analysed by their grade

	Daytime ward nurses	Ward sisters	Staff nurses	Enrolled nurses	Nursing assistants	Student nurses	Pupil nurses
	%	%	%	%	%	%	%
Part of their social caring role	46	50	53	41	38	70	65
Providing more comfort or basic care	28	20	28	27	39	15	4
Looking after patients when they are ill or need some medical attention	22	22	12	32	20	11	31
Other professional tasks	3	8	7	0	3	4	0
	100	100	100	100	100	100	100
Base: daytime ward nurses (reweighted)	324	213	58	75	129	53	48

Table 72   The part of their work liked the best by nurses aged under or over 40 analysed by grade*

	Daytime ward nurses		Registered nurses		Enrolled nurses		Nursing assistants	
	aged under 40	aged 40 or over	aged under 40	aged 40 or over	aged under 40	aged 40 or over	aged under 40	aged 40 or over
Part of their social caring role	% 54	% 34	% 61	% 39	% 51	% 31	% 42	% 33
Providing more comfort or basic care	23	36	21	24	20	33	35	45
Looking after patients when they are ill or need some medical attention	20	26	9	30	29	36	22	17
Other professional tasks	3	4	8	7	0	0	1	5
	100	100	100	100	100	100	100	100
Base: daytime ward nurses (reweighted)	193	130	92	73	35	40	70	59

*This analysis could not be carried out for the trainee nurses because only two of them were aged 40 or older.

103

nursing the best or second best was similar within each type of ward. However, chapter 2 shows that hardly any of the patients would have needed frequent medical attention or clinical nursing with the possible exception of patients in the non-ambulant and children's wards.

9.2 Further information on the nurses who most liked their clinical nursing work

Nurses who like the clinical nursing side of their work the best are of special interest because they may be more reluctant than others to accept a greater emphasis on the social caring aspects of their role.

The proportion of the nurses who liked their clinical role the best was higher amongst the enrolled (32%) and pupil nurses (31%) than amongst nurses in the other grades (see table 71). Also a greater proportion of the ward sisters and staff nurses aged 40 or over than of those who were younger enjoyed their clinical work the most (see table 72).

In the case of pupil nurses and the younger enrolled nurses, who were trained as pupils in subnormality nursing, it may be that their training syllabus, which has not been altered since it was introduced in 1964, places too much emphasis on clinical nursing.[1] The difference between the younger and older registered nurses (ward sisters and staff nurses) may also be related to differences in their training. A higher proportion of the older registered nurses, than of those aged under 40, were not qualified in subnormality nursing, and most of those who were had been trained before 1970 when the syllabus for students in subnormality nursing was altered to place more emphasis on the social aspects of caring.[1]

The proportion of the nurses who liked the clinical nursing side of their role the best was also noticeably higher amongst those in the acute sickness wards (47%) and the night nurses (36%) although clinical nursing would form a more important part of their work.

9.3 Views of the day staff on their role in the future

All the staff were given the opportunity to express their opinions on the way their work should develop in the future. The question which they were asked was "What are your views on the sort of work staff caring for the mentally handicapped should do in the future?" The answers were grouped into categories which are summarised in table 73 and shown in greater detail in table 74. About a quarter of the day staff did not give any views although they often commented that their opinions had been covered by more specific questions in the earlier parts of the interview. The percentages quoted in the tables are based on those staff who expressed views although they may not be completely representative of the views of all the staff.

9.4 Views on their social caring and clinical nursing roles

A clear majority of the nurses and hostel staff who expressed views on their role in the future felt that they should place a greater emphasis on their social caring role by developing their residents' potential abilities or by providing

---

[1]These points are considered more fully in chapter 12.

Table 73 A summary of the staff's views on the sort of work that they should carry out in caring for the mentally handicapped in the future

	Daytime ward nurses	Daytime hostel staff	Senior nursing staff	Ward sisters	Staff nurses	Enrolled nurses	Nursing assistants	Students	Pupils	Officers in charge	Deputies	Care assistants
	%72†	%70†	%57	%77	%80	%64	%69	%75	%78	%73	%70	%69
Place more emphasis on their social caring role*												
Maintain the role of clinical nursing or continue to provide the more traditional type of hospital care	8	6	10	11	14	5	4	17	5	7	2	7
Place more emphasis on community care	38	37	57	48	51	40	23	57	27	39	45	33
They should have better staffing levels and/or more facilities for the residents	30	17	14	28	33	28	30	28	37	13	15	18
Generally the staff should be given more training on all aspects of their work	13	17	15	19	27	12	7	19	5	22	25	12
The nurses or care staff should work more closely with other professional staff	6	7	22	11	10	5	3	13	0	8	8	6
Other views	23	24	14	19	22	21	26	17	29	19	17	28
Base: daytime ward and hostel staff and senior nursing staff who expressed views on their role in the future (reweighted)	240	221	97	184	49	58	77	47	41	101	53	125
Staff who expressed views on the future shown as a percentage of all the staff	74	78	86	86	84	77	60	89	85	88	90	71
Base: all daytime ward and hostel staff and senior nursing staff (reweighted)	324	285	113	213	58	75	129	53	48	115	59	177

*Table 74 gives further information on the answers which were combined to form the categories in this table.
†These percentages do not add up to 100 because some of the staff gave more than one answer.

105

a more homelike, family atmosphere in their units. Most of these staff saw this as involving an expansion of the sort of work they were aiming to carry out at present although they often implied that they needed better staffing levels to develop their role in this way. About a fifth of the nurses and a tenth of the hostel staff explicitly stated at this question that they needed better staff ratios in the future and in response to a specific question on their staff ratios slightly over half of the nurses and a third of the hostel staff said they were dissatisfied with the present staffing levels in their units.

Although the majority of the nurses said that more emphasis should be placed on their social caring role only a tenth of them directly stated or implied that too great an emphasis on clinical nursing was inhibiting the development of this type of care. This contrasts with the views held by a similar proportion (8%) of the nurses who emphasised that the more traditional type of nursing care would continue to be needed in the future. This included nurses who specifically stated that clinical nursing or qualified nurses would always be required and others who emphasised that the type of care which is at present provided by the hospitals would always be needed for lower grade patients. Most of the nurses with these views based them on criticisms of the care that would be provided by staff who were not trained in subnormality nursing, or scepticism about the scope for developing the abilities of the more severely handicapped patients. The annex to this chapter gives some examples of the views held by these nurses and also examples of the views of the nurses who felt that their clinical nursing role prevented them from placing more emphasis on social caring.

Generally the views expressed by the staff on the development of their social caring role were similar regardless of their grade, type of unit or age. One exception to this was that a slightly lower proportion of the senior nursing staff, than of the other nurses, said that in the future the patients should have a more homelike atmosphere or be taken on more outings. This may have reflected the fact that the senior nursing staff seemed to have relatively optimistic views on what the ward nurses were aiming to achieve at present (see chapter 8).

Possibly one of the most interesting results in this section is that the nurses who personally preferred their clinical nursing role were almost as likely as the others to consider that the social caring side of their work should be strengthened in the future. Two-thirds of these nurses said that the social caring side of their work should be developed whereas less than a tenth emphasised that the more traditional type of hospital nursing care would continue to be needed. This suggests that provided they personally had the opportunity to continue to give medical attention to mentally handicapped patients most of these nurses may accept that, in general, more emphasis should be placed on the social aspects of caring in the future.

9.5 Views on developing community care

Although the staff were not directly asked about community care, in replying to the question on the sort of work which they should do in the future, a third of the nurses and hostel staff stated that more emphasis should be placed on community care (see table 73). The main ways that they felt this should be achieved were by providing more hostels or group homes, providing more

Table 74 The staff's views on the sort of work that nurses and hostel staff should do in caring for the mentally handicapped in the future

	Daytime ward nurses	Daytime hostel staff	Senior nursing staff	Ward sisters	Officers in charge
	%	%	%	%	%
More emphasis should be placed on the staff's social caring role:—					
Concentrate on teaching basic skills (feeding, washing, dressing)	7	4	3	11	4
Develop the residents to their full potential (by education and training in social skills)	41	37	33	44	39
Use more behaviour modification programmes	2	3	4	5	2
Provide a more homelike, family atmosphere and spend more time with the residents	31	28	13	27	22
Take the residents on more outings (to football matches, bingo, pubs etc)	17	16	4	13	11
Place less emphasis on the clinical nursing role (and more emphasis on a teaching and social role)	9	9	14	14	23
Give staff more training on the social and educational side of their work	7	7	16	16	6
Staff who gave at least one of the above answers advocating placing more emphasis on social caring	72	70	57	77	73
Maintain the role of clinical nursing or continue to provide the more traditional type of hospital care:—					
clinical nursing or qualified nurses will always be needed	3	1	2	2	2
staff should be given more training on the clinical and medical side of their work	1	3	1	3	2
hospitals will always be needed for lower grade patients	5	2	7	8	3
staff who gave at least one of the above answers indicating maintaining the role of clinical nursing or of hospitals	8	6	10	11	7
More emphasis should be placed on community care:—					
There should be more hostels or group homes	18	26	10	26	26
The nursing or hostel staff should give more support to parents to enable them to care for mentally handicapped people at home	20	10	50	26	12
The general public should be made more aware of the needs of the mentally handicapped so that they will accept them in the community	10	10	11	13	10
Staff who gave at least one of the above answers indicating placing more emphasis on community care	38	37	57	48	39

(Continued overleaf)

Table 74   continued

	Daytime ward nurses	Daytime hostel staff	Senior nursing staff	Ward sisters	Officers in charge
	%	%	%	%	%
Other views:—					
Better staff: patient ratios are needed	22	12	8	20	8
More money should be spent on facilities for the mentally handicapped (eg on training centres)	12	6	7	14	7
Generally the staff should be given more training on all aspects of caring for the mentally handicapped	13	17	15	19	22
The nurses or care staff should work more closely with other professional staff	6	7	22	11	7
The hospitals or hostels should be run in a less rigid, hierarchical way	6	6	0	6	5
Higher grade residents should be separate from the lower grades and their different needs recognised	3	5	6	4	8
Staff should do less domestic or routine administrative work	1	7	1	2	1
Continue as at present or vague answers	6	4	3	2	2
Any other answers	7	5	4	5	4
Base: daytime ward and hostel staff and senior nursing staff who expressed views on their role in the future (reweighted)	240	221	97	184	101

support for parents and by educating the general public to understand and accept the mentally handicapped within the community. A particularly high proportion of the senior nursing staff (50%) said that the hospitals and nurses should give more assistance to parents to enable them to look after mentally handicapped people at home. Most of these nursing officers thought that qualified nurses based in hospitals for the mentally handicapped should provide domiciliary support for the parents often in conjunction with earlier diagnosis and assessments made by teams of staff from various professions. The type of service they suggested was broadly along the lines which were subsequently recommended by the National Development Group in 1977.

Annex to Chapter 9

The following examples illustrate the views expressed on their work in the future by the nurses who were most clearly (*a*) dissatisfied or (*b*) satisfied with their present links with clinical nursing. Although relatively few of the nurses expressed either of these views we cannot tell to what extent they would have been more widely supported if all the staff had been asked a specific question on this subject.

(*a*) Examples of the views stated by nurses who felt that too great an emphasis on clinical nursing was inhibiting the development of the social caring side of their work:—

"There should be more emphasis on social training rather than general nursing which is dealt with a lot in training courses. A lot of problems are of a social nature rather than medical and there should be more emphasis on this. The staff should be qualified in subnormality nursing whereas you can get SRNs in general nursing taking up a staff nurse post in subnormality. It's a specialist job but still they employ these people from other disciplines".

(A male charge nurse, aged 34, who qualified in subnormality nursing about 10 years ago.)

"All through my training it was stressed that patients should be made to feel that they were in a home rather than a hospital but it's impossible while we're running around in uniforms and being called nurse and I think there should be separate sick bays for patients who are ill".

(A female enrolled nurse, aged 25, who was enrolled in subnormality nursing 4 years ago after being a pupil nurse.)

"The staff should be more concerned with play therapy and the developmental needs of children and less with the clinical side".

(A female ward sister, aged 29, who qualified in subnormality nursing 2 years ago and is now working in a children's ward.)

(b) *Examples of the views stated by nurses who emphasised that the more traditional type of nursing care or qualified nurses would continue to be needed in the future:—*

"Trained nurses and the clinical side will always be needed. We want the patients out into the community but we realise this isn't possible if their families don't want them—they're not willing to accept them back".

(A female staff nurse, aged 55, who qualified in subnormality nursing (RNMS) five years ago.)

"If in the future they are going to send us the more difficult and highly dependent patients, they can't do without trained nurses. There are a lot of patients on this ward whom untrained people wouldn't be able to tell about physical illnesses and mental disturbances. I can't find the words to say how strongly I feel they are human beings; but where there is brain damage it's not right to push them beyond their limits. If we could have people to teach them to dance, wash and set their hair, that would help but I still say you've got to have people in the wards who know how to recognise subnormality and can deal with it. I'm convinced that a lot of the behaviour problems you get is because you've pushed them too far, taken them out of their security".

(A female ward sister, aged 54, who qualified in subnormality nursing over 30 years ago.)

"I think the staff should continue to be qualified nurses, otherwise the profession will go back to the workhouse days. There's a definite need for nursing staff to understand the signs of patients, be ready to deal with their disturbances—you can only get this with trained staff".

(A female staff nurse, aged 22, who had recently obtained her RNMS.)

"I feel that hospitals for the mentally handicapped are needed and have a great role to play although many of our patients could and should live in the community. My main criticism of Local Authority Social Services Departments is that they haven't built enough hostels and even if they had hostels I feel registered nurses are the only people who should run them, not care staff".

(A male charge nurse, aged 24 who qualified in subnormality nursing five years ago.)

10.   THE STAFF'S VIEWS ON THEIR RELATIONSHIP WITH OTHER PROFESSIONAL STAFF

The staff's views were sought on various issues connected with their relationship with staff in other professions. The two main objectives in obtaining this information were firstly to find out whether or not the nurses and hostel staff would like to have a closer working relationship with other professional staff and secondly to discover whether they were dissatisfied with the present role of the other professions.

10.1   Views on the role of staff from the occupational centres and school teachers

About half of the daytime ward nurses and two-thirds of the hostel staff felt that they would like to have more contact with staff from the occupational centres[1] and with school teachers (see table 75). Almost all of the other nurses and hostel staff were content with the amount of contact they had, and hardly any would have preferred this to be reduced.

Table 75   Views of the nursing and hostel staff on the amount of contact they have with staff from the occupational centres or with teachers

	Daytime ward nurses	Daytime hostel staff	Senior nursing staff†	Ward sisters	Officers in charge
	%	%	%	%	%
Staff from occupational centres The nursing or hostel staff felt that they would like—					
more contact	54	68	68	58	46
the same amount	45	32	32	41	53
less contact	1	0	0	1	1
with staff in this profession	100	100	100	100	100
*Base:*staff with residents who attend a centre (reweighted)*	*205*	*230*	*86*	*175*	*93*
Teachers from their residents' schools The nursing or hostel staff felt that they would like—					
more contact	47	66	57	52	48
the same amount	53	34	40	48	53
less contact	0	0	2	0	0
with staff in this profession	100	100	100	100	100
*Base:*staff who work with children who go to school (reweighted)*	*83*	*110*	*40*	*68*	*41*

*Throughout this chapter the tables are based only on daytime staff who have worked in their ward or hostel for at least three months (excluding trainee nurses) and senior nursing staff.
†In this table the senior nursing staff include both nursing officers responsible for wards who referred to the amount of contact they would personally like to have and the more senior nursing officers who referred to the amount of contact they would like their nurses to have.

[1]Throughout this chapter "occupational centres" is used to refer to any type of training centre, occupational, recreational or industrial therapy unit, or a sheltered workshop. This excludes the children's schools and teachers who are considered separately.

Slightly less than half of the hostel staff and only a quarter of the ward nurses thought that the occupational centres were aiming to provide their residents with some specific training as opposed to keeping them occupied[2] (see table 76). Despite this, almost all of the nurses and hostel staff felt that the occupational centres and schools provided a valuable service for their residents. However, at least a fifth of the staff in both groups were dissatisfied with the co-operation they received from the trainers or teaching staff (see table 77).

Table 76   Views of the nurses and hostel staff on the main aims of the occupational centres which their residents attended

The nursing or hostel staff felt that the occupational centres were mainly aiming to:	Daytime ward nurses	Daytime hostel staff	Nursing officers responsible for wards	Ward sisters	Officers in charge
	%	%	%	%	%
Provide their residents with some specific training*	27	45	53	26	46
Keep them occupied*	65	48	40	66	53
Occupy some of their residents but provide training for others	4	1	2	5	1
Do not know the centre's aims	5	7	5	3	0
	100	100	100	100	100
Base: day staff with residents who attended an occupational centre	205	230	59	175	93

*See footnote 2

10.2   Factors associated with dissatisfaction with the staff from the occupational centres or with school teachers

Some of the dissatisfaction amongst the nurses and hostel staff with the service or co-operation from the staff at the occupational centres seemed to stem from a lack of regular discussion about the progress of their residents with these staff. The proportions of the nurses and hostel staff who were dissatisfied were much higher amongst those who had not taken part in these discussions for six months or longer than amongst those who had been involved in them in the previous four weeks (see table 78). This applied to both the trained staff and the nursing and care assistants. It was suggested in chapter 6 that the work of the nursing and care assistants, as well as of the more senior staff, might be of greater value if they had more frequent discussions with staff from the occupational centres. The evidence here that taking part in such discussions was associated with greater confidence, amongst both the junior and the more senior staff, in the service provided by the centres again indicates the value of involving all levels of staff in this type of discussion.

[2]The staff were asked to select between these alternative aims so that each staff member was free to place his own interpretation on "specific training" and "keep them occupied".

Table 77 Views of the nurses and hostel staff on the value of the service provided by staff from the occupational centres and school teachers and the co-operation they receive from these staff

	Daytime ward nurses	Daytime hostel staff	Senior nursing staff	Ward sisters	Officers in charge
Staff from occupational centres	%	%	%	%	%
(i) The nursing or hostel staff felt that the service provided by these staff was:					
very valuable	60	66	68	56	61
fairly valuable	30	27	27	33	29
of little value	10	7	5	11	10
	100	100	100	100	100
(ii) Co-operation: the nursing or hostel staff were:					
satisfied	73	63	87	71	71
dissatisfied	27	37	13	29	29
with the co-operation from these staff	— 100	— 100	— 100	— 100	— 100
Base: staff with residents who attend a centre (reweighted)	*177*	*170*	*86*	*175*	*93*
Teachers from their residents' schools					
(i) The nursing or hostel staff felt that the service provided by these staff was:					
very valuable	70	72	60	66	77
fairly valuable	24	24	30	24	23
of little value	7	4	10	10	0
	100	100	100	100	100
(ii) Co-operation: the nursing or hostel staff were:					
satisfied	80	62	74	84	81
dissatisfied	20	38	26	16	19
with the co-operation from these staff	— 100	— 100	— 100	— 100	— 100
Base: staff who work with children who go to school (reweighted)	*83*	*110*	*40*	*68*	*41*

The staff's views on the main aims of the occupational centres which their residents attended were related to their satisfaction with the service provided by the centres. There was more dissatisfaction amongst the nurses or hostel staff who believed that the centres were mainly concerned to keep their residents occupied than amongst those who held that the centres were aiming to provide a specific training (see table 79). The actual objectives of the staff from the centres are not known and we cannot tell whether this dissatisfaction was justified or whether it stemmed from misconceptions, possibly due to a lack of communications between the two staff groups, about what the centres were aiming to achieve.

Table 78 The relationship between the time since last discussing a resident's progress with staff from the occupational centres and satisfaction with the service provided by these staff

The proportion of the nurses or hostel staff who felt that staff in the occupational centres:	Daytime ward nurses who last discussed a resident's progress with staff from the centres:		Daytime hostel staff who last discussed a resident's progress with staff from the centres:	
	within the previous 4 weeks*	at least 6 months ago*	within the previous 4 weeks*	at least 6 months ago*
	%	%	%	%
provided a valuable service and were satisfied with their co-operation	83	56	82	38
provided a service that was of little value or were dissatisfied with their co-operation	17	44	18	62
	100	100	100	100
Base: daytime staff with residents who attended an occupational centre (reweighted)	*64*	*81*	*74*	*73*

Only a few of the staff had last had this type of discussion between 4 weeks and 6 months ago so separate percentages could not be calculated for these groups.

Table 79 The relationship between the staff's views on the aims of the occupational centres which their residents attend and their satisfaction with the service provided by staff from the centres

The proportion of the nurses or hostel staff who felt that staff in the occupational centres:	Daytime ward nurses who felt that the occupational centres mainly aimed to:		Daytime hostel staff who felt that the occupational centres mainly aimed to:	
	provide some specific training	keep the residents occupied	provide some specific training	keep the residents occupied
	%	%	%	%
provided a valuable service and were satisfied with their co-operation	82	60	75	49
provided a service that was of little value or were dissatisfied with their co-operation	18	40	25	51
	100	100	100	100
Base: daytime staff with residents who attended an occupational centre (reweighted)	*49*	*117*	*75*	*88*

A similar analysis concerned with staff who were dissatisfied with the role of school teachers did not uncover any factors which were clearly associated with this dissatisfaction. However the staff were not asked for their views on what the teachers were aiming to achieve.

114

10.3 Views on the role of other professional staff

The staff's views on the role of the other professional staff were obtained only from the trained nurses, officers in charge and deputies because the pilot work for the survey indicated that the nursing and care assistants generally had little experience of their work.

Table 80 Views of the trained nurses and senior hostel staff on the amount of contact they have with members of specified professions

	Trained nurses— ward nurses on day shifts	Officers in charge and deputies	Senior nursing staff	Ward sisters	Officers in charge
	%	%	%	%	%
(a) Consultant pyschiatrists for the mentally handicapped The nursing or hostel staff felt that they would like—					
more contact	57	63	49	50	54
the same amount	43	33	49	50	43
less contact	0	4	1	1	3
with staff in this profession	—	—	—	—	—
	100	100	100	100	100
(b) Ward doctors or GPs The nursing or hostel staff felt that they would like—					
more contact	26	31	42	18	31
the same amount	72	68	58	78	69
less contact	2	1	0	3	0
with staff in this profession	—	—	—	—	—
	100	100	100	100	100
(c) Social workers The nursing or hostel staff felt that they would like—					
more contact	64	70	72	65	66
the same amount	34	27	24	32	30
less contact	2	3	4	3	4
with staff in this profession	—	—	—	—	—
	100	100	100	100	100
(d) Psychologists The nursing or hostel staff felt that they would like—					
more contact	65	62	71	61	53
the same amount	34	36	28	35	45
less contact	2	2	1	4	2
with staff in this profession	—	—	—	—	—
	100	100	100	100	100
Base: day staff and senior nursing staff (reweighted)	*155*	*102*	*85**	*195*	*107*

*In parts (a), (b) and (d) the senior nursing staff includes both nursing officers responsible for wards who referred to the amount of contact they would personally like to have and the more senior nursing officers who referred to the amount of contact they would like their nurses to have. Part (c) is based only on the (46) nursing officers responsible for wards.

115

The majority of the trained ward nurses, officers in charge and deputies felt that they should have more contact with consultants, social workers and psychologists but only slightly under a third felt that they needed more contact with ward doctors or GPs (see table 80). Hardly any of the staff would have preferred to have had less contact with any of these professions.

Table 81 **Views of the trained nurses and senior hostel staff on the value of the service provided by staff in specified professions and the co-operation they receive from these staff**

	Trained nurses— ward nurses on day shifts	Officers in charge and deputies	Senior nursing staff	Ward sisters	Officers in charge
	%	%	%	%	%
(a) Consultant psychiatrists for the mentally handicapped					
(i) The nursing or hostel staff felt that recommendations made by consultants about training or social care were—					
very valuable	45	34	41	49	38
fairly valuable	46	60	41	40	59
of little value	9	6	19	11	3
	100	100	100	100	100
(ii) Co-operation: the nursing or hostel staff were—					
satisfied	78	66	75	72	67
dissatisfied	22	34	25	28	33
with the co-operation	—	—	—	—	—
from consultants	100	100	100	100	100
(b) Ward doctors of GPs					
(i) The nurses felt that recommendations made by ward doctors or GPs about training or social care were—					
very valuable	58	*	37	53	*
fairly valuable	38		39	40	
of little value	4		24	7	
	100		100	100	
(ii) Co-operation: the nursing or hostel staff were—					
satisfied	93	87	91	93	83
dissatisfied	7	13	9	7	17
with the co-operation	—	—	—	—	—
from ward doctors or GPs	100	100	100	100	100

*This applied to only a few of the hostel staff.

Table 81 Continued

	Trained nurses—ward nurses on day shifts	Officers in charge and deputies	Senior nursing staff	Ward sisters	Officers in charge
	%	%	%	%	%
(c) Social workers					
(i) The nursing or hostel staff felt that the service provided by social workers was—					
very valuable	38	37	50†	40	38
fairly valuable	36	32	26	32	29
of little value	25	31	24	28	34
	100	100	100	100	100
(ii) Co-operation: the nursing or hostel staff were—					
satisfied	66	55	73†	61	54
dissatisfied	34	45	27	39	46
with the co-operation from social workers	100	100	100	100	100
(d) Psychologists					
(i) The nursing or hostel staff felt that recommendations made by psychologists about training or social care were—					
very valuable	35	41	50	32	60
fairly valuable	51	54	38	51	30
of little value	15	5	12	17	10
	100	100	100	100	100
(ii) Co-operation: the nursing or hostel staff were—					
satisfied	55	47	72	50	50
dissatisfied	45	53	28	50	50
with the co-operation from psychologists	100	100	100	100	100

Approximate (reweighted) bases:**
for (i) Nursing and hostel staff who had been given recommendations on training or social care by the specified professional staff (b & d) 57 (a & d) 24 46   (b & d) 83 (a & d) 30
(a & c) 94 (c) 97   (a & c) 146 (c) 104
for (ii) Nursing and hostel staff who felt that this applied to them 103 (a & d) 70 65   (a & b) 194 (a & d) 64
(b & c) 96   (c & d) 143 (b & c) 103

†*Senior nursing officers were not asked about the value of the service provided by social workers and so these percentages are solely based on nursing officers.*
***These bases varied according to the profession. The actual bases were always equal to or greater than the numbers shown in the table.*

The nurses and hostel staff generally seemed to be satisfied with the service provided by the medical staff and consultants although a fifth of the trained nurses and a third of the senior hostel staff were dissatisfied with the co-operation from consultants (see table 81). There was rather more discontent with the co-operation obtained from psychologists and social workers in that half of the ward sisters and officers in charge expressed dissatisfaction in connection with psychologists and these proportions were only marginally lower with respect to social workers.

10.4 Factors associated with dissatisfaction with consultants, social workers or psychologists

Half of the ward sisters and a third of the nursing officers were dissatisfied with the amount of influence they had over deciding which patients should be admitted to, or transferred from, their wards. This dissatisfaction was closely related to the extent to which they felt they were actually involved in making this type of decision on individual patients (see table 82)—a result which is consistent with a comparable study on all grades of nurses by Moores et al (1977a). Most of the officers in charge had more influence than the nurses over these decisions on individual residents, but within the group of officers in charge there was a clear relationship between their amount of influence and their satisfaction. This dissatisfaction can be seen as an indirect criticism of the present role of some of the consultants within the hospitals, and of social workers and senior social services staff within the hostels, because it was seen in chapter 6 that, in the units in which the ward sisters or officers in charge were not consulted, consultants or social workers usually made these decisions.

The proportion of trained nurses and senior hostel staff who were dissatisfied with the co-operation from psychologists was much greater amongst those who had not had a discussion with a psychologist about any of their residents for at least six months than amongst those who talked to a psychologist more recently (see table 83). As the majority of the former group had never talked to a psychologist about any of their residents, their adverse views on psychologists did not seem to be based on direct experience of their work. More recent contact with consultants or social workers was only marginally related to nurses or hostel staff being more satisfied with their co-operation or service.

It is sometimes suggested that a lack of co-operation between nurses and other professional staff may partly stem from nurses having a more pessimistic view, than other professional staff, of the potential abilities of their patients (see for example Jones, 1975 pp 123/4). However, no relationships were found between the general attitudes and aims of the nurses or hostel staff, on the one hand, and whether or not they were dissatisfied with the co-operation from consultants, psychologists or social workers on the other hand.

10.5 Views of the senior nursing staff on additional tasks which should be carried out by nurses instead of by other professional staff

In reply to the question "Do you think there are any tasks or responsibilities which are currently carried out by staff in different professions which should be carried out by nursing staff?". Half of the senior nursing staff suggested at least one additional task which they considered that nurses should do (see

Table 82 The extent of satisfaction amongst the senior ward and hostel staff with the influence they had over which residents should be admitted to or transferred from their units, analysed by their involvement in making decisions on individual residents

The proportion of these staff who were:	All nursing officers	All ward sisters	WARD SISTERS AND NURSING OFFICERS Scores on participation in decisions* scale			
			0–1	2–3	4–5	6–7
	%	%	%	%	%	%
satisfied	65	49	26	38	59	93
dissatisfied	35	51	74	62	41	7
with the influence they had over which patients should be admitted to or discharged from their ward(s)	100	100	100	100	100	100
Base: ward sisters and nursing officers† responsible for wards (reweighted)	*48*	*191*	*38*	*54*	*73*	*41*

The proportion of these staff who were:	All officers in charge	OFFICERS IN CHARGE Scores on participation in decisions* scale		
		0–3	4–5	6–7
	%	%	%	%
satisfied	78	55	79	88
dissatisfied	22	45	21	12
with the influence they had over which residents should be admitted to or discharged from their hostel	100	100	100	100
Base: officers in charge†	*101*	*20*	*39*	*42*

Higher scores on this scale indicated that the staff took part in making more decisions on individual residents and were more likely to have recently attended case conferences and staff discussions.
†*Excluding a few staff who said this was not applicable.*

table 84). Most of these nursing officers said that their nurses should make a greater contribution to the work carried out in the occupational centres or the schools. Generally they envisaged this as a way of expanding or improving the occupational or educational facilities and were not suggesting that the nurses should replace the existing staff. In considering these views it is interesting to note that about half of the ward nurses said that the occupational centres which their patients attended were partly or wholly staffed by nurses.[3]

Only a tenth of the nursing officers said that nurses should provide the type of advice and support to relatives which at present is given by social workers or health visitors. However it was seen previously that at least half of the nursing officers felt that more domiciliary support should be given to relatives and in most cases suggested that their nurses should contribute to expanding this service.

[3]Five per cent. of all the nurses were working in an occupational centre (table 31).

Table 83 The relationship between the time since last talking to a psychologist about one of their residents and the staff's views on the co-operation they received from psychologists

The proportion of these nursing and hostel staff who were:	TRAINED NURSES who last talked to a psychologist about a resident		OFFICERS IN CHARGE AND DEPUTIES who last talked to a psychologist about a resident	
	within the previous 6 months†	at least 6 months ago†	within the previous 6 months†	at least 6 months ago†
	%	%	%	%
satisfied	71	39	82	20
dissatisfied	29	61	18	80
with the co-operation from	—	—	—	—
psychologists	100	100	100	100
Base: daytime ward nurses and hostel staff* (reweighted)	54	41	24	35

*Excluding staff who felt that this was not applicable.
†The time period within the previous 6 months was used because only a few of the staff had talked to a psychologist within the previous 4 weeks.

Table 84 Tasks or responsibilities which the senior nursing staff felt should be carried out by nurses instead of by staff in other professions

Tasks or responsibility	Senior nursing staff
	%
Some of the work carried out by staff in occupational centres	26
Some of the work carried out by teachers in the patients' schools	15
Providing the support and advice which at present is given by social workers or health visitors to families caring for a mentally handicapped child in the community	9
Assisting with physiotherapy or speech therapy (usually by working under the supervision of trained therapists)	8
Some of the responsibilities which are held by consultants at present	5
Other miscellaneous tasks	7
At least one of the above tasks	50
Base: all senior nursing staff (reweighted)	113

10.6 Conclusions on the staff's relationship with other professional staff

At least half of the nursing and hostel staff seemed to be in favour of working more closely with staff in all but one of the professions covered by the survey. The exception was ward doctors or GPs with whom most of the staff felt they had sufficient contact at present.

Two factors which were found to be related to dissatisfaction with the present role or service provided by other professional staff were firstly a lack of regular discussions with them (especially with respect to staff from the training centres and psychologists) and secondly a lack of influence over decisions on individual residents. Thus, although the staff were generally in favour of more contact with other professions, this may only lead to greater co-operation if it resulted in the senior ward and hostel staff being more regularly involved in making decisions on, for example, the admission or transfer of a resident.

11 THE STAFF'S VIEWS ON THEIR CAREERS

Any proposals for the future role and training of staff who care for the mentally handicapped need to take into account the staff's own career aims. Thus it is important to know whether nurses employed on this work see their careers as being linked primarily to the mainstream of nursing or specifically to the care of the mentally handicapped. This chapter is concerned with the reasons staff gave for starting to work with the mentally handicapped, the kind of work they expected or wanted to do in the future, and how they saw their career prospects.

11.1   Reasons for first working with the mentally handicapped

Information on reasons for first working with the mentally handicapped was obtained only from staff with less than six years' experience of this work (ie from 59% of all the nurses and 69% of all the hostel staff). Staff with six years or more experience were excluded because their reasons might be of less relevance to present recruitment policies even if they were able to remember correctly their motivation. Nevertheless, it cannot be assumed that the recently recruited[1] staff were always able to recall the reasons which had actually influenced them, and their answers may to some extent reflect the way they currently see their work rather than the way they had expected it to be before they started working with the mentally handicapped.

Recently recruited staff were asked to select from a set of 12 cards those which described their reason(s) for taking their first job which involved caring for the mentally handicapped.

The majority of these nurses and hostel staff indicated that they had mainly wanted a job which would involve caring for people or that they were specifically interested in working with the mentally handicapped or with children (see table 85).

About a third of the nurses and slightly over a quarter of the hostel staff had previously worked as nurses caring for other types of patients but smaller proportions of both groups (a quarter of the nurses and a tenth of the hostel staff) said they started to work with the mentally handicapped mainly because they wanted to do or continue doing a nursing job. Pilot work for the survey indicated that the staff who selected "wanting to do a nursing job" as their main reason had generally been attracted by the clinical nursing role rather than by the idea of nursing the mentally handicapped in particular.

Only a tenth of the staff said that their main reason for initially working with the mentally handicapped was the convenience of the hours or the fact

---

[1]Throughout this chapter staff with less than 6 year's experience of working with the mentally handicapped are referred to as having been "recently recruited" although some of them may have been recruited more than 6 years ago.

Table 85   The main reason given by recently recruited staff for starting to work with the mentally handicapped

Main reason	All nurses with less than 6 years' experience*	All hostel staff with less than 6 years' experience*	Students	Pupils	Nursing assistants	Care assistants
	%	%	%	%	%	%
Wanting a job that involved caring for people	48	57	49	51	52	57
Specifically interested in working with the mentally handicapped (because they had been a voluntary worker, or had a relative who had worked with the mentally handicapped, or a relative who was mentally handicapped)	8	11	14	13	7	11
Wanting to work with children (aged under 16)	2	5	1	2	3	6
	58	73	64	66	62	74
Wanting to do (or continue doing) a nursing job	23	9	21	24	21	11
Convenience: of the hours and shifts or of living close to a hospital or hostel	10	13	6	2	12	14
Any of the other specified reasons (boredom with other kinds of work, looking for any job, attracted by the pay or by a job which provided accommodation)	4	2	5	6	3	2
None of the above reasons applied	4	2	4	3	2	1
	100	100	100	100	100	100
Base: staff who had worked with the mentally handicapped for less than 6 years (reweighted)	*333*	*223*	*81*	*63*	*180*	*178*

Relatively few of the trained nurses or more senior hostel staff had worked with the mentally handicapped for less than six years so that separate percentages could not be shown for staff in the more senior grades.

that a hospital or hostel was close to their home. However, about 40% of the nursing and care assistants, but only a tenth of the trainee nurses, said that convenience was a contributory factor. This is consistent with other results which show that, compared with the trainees, recently recruited nursing and care assistants were more likely to have lived near to their first hospital or hostel and tended to be older, married female staff with young children, and were often working part-time (see table 86). Similarly a relatively higher proportion of the nursing and care assistants had started working with the mentally handicapped immediately after being housewives whereas relatively more of the trainees had come from full-time education. However, the majority of the staff in all these grades had started working with the mentally handicapped immediately after being in other paid work (see table 87). Thus, although the majority of the trainees were aged under 25, most of them had done some other type of work after leaving school before they started working with the mentally handicapped. This is consistent with the results in the Briggs report which show that women tend to enter psychiatric or subnormality nursing at a slightly older age than other types of nursing.

123

Table 86 Circumstances of recently recruited staff

	All nurses with less than 6 years' experience	All hostel staff with less than 6 years' experience	Students	Pupils	Nursing assistants	Care assistants
Proximity to their first hospital or hostel	%	%	%	%	%	%
At the time of applying for their first job they were living: within daily travelling distance from the hospital or hostel	82	85	57	62	94	90
elsewhere in the UK	9	15	20	18	3	10
abroad	9	1	24	21	2	1
	100	100	100	100	100	100
Sex and family situation (at time of interview)						
Male	28	14	46	35	18	7
Female—single	19	22	36	43	13	25
Female—married, widowed, divorced or separated and without any children	8	11	11	13	4	10
Female—married, widowed, divorced or separated with a child aged under 16	34	31	7	6	51	36
Female—married, widowed, divorced or separated with youngest child aged over 16	11	22	0	3	14	22
	100	100	100	100	100	100
Age (at time of interview)						
16–29	49	39	87	84	36	41
30–39	26	17	11	13	32	18
40 or older	25	44	1	3	32	42
	100	100	100	100	100	100
Hours worked (at time of interview)						
Full time (at least 40 hours a week)	65	55	94	95	51	46
Part time (less than 40 hours a week)	35	45	6	5	49	54
	100	100	100	100	100	100
Base: staff who had worked with the mentally handicapped for less than six years (reweighted)	*333*	*222*	*81*	*63*	*180*	*178*

11.2 Career aspirations

Possibly the most crucial information concerning the staff's career aspirations is firstly whether they expected to continue to work with the mentally handicapped and secondly, for the nurses only, whether they thought they would ever like to transfer to other types of nursing. Throughout this section it is important to note the distinction between staff's views on what they *expected* to do in the future and their views on the sort of work they would *like* to do or would seriously think of doing if it was possible for them to do so.

The type of work staff expected to be doing in five years' time. In response to the question, "In five years' time do you think you will still be working with the mentally handicapped or do you think you will be doing something else?"

124

Table 87 The employment situation of recently recruited staff immediately prior to their first job caring for the mentally handicapped

	All nurses with less than 6 years' experience	All hostel staff with less than 6 years' experience	Students	Pupils	Nursing assistants	Care assistants
	%	%	%	%	%	%
Paid work (for over 10 hours a week)	62	64	63	61	56	61
Housewife	18	18	4	3	27	21
Full-time education	12	8	25	24	7	9
Unemployed and actively seeking work	6	6	6	8	7	6
Other answers	3	3	3	5	3	3
	100	100	100	100	100	100
Base: staff who had worked with the mentally handicapped for less than six years (reweighted)	*333*	*222*	*81*	*63*	*180*	*178*

about two-thirds of the nurses and hostel staff said they expected to continue to be working with the mentally handicapped (table 88). Of the other staff who felt able to predict what they would be doing, most expected to have retired or stopped working for domestic reasons. Only about a tenth of all the staff expected to be working in a different type of job and almost half of these thought they would have changed jobs within the next six months. However, 90 % of all staff thought they would still be working with the mentally handicapped in six months' time since very few of them expected to retire or leave for domestic reasons within this period.

11.3 Nurses who were interested in transferring to other types of nursing

Although the results in the previous section show that most of the nurses who expected to be employed in five years' time thought their careers would continue to be in caring for the mentally handicapped, there was considerable interest amongst nurses in the possibility of transferring to other types of nursing. Answers to the question, "In the future, do you think you would ever like to transfer to a different type of nursing, that is other than with mentally handicapped patients in a hospital?" indicated that about a third of the nurses thought they might like to do so (excluding those who were solely interested in community nursing—see table 89). A noticeably higher proportion of the trainees (about a half), than of the other nurses, thought they would like to make this type of transfer; a point which must be of some concern if their present training is considered to be mainly enabling them to provide social care for the mentally handicapped rather than developing their clinical nursing skills.

A fifth of the student nurses and slightly lower proportions of ward sisters and staff nurses said they might like to transfer to community nursing in the future. This suggests that it would be possible to recruit qualified subnormality nurses to work in the community if, in the future, the hospitals or community health teams were to provide more support to families looking after mentally handicapped people in their own homes.

125

Table 88 The type of work staff expected to be doing in five years' time analysed by their grade

	All nursing staff	All hostel staff	Senior nursing staff	Ward sisters	Staff nurses	Enrolled nurses	Students	Pupils	Nursing assistants	Officers in charge	Deputy officers in charge	Care assistants
	%	%	%	%	%	%	%	%	%	%	%	%
Working with the mentally handicapped	63	66	66	67	55	60	63	59	66	68	67	65
Working in a different type of job	11	6	3	8	18	8	14	23	10	8	5	7
Retired	11	6	19	13	12	18	0	0	9	8	10	4
No longer working for domestic or other reasons	6	13	6	4	7	3	8	2	7	8	5	16
Did not know what they would be doing in five years' time	10	9	7	9	8	11	16	16	8	8	12	8
	100	100	100	100	100	100	100	100	100	100	100	100
Base: all nursing and hostel staff (reweighted)	563	324	113	290	97	123	89	64	235	115	59	216

126

Table 89 The proportion of nurses who would like to transfer to other types of nursing in the future

	All nursing staff	Senior nursing staff	Ward sisters	Staff nurses	Enrolled nurses	Nursing assistants	Students	Pupils
	%	%	%	%	%	%	%	%
Proportion of the nurses who thought they—								
might like to transfer to—								
general nursing	19	14	14	16	16	19	25	38
psychiatric nursing	13	4	15	13	15	8	33	23
geriatric nursing	7	2	6	8	10	7	3	8
sick children's nursing	8	1	4	5	8	8	12	14
other specialities	4	3	6	3	3	3	7	6
would like to transfer to any of the above types of nursing	32	17	30	30	31	29	46	52
would not like to transfer to any other type of nursing (except possibly to community nursing)	68	83	70	70	69	71	54	48
	100	100	100	100	100	100	100	100
Proportion who thought they might like to transfer to community nursing	10	3	13	16	11	7	21	11
Base: all nurses except for those who expected to retire within six months (reweighted)	*550*	*109*	*282*	*197*	*118*	*229*	*89*	*64*

127

Table 90 The proportion of nurses who would seriously think of working in a hostel or home for the mentally handicapped run by a local authority or voluntary society

	All nursing staff	Senior nursing staff	Ward sisters	Staff nurses	Enrolled nurses	Nursing assistants	Students	Pupils
	%	%	%	%	%	%	%	%
The proportion of nurses who—								
would	53	38	54	52	55	50	66	59
would not	41	58	42	45	36	43	27	34
did not know if they would	6	4	4	3	9	7	7	6
seriously think of working in this type of hostel or home	100	100	100	100	100	100	100	100
Base: all nurses except for those who expected to retire within six months (reweighted)	*550*	*109*	*282*	*97*	*118*	*229*	*89*	*64*

11.4 Nurses who would consider working in hostels for the mentally handicapped

In reply to the question, "In the future, would you ever seriously think of working in a hostel or home for the mentally handicapped run by a local authority or voluntary society?" slightly over half of the nurses said they would consider doing this type of work (see table 90). This suggests that it should be possible to continue to recruit a substantial proportion of the new staff to work in local authority hostels from nurses with experience of working in sub-normality hospitals.

11.5 Hostel staff who would consider working in hospitals for the mentally handicapped

In contrast to the general interest in working in hostels amongst all grades of nurses, only a tenth of the officers in charge but a higher proportion of the care assistants (40%) said they would seriously think of working in a hospital for the mentally handicapped in the future (see table 91).

Table 91 The proportion of hostel staff who would seriously think of working in a hospital for the mentally handicapped

	All hostel staff	Officers in charge	Deputies	Care assistants
The proportion of hostel staff who—	%	%	%	%
would	33	10	22	41
would not	63	86	74	55
did not know if they would	3	4	3	3
seriously think of working in a hospital for the mentally handicapped	100	100	100	100
Base: all hostel staff except for those who expected to retire within six months (reweighted)	*322*	*49*	*58*	*215*

11.6 Staff's views on their promotion opportunities

The staff's views on their promotion prospects were sought to discover whether there appeared to be any general problems related to the career structures which might discourage people from starting or continuing to work with the mentally handicapped.

About 60% of all the nurses and hostel staff who worked full-time were satisfied with their chances of promotion (table 92). The majority of the remaining 40% of full-time staff and half of those who worked part-time felt that promotion opportunities were not applicable to them but this may have reflected an awareness of their lack of promotion outlets (for example nursing assistants who knew they would not be accepted as trainees), rather than a lack of interest in career opportunities.

129

Although only a few (6%) of the hostel staff were expecting to do a different type of work within the next five years, slightly over half of these staff were dissatisfied with their present promotion opportunities, as compared with less than a fifth of those who expected to continue to work with the mentally handicapped. Amongst the nurses there was not a clear relationship between dissatisfaction with their chances of promotion and expecting to do a different type of work.

About a third of the nurses and a quarter of the hostel staff who expected to continue to work with the mentally handicapped for at least five years thought they would be promoted to a more senior grade within this time (see table 93). Not surprisingly this included almost all of the students and pupils as they would have completed their training within this period.

There was not a straightforward relationship between the staff's promotion expectations and whether or not they were satisfied with their promotion prospects. On the one hand, somewhat surprisingly, staff who expected to be promoted within the next five years were slightly more likely, than the others, to be dissatisfied with their chances of promotion (possibly partly because they felt they should have been promoted more quickly). On the other hand, staff who thought they would be in the same grade in five years' time were more likely to feel that chances of promotion were not applicable to them (particularly nursing assistants and officers in charge).

Lower proportions of the enrolled nurses, nursing and care assistants and officers in charge, than of staff in the other grades, expected to be promoted within the next five years and staff in these grades were also more likely to feel that promotion was not applicable to them or to be dissatisfied with their prospects. With respect to the enrolled nurses and nursing and care assistants this would appear to be a reflection of their present situation in that without further training most of them would not be considered to be eligible for promotion.[2] The fact that a relatively low proportion of the officers in charge expected to be in a more senior grade in five years' time may have partly stemmed from there not being a clear channel for promoting them within the same type of work. Only a few of the officers in charge said they had a person in charge of them who was solely responsible for services for the mentally handicapped whereas in most of the hospitals the ward sisters could become nursing officers and continue to be responsible only for mentally handicapped patients.

11.7   Discussion on the staff's careers

In many respects the careers of the nurses seemed to be more closely linked to providing social care for the mentally handicapped than to doing clinical nursing. Recently recruited nurses were more likely to have been mainly attracted by the opportunity to do a caring job rather than by the opportunity to become, or continue to be, a nurse. Similarly the vast majority of the nurses who expected to be in employment in five years' time thought they would still be working with the mentally handicapped.

---

[2]Except for a few of the enrolled nurses who could become senior enrolled nurses, and a few of the care assistants, who held a nursing or social work qualification.

Table 92 Satisfaction with their chances of promotion analysed by grade, for staff who worked full-time

	All nurses	All hostel staff	Senior nursing staff	Ward sisters	Staff nurses	Enrolled nurses	Nursing assistants	Students	Pupils	Officers in charge	Deputies	Care assistants
Very or fairly satisfied	%59	%64	%75	%73	%56	%50	%46	%75	%77	%55	%70	%65
A little or very dissatisfied	18	22	12	13	31	24	14	19	15	18	12	30
Staff who said that chances of promotion were not applicable to them	24	14	14	15	13	26	41	5	8	27	18	5
	100	100	100	100	100	100	100	100	100	100	100	100
Base: all staff who worked full-time (ie at least 40 hours a week)	361	203	72	260	55	85	117	68	58	108	57	100

131

Table 93 The staff's views on their promotion prospects during the next five years, for all staff who expected to continue to work with the mentally handicapped over this period

	All nurses	All hostel staff	Senior nursing staff	Ward sisters	Staff nurses	Enrolled nurses	Nursing assistants	Students	Pupils	Officers in charge	Deputies	Care assistants
	%	%	%	%	%	%	%	%	%	%	%	%
In five years' time the staff expected—												
to be promoted to a more senior grade	36	23	50	33	48	20	21	95	97	22	47	17
to be in the same grade	59	58	46	62	44	76	74	0	0	66	24	66
could not say which grade they expected to be or not in a comparable grade	5	19	4	5	8	4	5	5	3	12	29*	17
	100	100	100	100	100	100	100	100	100	100	100	100
Base: all staff who expected to still be working with the mentally handicapped in five years' time (reweighted)	356	211	73	193	53	74	155	56	37	78	39	139

*Most of these deputy officers in charge expected to become (field) social workers.

Nevertheless there were two ways in which the careers of a considerable proportion of the nurses were linked to, or potentially linked to, other types of nursing: firstly in that about 40% of the nurses had previously worked with other types of patients, and secondly in that a third of the nurses thought they would like to transfer to other types of nursing in the future. The first point suggests that if the training and career structures of the nurses ceased to be linked to other types of nursing, then, one numerically important source of recruitment might dwindle. However, it is not possible to say whether other suitable people would be attracted to working in the hospitals for the mentally handicapped if they felt the job was more closely linked to residential social work than to clinical nursing. There was no evidence to suggest that nurses with previous experience of other types of nursing placed less emphasis, than the other nurses, on the social caring side of their work, nor was the interest in transferring to other types of nursing confined to those who were most attached to the clinical side of their present work. The extent of interest in the possibility of transferring to other types of nursing suggests that some of the present nurses may be disappointed with any proposals which would make this more difficult for them in the future. However, it is possible that even in the present circumstances nurses would find it difficult to make this type of transfer unless they had additional nursing qualifications.

A lack of career opportunities for the enrolled nurses and nursing and care assistants seemed to lead to a relatively higher proportion of the staff in these grades feeling that chances of promotion were inapplicable to them or to dissatisfaction with their prospects. Although the background information on the recently recruited nursing and care assistants suggests that many of them may not be prepared to move to a different hospital or hostel for training or promotion, they may be interested in developing their careers in other ways.

12 TRAINING IN THE CARE OF THE MENTALLY HANDICAPPED

One of the most important issues for consideration by the Jay Committee centred on what type of training staff should receive and whether the present training for nurses places sufficient emphasis on the social aspects of caring. This chapter is concerned firstly with the subjects in which staff had received some training and secondly with the views of qualified staff on the adequacy of their training. Because staff's views on their training may partly reflect their own career interests, it was necessary to examine whether there were any differences in the type of care they provided which may have resulted from differences in their formal training.

12.1 Basic training given to nursing and care assistants

Over 80% of the nursing assistants, but just over half of the care assistants, said they had been given some training or advice on basic ways of caring for their residents, for example in washing or dressing them or dealing with incontinence (see table 94). However, in many of the adult hostels the care assistants may not need this type of training because almost all of the residents could look after themselves.

Only slightly over half of the nursing and care assistants said they had received some training or advice on ways of dealing with difficult behaviour in residents (the examples used in the question were aggressive or destructive behaviour). Since most of the wards and hostels contained at least one resident who was considered to have a behaviour problem (see chapter 3), this subject appears to be relatively neglected in the training given to the assistants.

Table 94 Basic training or advice given to nursing and care assistants

	Nursing assistants	Care assistants
Training or advice on ways of feeding, washing or dressing residents or ways of changing incontinent residents	%	%
Had been given this type of training or advice:		
by the ward sister or officer in charge of their unit	66	37
on an induction course (or in-service training)	29	7
in any other way	18	19
Had been given this training or advice in at least one of these ways	84†	58†
Had not been given this type of training or advice	16	42
	100	100
Training or advice on ways of dealing with difficult behaviour in residents—for example, aggressive or destructive behaviour		
Had been given this type of training or advice:		
by the ward sister or officer in charge of their unit	51	47
on an induction course (or in-service training)	11	6
in any other way	11	12
Had been given this training or advice in at least one of these ways	60†	57†
Had not been given this type of training or advice	40	43
	100	100
Base: nursing assistants working on wards and all care assistants*	*209*	*187*

*Excluding a few care assistants who were qualified in subnormality nursing or in social work.
†Some of the staff had received this training in more than one way.

Table 95 Training received on the use of behaviour modification programmes by staff who had worked in their ward or hostel for at least 3 months

	Daytime ward nurses	Daytime hostel staff	Senior nursing staff	Ward sisters	Staff nurses	Enrolled nurses	Nursing assistants	Officers in charge	Deputies	Care assistants
	%	%	%	%	%	%	%	%	%	%
Proportion of the staff who—										
had received some training or advice on ways of carrying out or designing behaviour modification programmes	41	30	54	50	46	42	33	46	33	24
had not received this type of training	57	69	46	50	53	58	63	53	65	75
did not know	2	1	0	0	1	0	4	1	2	1
	100	100	100	100	100	100	100	100	100	100
Base: daytime ward nurses and hostel staff who had worked in their ward or hostel for at least three months* and senior nursing staff (reweighted)	234	271	113	195	48	66	106	97	57	177

*The question on training in behaviour modification programmes was asked within the context of obtaining other information on the way the units were run so staff who had worked in their ward or hostel for less than three months (and the trainees) were excluded because they were not expected to be fully familiar with the running of the units.

Table 96 The nurses' experience of the type of work carried out in hostels run by local authorities or voluntary organisations

	Daytime ward nurses	Senior nursing staff	Ward sisters	Staff nurses	Enrolled nurses	Nursing assistants	Students	Pupils
	%	%	%	%	%	%	%	%
Had previously worked in a hostel*	2	3	6	7	0	0	6	0
Had not worked in a hostel but had visited at least one hostel	53	81	75	79	57	30	73	50
Had not visited any hostels but had been told about the type of work they carry out	15	4	10	4	21	18	8	23
Had not been told about the work carried out in hostels and had no direct experience of their work	30	11	9	9	22	52	13	27
	100	100	100	100	100	100	100	100
Base: daytime ward nurses and senior nursing staff (reweighted)	324	113	213	58	75	129	53	48

*This table only refers to experience of hostels run by local authorities or voluntary organisations and so excludes the nurses' experience of hostels which are run by hospitals.

Assistants had mainly been given their training or advice on basic care and behaviour problems by their ward sister or officer in charge rather than through an induction course or in any other way.

12.2 Training on the use of behaviour modification programmes

It was seen in chapter 4 that, according to the staff, behaviour modification programmes were used with some of the residents from about a third of the wards and a fifth of the hostels. A slightly higher proportion of the nurses (41 %) than of the hostel staff (30 %) had received some training or advice on the use of these techniques (see table 95). The proportion of nurses who had been given this type of training was noticeably higher amongst the registered nurses who had trained as students in subnormality nursing since 1970 (about two-thirds) than amongst those with other types of training or the nursing assistants.

12.3 Experience of other types of residential accommodation for the mentally handicapped

If nurses knew something of the work carried out in hostels, it might assist them to assess whether their patients could live more independently, possibly within a hostel. Registered nurses were the most likely, and nursing assistants the least likely, to have had some direct experience of the work carried out in hostels run by local authorities or voluntary organisations. About 80% of the registered nurses, but only 30% of the nursing assistants, had worked in or visited a hostel; half of the nursing assistants said they had never been told about the work carried out in hostels (see table 96).

The corresponding results for the hostel staff show that the proportion of them who had either worked in or visited a subnormality hospital (79%—see table 97) was much higher than the proportion of nurses with direct experience of hostels (55%).

Table 97 The hostel staff's experience of the type of work carried out in hospitals for the mentally handicapped

	Daytime hostel staff	Officers in charge	Deputies	Care assistants
	%	%	%	%
Had previously worked as a nurse in a hospital for the mentally handicapped	21	43	29	11
Had not worked in subnormality nursing but had visited at least one hospital	58	55	62	58
Had not visited any hospitals for the mentally handicapped but had been told about the type of work they carry out	10	1	5	14
Had not been told about the type of work carried out in hospitals for the mentally handicapped and had no direct experience of their work	11	2	3	16
	100	100	100	100
Base: daytime hostel staff (reweighted)	*285*	*115*	*59*	*177*

12.4 The experience of staff in children's units of looking after children who are not handicapped

It may well be desirable for staff in children's units to have some experience of working with, or bringing up, children who are not mentally or physically handicapped so that they would have some insight into children's normal behaviour and development.

The majority of the staff in both the children's wards and hostels had had some experience of looking after "normal" children either through working in a nursery or children's home, for example, or bringing up children of their own (see table 98).

It appeared that the hospitals were to some extent able to recruit staff to the children's wards who were particularly interested in working with children since half of the nurses in these wards said they had chosen to work with children and had not simply been allocated to a children's ward by the hospital. By contrast, within the hospitals which had adult and children's wards, only a sixth of the nurses in the adult wards said they had chosen to work with adults.

Table 98   Previous experience of staff in children's units of working with children who are not handicapped

	Daytime nurses in children's wards	Daytime care staff in children's hostels
	%	%
Had previously worked for at least four weeks with children who were not handicapped mentally or physically, for example in a nursery, a school or a children's home	26	56
Had not worked for four weeks with "normal" children but did have at least one child of his or her own	45	25
Had not worked for four weeks with "normal" children and did not have any children of his or her own	29	19
	100	100
Base: all daytime ward or hostel staff except for trainee nurses (reweighted)	33	76

12.5 Subjects included in the training received by recently qualified staff

Staff who had obtained a formal qualification in subnormality nursing or social work since 1970, and the second and third year trainee nurses, were asked to select from a set of 14 cards those which described subjects covered during their training. The vast majority of the nurses considered they had been given some training on almost all of these subjects, whereas the training given to staff who had attended social work courses frequently did not seem to have covered topics which were specifically related to providing basic care or medical care for the mentally handicapped (see table 99). To some extent this latter finding was not surprising because most of the social work courses provided a

138

Table 99   Subjects included in the training of staff who have qualified in subnormality nursing or social work since 1970 or are currently in their second or third year as trainees

The proportion of these staff who considered that the following subjects had been included in their training:—	Staff who have received training		
	to become registered nurses*	to become enrolled nurses†	on a social work course**
	%	%	%
The educational and training side of the work eg teaching residents to wash or feed themselves, or teaching reading or writing, preparing them to go to work	97	88	46
Ways of enabling residents to develop emotionally and psychologically and helping them to make more choices for themselves eg ways of making them aware of opportunities of developing their self-awareness	81	63	79
Ways of providing a homelike atmosphere for residents	89	82	68
The sort of games and other recreational activities they could do with the residents	92	87	46
Basic ways of caring for residents eg how to wash, bath, dress, toilet them	97	90	29
Ways of dealing with difficult behaviour in residents eg aggressive or destructive behaviour	96	97	46
Knowledge of clinical nursing eg ways of looking after residents with a physical illness, giving injections, treating bedsores	98	98	21
Knowledge of the cause of mental handicap and of genetics	97	95	75
The development and growth of normal children	92	73	96
Knowledge of the use of personal relationships eg the use of group dynamics or staff-resident relationships	72	63	82
Ways of helping parents to care for the mentally handicapped in their own homes	52	37	39
The sort of work carried out by staff in other professions	70	46	82
Knowledge of the Mental Health Acts and the legal rights of patients/residents	97	91	75
Ways of training or supporting other nursing or care staff	73	37	50
Base: staff who have qualified in subnormality nursing or social work since 1970 or are in their second or third year as trainees (reweighted)	*137*	*51*	*28*

About a third of these nurses were ward sisters, a quarter were staff nurses and the remainder were second or third year students.
†*About two-thirds of these nurses were enrolled and a third were second year pupils.*
**These staff were all officers in charge because only a few of the other hostel staff had obtained a social work qualification since 1970.*

qualification in all types of residential social work with adults or children rather than a specialised training in caring for the mentally handicapped.[1] Nevertheless it may be of concern that almost half of the officers in charge who had recently obtained a social work qualification felt that their course had not covered the educational and training side of their work or the sort of games and activities they could undertake with the residents.

Training in ways of helping parents to care for the mentally handicapped within their own homes appeared to have been relatively neglected in both the nursing and the social work training courses. Only half of the staff who had recently trained as students and about a third of those who had trained as pupils or on a social work course considered that this topic had been included in their training. This implies that more emphasis would need to be placed on training in this area if staff were to be involved in providing more assistance to parents along the lines suggested by many of the senior nursing staff in chapter 9.

12.6 Views of recently qualified staff and trainee nurses on their training

Recently qualified staff and second or third year trainees were asked to reconsider the 14 cards describing training topics and to select from them the two on which they would have preferred more emphasis in their training and the two on which they would have preferred less emphasis.

There was no general consensus amongst staff on how the emphasis on various parts of their training could be improved, and almost a third of them felt that none of the subjects should be given less emphasis. However, the proportion of nurses who would have preferred greater emphasis on at least one of the four subjects which were most closely related to their social caring role was noticeably higher than the proportion who felt that less emphasis was needed on any of these topics (see table 100). This particularly applied to nurses who had trained as students of whom slightly over a third would have preferred more emphasis on the educational or training side of their work and on ways of enabling their patients to develop emotionally or psychologically and helping them to make more choices for themselves.

Of the officers in charge who had attended a social work training course since 1970, relatively high proportions would have preferred more emphasis on ways of enabling their residents to develop emotionally or psychologically or on the use of personal relationships (for example through training in group dynamics). Although it was seen in the previous section that only about half of the officers in charge considered that their course had covered the educational and training side of their work or the type of activities they could do with the residents, hardly any of them felt that these topics needed more emphasis.

12.7 Views of senior nursing staff on the present syllabus for student nurses

In reply to the question "Are there any subject areas which you think should be given more emphasis in the training of student nurses?" two-thirds of the senior nursing staff suggested at least one subject on which they felt more

---

[1]It was seen in table 16 that the most frequently held social work qualifications were the CRSW for residential work with adults or the equivalent qualification in residential work with children (the CRCCYP).

Table 100 Views of staff who have qualified since 1970 and of second or third year trainees on the subjects which should have been given (a) more or (b) less emphasis in their training

	(a) The two subjects on which more emphasis would have been preferred by staff who have received training:			(b) The two subjects on which less emphasis would have been preferred by staff who have received training:		
	to become registered nurses*	to become enrolled nurses*	on a social work course*	to become registered nurses	to become enrolled nurses	on a social work course
	%	%	%	%	%	%
The educational and training side of the work eg teaching patients/residents to wash or feed themselves, or teaching reading or writing, preparing them to go to work	34	26	4	7	4	0
Ways of enabling patients/residents to develop emotionally and psychologically and helping them to make more choices for themselves eg ways of making them aware of opportunities or developing their self-awareness	38	28	44	2	2	0
Ways of providing a homelike atmosphere for patients/residents	11	6	4	5	10	11
The sort of games and other recreational activities they could do with the patients/residents	12	11	4	7	15	22
ANY OF THE FOUR AREAS ABOVE—ON THE SOCIAL CARING SIDE OF THEIR WORK	72	49	48	17	25	33
Basic ways of caring for patients/residents eg how to wash, bath, dress, toilet them	8	9	0	19	13	15
Ways of dealing with difficult behaviour in patients/residents eg aggressive or destructive behaviour	17	29	30	2	2	0
Knowledge of clinical nursing eg ways of looking after patients/ residents with a physical illness, giving injections, treating bedsores	15	24	0	13	13	22
Knowledge of the cause of mental handicap and of genetics	12	15	3	11	6	15
The development and growth of normal children	5	1	4	10	13	15
Knowledge of the use of personal relationships eg the use of group dynamics or staff-resident relationships	12	4	37	4	10	0
Ways of helping parents to care for the mentally handicapped in their own homes	24	22	7	4	2	4
The sort of work carried out by staff in other professions	5	4	4	19	27	19
Knowledge of the Mental Health Acts and the legal rights of patients/residents	2	10	19	16	21	11
Ways of training or supporting other nursing or care staff	6	5	15	2	6	0
Would not have preferred less emphasis on any of these training areas				31	27	30
Base: staff who have qualified in subnormality nursing or social work since 1970 or are in their second or third year as trainees	137	51	28	137	51	28

*The notes on table 99 give further information on the present grades of these staff.

141

emphasis was required. The topics which were the most frequently mentioned related to ways of teaching the patients and developing their abilities and of assisting mentally handicapped people to live with their families in the community (see table 101). These views seem to be generally consistent with those of the nurses who have recently been trained as students and with the previous finding that only half of these nurses considered that ways of giving parents this type of assistance had been included in their training.

In response to a similar question on subjects which should be given less emphasis on the student nurses' syllabus, about half of the senior nursing staff who expressed a view did not think there were any subjects on which less emphasis should be placed. Most of the other nursing officers felt that less emphasis was needed on subjects related to the clinical or medical aspects of the work. This seems to contrast with the views expressed by nurses who have recently been trained as students in that only slightly above a tenth of them selected clinical nursing as one of the two training asrcas on which thcy would havc preferred less emphasis. However we cannot tell whether this does represent a difference between the views of senior nursing staff and nurses who had recently been in training as it may be partly related to differences in the wording and form of the questions.

Table 101 **Views of the senior nursing staff on the subjects which should be given more, or less, emphasis in the present training syllabus for students**

(a) The proportion who suggested that **more emphasis** should be placed on:	Senior nursing staff
	%
Ways of teaching the patients and developing their potential abilities	38
Ways of caring for the mentally handicapped in the community (including the role of social workers in the community)	24
Behaviour modification techniques	11
Clinical or medical aspects of caring for the mentally handicapped	13
Psychiatric aspects of caring for the mentally handicapped (for example, ways of caring for patients who are mentally ill or emotionally disturbed)	8
Ward management	4
Any other subject	13
The proportion who felt that:	%
more emphasis was needed on at least one of these subjects	68
there were no subjects which needed more emphasis	17
did not know	15
	100
(b) The proportion who suggested that **less emphasis** should be placed on:	%
The clinical or medical aspects of their work	33
Any other subject	8
The proportion who felt that:	%
less emphasis was needed on at least one of these subjects	41
there were no subjects which needed less emphasis	44
did not know	15
	100
Base: all senior nursing staff (reweighted)	*113*

Table 102   The age of the daytime ward nurses analysed by their type of qualification or training

Age	TYPE OF QUALIFICATION OR TRAINING				
	RNMS* obtained from 1971–76 and 2nd/3rd year students	RNMS* obtained prior to 1971	Registered nurse but not qualified in subnormality nursing	SEN(MS)† obtained after training as pupils and 2nd year pupils	SEN(MS)† obtained by experience and SENs not qualified in subnormality nursing
	%	%	%	%	%
less than 25	28	0	0	42	8
25–29	41	11	21	21	5
30–39	20	33	15	18	8
40–49	8	29	26	8	29
50 or older	3	27	39	12	50
	100	100	100	100	100
Base: qualified nurses and 2nd/3rd year trainees who worked on the wards in the daytime (reweighted)	93	68	39		38

*Registered nurse for the mentally subnormal or the equivalent Scottish qualification (RNMD).
†Enrolled nurse for the mentally subnormal.

Table 103 The part of their work which the daytime ward nurses liked the best, analysed by their type of qualification or training

Part of their work they liked best:	TYPE OF QUALIFICATION OR TRAINING				
	RNMS obtained from 1971–76 and 2nd/3rd year students	RNMS obtained prior to 1971	Registered nurse but not qualified in subnormality nursing	SEN(MS) obtained after training as a pupil and 2nd year pupils	SEN(MS) obtained by experience and SENs not qualified in subnormality nursing
	%	%	%	%	%
part of their social caring role (encouraging the residents to be more independent, teaching or training, or taking part in activities with them)	63	53	36	48	38
providing more comfort or basic care for their residents	19	24	25	26	22
looking after residents when they are ill or need some medical attention	10	15	37	26	41
other professional tasks	9	8	3	0	0
	100	100	100	100	100
Base: qualified nurses and 2nd/3rd year trainees who worked on the wards in the daytime (reweighted)	93	68	39	51	38

12.8 The relationship between the formal training received by staff, their attitudes and the type of care they provided

The attitudes and work of the daytime ward and hostel staff who had a recognised nursing or social work qualification were analysed by the type of formal training they had had to see whether there were differences in their attitudes or work which might have stemmed from their training.

Registered nurses For this purpose the registered nurses were divided into three groups: those who had become qualified in subnormality nursing in 1971 or subsequently (who were considered together with the second and third year students); those who were registered in subnormality nursing prior to 1971; and those who were not qualified in subnormality nursing. As most of the nurses in the first group were aged under 30 whereas the others were usually older (see table 102), it is not possible to tell whether any differences between the first group and the other two are related to age rather than to differences in their training.

There were no appreciable differences between the three groups in the amount of time which they had spent in teaching or playing with their patients or the number of restrictions in their wards although there were two ways in which their attitudes seemed to be related to their training. Firstly, a higher proportion of the registered nurses who were not qualified in subnormality nursing, than of the others, preferred the clinical side of their work to the social caring side (see table 103). Secondly, compared with the other registered nurses, those who had been in training since 1970 had slightly more optimistic attitudes towards the potential capacities of mentally handicapped people. However, the previous results suggest that in practice, possibly because of their lack of experience, this did not result in the recently trained nurses spending more time on teaching their patients or encouraging them to live more independently.

Enrolled nurses In order to consider the training given to the enrolled nurses it is necessary to distinguish between those who had trained as pupils in subnormality nursing and those who had become enrolled because of their experience as nursing assistants prior to 1968 or through training in another type of nursing. Because the syllabus for pupils in subnormality nursing was introduced in 1964, the enrolled nurses who have trained as pupils tend to be much younger than the other enrolled nurses (see table 102).

There were generally only minor differences between the two groups of enrolled nurses[2] in the time that they spent on the social caring side of their work or in their general attitudes towards the potential abilities of mentally handicapped people. However, a slightly lower proportion of the nurses who had trained as pupils (26%) than of the others (41%) preferred the clinical nursing side of their work to the social caring side.

It has previously been noted that, in comparison with the registered nurses, the enrolled nurses tended to have a more pessimistic view of the potential abilities of mentally handicapped people (chapter 7) and that a higher proportion of them preferred the clinical nursing side of their work to the social caring

---

[2]The second year pupil nurses were included with the enrolled nurses who had trained as pupils for this analysis.

side (chapter 9). These differences persisted, but to a lesser extent, when attention was confined to the nurses who have recently trained as students or pupils. They may partly stem from the training nurses receive because the syllabus for students was changed in 1970 to place more emphasis on the social aspects of caring whereas the syllabus for pupils has not been revised since its introduction in 1964. The notes on the pupils' syllabus state that one of the two principles which were carefully considered in its preparation was "that as far as is practicable the training of pupil nurses in psychiatric hospitals should be in line with training based on general, geriatric, or specialised acute hospitals". This, in conjunction with the above results, suggests that, for subnormality work the pupils' training may place too great an emphasis on clinical nursing and basic care and insufficient emphasis on the scope for developing their patients' abilities. Although it was seen previously that only a few of the nurses who had trained as pupils felt that their training placed too much emphasis on clinical nursing, this may be the result of their liking this part of their work coupled with an interest in the possibility of transferring to other types of nursing in the future.

Officers in charge The time that officers in charge devoted to the social caring side of their work, the number of restrictions in their hostels, and their general attitudes were not consistently related to whether or not they had obtained a recognised training qualification, nor were they related to whether their qualification was in nursing or social work. The small group of officers in charge who were qualified in both nursing and social work were of special interest because of suggestions that this may be the best combination of training for staff who care for the mentally handicapped (Tizard, 1975 and Jones, 1975). Although the numbers involved (only 10 officers in charge) were too small to support any firm conclusions on this issue, it is interesting to note that these officers were more optimistic about the potential abilities of the mentally handicapped than the others and were more likely to consider that their most important aim was to enable their residents to live more independently in society.

12.9 Further training received by qualified staff

To discover whether there were opportunities for trained staff to extend their knowledge or bring it more up to date, nurses who were qualified after being trainees in subnormality nursing and qualified hostel staff were asked whether they had attended any refresher courses or been given any further training. There seemed to be a distinction between, on the one hand, registered nurses and qualified hostel staff of whom half or more had received some further training and, on the other hand, the enrolled nurses very few of whom had attended this type of course (see table 104). Although about half of the courses which the registered nurses had attended were connected with the management of wards, they presumably would have included opportunities to discuss current ideas on the type of care required by their patients. Most of the other courses were either on general developments in the type of care needed within the hospitals or hostels, or on the use of specific techniques, for example behaviour modification methods, group dynamics and the nursing of geriatric patients.

Table 104 Proportion of the staff who had been formally trained in subnormality nursing or social work who had attended a refresher course or been given some further training

Since qualifying in subnormality nursing or social work they:	Senior nursing staff	Ward sisters	Staff nurses	Enrolled nurses*	Officers in charge
	%	%	%	%	%
had attended a refresher course or received some further training	88	81	50	11	60
had not attended this type of course	12	19	50	89	40
	100	100	100	100	100
Base: all staff who had been formally trained in subnormality nursing or social work (reweighted)	82	223	67	43	54

*This is based only on the enrolled nurses who had qualified after training as pupils.

About three-quarters of the registered nurses and officers in charge and slightly fewer of the enrolled nurses said that there were further training courses which staff from their hospital or hostel could attend. The reasons for not having attended a course which were most frequently given by staff who said that courses were available were that they had not had sufficient experience since qualifying (particularly the enrolled nurses) or that they were too busy or short-staffed (particularly the officers in charge). Although several enrolled nurses felt that they did not have sufficient experience to attend a course, comparing them with the registered nurses with a similar or shorter amount of experience (ie those who qualified since 1970) shows that 65% of the latter compared with only 11% of the former had received some further training.

12.10 Summary on training in the care of the mentally handicapped

There appears to be scope for improving the training given to all levels of staff, particularly in the areas of education and training of mentally handicapped people, and assisting families to care for the mentally handicapped in the community if this latter is to form a more important part of their work in the future.

It has been noted previously that nursing and care assistants and enrolled nurses tended to be more pessimistic than other staff about the potential abilities of the mentally handicapped (chapter 7). Staff in these grades were also less likely than registered nurses or more senior hostel staff to have been given some training or advice on the use of behaviour modification programmes or to have visited alternative types of residential accommodation for the mentally handicapped. With respect to the nursing and care assistants this seems to be related to a general lack of training for staff in their grades. Their training on ways of helping with basic care had usually been given by their ward sister or officer in charge rather than on an induction course and almost half of the assistants said they had not received any training or advice on ways of dealing with behaviour problems.

It is questionable whether the enrolled nurses receive sufficient training on the scope for developing the full potential of their patients or on the scope for community care. The stronger interest in clinical nursing amongst enrolled nurses than amongst registered nurses appears to stem partly from their formal training placing perhaps undue enphasis on basic nursing, including clinical and medical aspects, which seems to form a relatively minor part of their work. In addition hardly any of the enrolled nurses who had trained as pupils had subsequently attended a referesher course or been given any further training after they had qualified.

The changes in the syllabus for student nurses in 1970 may have led to the recently trained nurses having a slightly more optimistic view of the scope for developing the abilities of mentally handicapped people but, in practice, they do not seem to spend more time on teaching their patients or encouraging them to be more independent. The majority of the nurses who had trained as students since 1970 would have preferred their training to have placed more emphasis on the educational or training side of their work or on ways of helping their patients to become more independent emotionally or psychologically. Almost half of the senior nursing staff who expressed a view on this issue felt that the students' syllabus placed too much emphasis on the medical or clinical aspects of their work although only a few of the nurses who had recently trained as students would have preferred less training in clinical nursing.

There was no evidence to suggest that the type of care provided in the hostels was related to whether or not the officers in charge had obtained a recognised training qualification, or to whether they were qualified in nursing or social work. It was of concern to find that about half of the hostel staff who had recently qualified on a social work course felt that the educational or training side of their work and the type of activities they could do with the residents had not been covered in their course. This presumably resulted from most of the social work courses providing a qualification in all types of residential care for adults or children and not a specialised training in working with the mentally handicapped.

References

ANDEBERG M. *Cluster Analysis*, Academic Press (1973).

ANDRON L and STURM M. Is "I do" in the repertoire of the retarded? A study of the functioning of married retarded couples, *Mental Retardation*, 11, pp 31–34 (1973).

BEALE E M C. Euclidean cluster analysis, *Bulletin of the International Statistical Institute*, No 43, Book 2, pp 92–94.

BONE M, SPAIN B and MARTIN F. *Plans and provision for the Mentally Handicapped*, Alan and Unwin (1972).

THE BRIGGS REPORT, *Report of the Committee on Nursing*, HMSO, 1972.

COMMUNITY CARE, Sharing the sex secret: sex education for the mentally handicapped, 7 July 1976.

CRAFT A and M. Subnormality in marriage, *Social Work Today*, Vol 7 No 4 pp 98–101 (1976).

CRAFT M. The sexual problems of the disabled: psychological aspects, *Royal Society of Health Journal*, London Vol 96, No 3 pp 110–113 (1976).

DHSS. *Better services for the mentally handicapped*, 1971, HMSO.

DHSS. *Census of Residential Accommodation 1970, part II*, Residential accommodation for the mentally ill and the mentally handicapped by M MORGAN, HMSO.

DHSS. *Statistical and Research Report Series No 3*, Census of Mentally handicapped patients, in hospitals in England and Wales at the end of 1970, HMSO.

DHSS. *Statistical Report Series No 10*, Facilities and Services of Psychiatric Hospitals in England and Wales, 1969.

DHSS. *Statistical and Research Report Services*, Facilities and services of mental illness and mental handicap hospitals in England 1976, HMSO.

DURWARD L and WHATMORE R. *Testing Measures of the quality of residential care: A pilot study*, Wessex Health Care Evaluation Research Team, Report No 11 (1975).

EVERITT B. *Cluster Analysis: an SSRC review of current research*, Heinemann (1974).

FRIEDMAN H P and RUBIN J. On some invariant criteria for grouping data, *Journal of the American Statistical Association*, V 62, pp 1159–1178, (1967).

GENERAL HOUSEHOLD SURVEY, Reports for years 1971–76, OPCS, HMSO.

GLOSSOP C, FELCE D, SMITH J and KUSHLICK A. Contacts made by "external professionals" with clients resident in locally based and "traditional" hospital units, Wessex Health Care Evaluation Research Team, *Report No 127* (1977).

GRANT G and MOORES B. Comparisons of patient activities in two hospitals for the mentally handicapped. *Apex*, Vol 4 No 2 (1976).

GOFFMAN E. *Asylums: Essays on the social situation of mental patients and other inmates*, New York: Doubleday (1961).

JONES K. *Opening the door*, Routledge (1975).

KIERNAN and WOODFORD (editors). *Behaviour modification with the severely retarded*, Associated Science Publisher, Elsvier (1975).

149

KING R. Alternatives to the hospital for the residential care of the mentally retarded, in *Roots of Evaluation*—editors J Wing and H Hafner, Oxford University Press (1973).

KING R, RAYNES N and TIZARD J. *Patterns of Residential care*, Routledge (1971).

KUSHLICK A, Evaluation of residential services for mentally handicapped children in *Roots of Evaluation*—editors J Wing and H Hafner, Oxford University Press (1973).

KUSHLICK A, BLUNDEN R, and COX S. *Psychological Medicine* 3, 1973, pp 446–478.

KUSHLICK A, PALMER J, FELCE D and SMITH J, Summary of current research in mental handicap work 1977, Wessex Health Care Evaluation Research Team, Report No 126.

MOORES B and GRANT G, Feelings of alienation among nursing staff in hospitals for the mentally handicapped, *Int J Nurs Stud*. Vol 14, pp 5–12 (1977).

MOORES B and GRANT G. Optimists and pessimists: Attitudes of nursing staff towards the development potential of mentally handicapped patients in their charge, *Int J Nursing Studies*, Vol 14, pp 13–18 (1977).

MORRIS P, *Put Away: A sociological study of institutions for the mentally retarded*, Routledge, (1969).

NATIONAL DEVELOPMENT GROUP for the Mentally Handicapped, *Mentally Handicapped Children: a plan for action*, (available from Room C411, DHSS, Alexander Fleming House, Elephant and Castle, London SE1 6BY) (1977).

PALLISTER P D and PERRY R, Reflections on marriage for the retarded: The case for voluntary sterilisation, *Hosp Commun Psychiat*, Vol 24, pp 172–174 (1973).

PERKINS C. Mental handicap—a case for counselling, *Youth Counselling Bulletin*, Leicester Vol 2, No 1, pp 7–8 (1976).

PRICES AND INCOMES BOARD REPORT No 60, Pay of nurses and midwives in the National Health Service, HMSO, (1968).

RAYNES N, PRATT M and ROSES S, Aides' involvement in decision-making and the quality of care in institutional settings, Amer, J Ment Defic, Vol 81, No 6, pp 570–577 (1977).

SADLER J and WHITWORTH T. *Reserves of Nurses*, OPCS HMSO (1975).

THE SALMON REPORT. *Report of the Committee on Senior Nursing Staff Structure*, HMSO, 1966.

THOMAS M and MORTON-WILLIAMS J. Overseas nurses in Britain, *PEP Broadsheet*, 1972, p 539.

TIZARD J in *Varieties of residential experience*—editors Tizard, Sinclair and Clarke, Routledge, 1975.

WANDSWORTH SOCIAL SERVICES DEPARTMENT, Research and Planning Section: Project 74, *Clearing House for local authority social services research* No 1, (1977).

WISHART D. *Clustan 1B. User Manual* Modified by the SIA Management Science Department (1970).

APPENDIX A—SAMPLING REPORT by Denise Lievesley

A.1 Sample requirements

The sample was intended to provide information about all grades of nursing staff working with mentally handicapped patients, and care staff in local authority hostels for the mentally handicapped, and to allow comparisons to be made between hospital wards and local authority hostels, concerning the type of patients and the way the units were run.

These aims were achieved by selecting representative samples of—

(a) wards and hostels

(b) staff working in selected wards and hostels

(c) nurses within the selected hospitals who were not working on wards (eg nurses in recreational units).

Information on the selected wards and hostels could then be linked to the answers from staff within them. The combination of (b) and (c) provided representative samples of all hospital nursing staff and all hostel care staff.

The intended sample sizes were approximately—

(i) 55 hospitals and 300 wards

(ii) 100 hostels

(iii) 1,050 nursing staff and 400 hostel staff.

A.2 Sampling frames

Lists were provided by the Department of Health and Social Security and the Scottish Department of Home and Health covering, throughout Great Britain, all the NHS hospitals for the mentally handicapped and any other NHS hospitals which were known to have units or wards for the mentally handicapped. These contained 282 hospitals, most of which catered solely for the mentally handicapped, but 47 of the hospitals contained other types of patients.

The DHSS and SHHD also provided lists of local authority hostels for the mentally handicapped in England and Scotland. These were extended to Wales and updated by directly contacting local authorities. Hostels or group homes (for the mentally handicapped) which did not have any resident care staff were excluded from the survey. The sampling frame contained 410 hostels.

A.3 Selection of hospitals and hostels

It was necessary to select hostels and the smaller hospitals in groups which were geographically clustered in order to provide economic workloads for the interviewers. The initial stage in the sampling procedure was, therefore, to form groups of hospitals and hostels, the most common grouping consisting of 2 hostels and 1 hospital. The 208 resulting groups were ordered by county within standard region and a quarter of them were selected on a systematic random basis.

Hostels All the hostels in the selected geographical groups were included in the survey and an additional sample was drawn of hostels which had opened since the sampling frame was compiled. The sample of hostels does not require any re-weighting since all hostels had the same chance of selection. A total of 108 eligible hostels were selected of which all but 5 agreed to participate in the survey. Eight of the participating hostels contained 3 or more patients who were not mentally handicapped (they were usually considered to be mentally ill or disturbed). The staff from these 8 hostels were included in the survey but, because the survey was primarily concerned with mentally handicapped residents, information was not collected on their residents' abilities.

151

Hospitals An additional sampling procedure was carried out in order to give hospitals chances of selection which varied according to their size, so that the larger hospitals had a greater chance of selection than the smaller ones. This meant that the variation in the number of interviews per hospital could be reduced. It also had the advantage that the wards and staff from larger hospitals were not drawn from only one or two examples of such hospitals. Where possible hospitals in the selected geographical groups were included in the sample so that the majority of the selected hostels were within reasonable travelling distance of a sampled hospital. Fifty-seven hospitals were selected of which all but one agreed to participate in the survey.

A.4 Selection of wards and staff

Wards A random sample of wards[1] was drawn from within the selected hospitals with the probability of selection inversely proportional to the probability of selection of the hospital, where this was possible. Thus wards in the larger hospitals had a lower chance of being selected than the wards in the smaller hospitals. In this way each ward had the same overall chance of being selected except for the wards in the 7 smallest hospitals. Because the probability of selecting the smallest hospitals was very low it was necessary to apply a separate reweighting factor to their wards in order to give them the same weight as wards in the other hospitals.

Table A1 Probability of selecting hospitals and wards

Size stratum	Size of* hospital	Probability of selecting hospital	Total No. of hospitals selected	Probability of selecting wards	Total No. of wards selected
A	0–19	1/24	3	1/1	3
B	20–49	1/12	4	1/1	6
C	50–149	1/4	17	1/1·5	83
D	150–449	1/2	23	1/3	126
E	449+	3/4	9	1/4·5	81

*Estimated number of eligible staff.

A sample of 299 wards was drawn from the 56 participating hospitals and, after reweighting wards in the 7 smallest hospitals, the reweighted sample size was 311 wards (excluding two wards where we were unable to carry out interviews with the ward sisters on the abilities of the patients). This included 9 acute sickness wards which were for patients who required operations or other medical treatment. Nursing staff from the acute sickness wards were included in the survey but no information was collected on the abilities of their patients or the way their wards were run.

Nursing staff Two samples of nursing staff were selected: one of nurses who were allocated to the selected wards, and the other of nurses who had not been allocated to wards (eg nurses working in recreational units) and senior nursing staff. In order to include sufficient numbers of trained nurses the probability of selecting the nurses varied according to their grade. Thus the probability of selection took into account the grade of the nurse, the probability of selection of the hospital and (where appropriate) the probability of selection of the ward.

Ward orderlies, maintenance staff and staff working fewer than ten hours per week were not included in the survey. Nursing staff who were training in other nursing specialities, but temporarily working in the selected hospitals, were also excluded. The response rates and the number of interviews carried out with the various grades of staff are given in table 1.1 in chapter 1.

---

[1]Wards refer to all wards and other residential units in hospitals.

Hostel staff The probability of selecting the hostel staff was the same in each hostel because all hostels had the same chance of being selected. Domestic and maintenance staff and staff working fewer than 10 hours a week were excluded. Since separate analyses were to be conducted on the sample of officers in charge we required a sample of this category which was larger than would have been achieved by proportionate sampling. We therefore included all the officers in charge of the selected hostels, but only 3 in 7 of the deputies and other care staff.

A.5 Reweighting

It was necessary to apply a separate reweighting factor to senior nursing staff and ward sisters in the 7 smallest hospitals so that they would have the same weight as the staff in these grades in the other hospitals. This was required partly because the probability of selecting the smallest hospitals has been so low and partly because of the need to include in the sample a higher proportion of the senior nursing staff and ward sisters than of the other nursing grades. The reweighted sample sizes for each grade after carrying out this process are shown in column (ii) of table A.2. This column shows the base numbers used in tables which make comparisons between grades.

Column (iii) of table A.2 shows the correction factors which have been used to reweight the results in any analyses which combine staff grades with differing selection probabilities. Multiplying the number on column (ii) by the factor in column (iii) produces the reweighted numbers of the staff in each grade for tables in which all the

Table A.2   The sample sizes after reweighting

For nursing staff	(i) Numbers interviewed	(ii) Reweighted sample size for analysis by grades	(iii) Correction factor for analysis of all nursing staff	(iv) Reweighted sample size for analysis of all nursing staff = (ii) × (iii)
Senior nursing staff (ie above the grade of ward sister)	95	113	1/4	29
Ward sisters/charge nurses	264	290	1/4	72
Staff nurses (including deputy sisters/charge nurses)	97	97	1/2	49
Enrolled nurses (including senior enrolled nurses)	123	123	5/6	102
Student nurses	89	89	1/2	45
Pupil nurses	64	64	1/2	32
Nursing assistants	235	235	1	235
Total	967			563

For hostel staff	(i) Numbers interviewed	(ii) Sample size for analysis by grades	(iii) Correction factor for analysis of all hostel staff	(iv) Reweighted sample size for analysis of all hostel staff = (ii) × (iii)
Officers in charge	115	115	3/7	49
Deputy officers in charge	59	59	1	59
Other care staff	216	216	1	216
Total	390			324

hospital or all the hostel staff are combined (see column (iv)). The reweighted total sample of nursing staff is 563 individuals and in the sample of hostel staff the reweighted total is 324 individuals.

The overall probability of selection of the hostel staff was much higher than of the nurses and consequently it is inappropriate to carry out any analyses which combine the hostel with the nursing staff.

A.6 Sample validation

Table A.3 shows that the sample of staff had a similar distribution by grade to the total distribution for all staff in England in 1975. Any differences may be partly due to slightly different distributions of staff in Scotland and Wales and partly to the exclusion from the survey of a few staff who worked for less than 10 hours a week who were mainly nursing or care assistants.

Table A.3 Distribution of the staff grades in the sample compared with the total national distribution for England

Nursing staff	Sample (England, Scotland and Wales) 1976	Total population (England) 1975
	%	%
Senior staff	5	3
Ward sisters	13	13
Staff nurses	9	7
Enrolled nurses	18	19
Nursing assistants	42	44
Trainee nurses	14	14
	100	100
Total—all grades	563	23,981

Hostel staff	Sample (England Scotland and Wales) 1976	Total population (England) 1975
	%	%
Officers in charge	15	14
Deputy officers in charge	18	14
Other care staff	66	71
	100	100
Total—all grades	324	2,640

A.7 Sampling errors—introduction

Sampling error stems from the selected sample not being completey representative of the total population. It is important to remember, however, that it is only one of the factors which affects the precision of results obtained in any survey. The other sources of inaccuracy inculding, for example, non-response and recording errors, cannot be quantified.

154

Sampling errors show the amount by which the values found for a given sample size can be expected to differ from the true value for the total population from which the sample was selected. With a simple random sample the formula for calculating the sampling error of a percentage p, is

$$\text{sampling error, s.e (p)} = \sqrt{\frac{p\,(100{-}p)}{n}}$$

where n is the achieved number of cases in the sample. Unfortunately, this formula is often a poor approximation when a complex sample design, such as this, has been used. The clustering of the sample, necessary to keep interview costs sufficiently low, may lead to an increase in the sampling error which is only partly compensated for by the effect of regional stratification. The formulae which were used to calculate the sampling errors for this complex sample design are based on a method described by Kish et al.[2][3]

It is not feasible to calculate exact sampling errors for every published result because of the excessive computation which would be required. Tables A.4–A.6 show the sampling errors which have been computed for the nursing and hostel staff and the residents for a selection of results.[3]

Once the sampling errors are known the confidence intervals can be obtained for a percentage, p, using the formula p $\pm$ 1.96 s.e (p). There is a probability of less than 5 chances in 100 that the true value for the total population lies outside this range. For example, from table A.4 it can be seen that there is a 95% probability that the proportion of all the hospital nurses who are female is between 66% and 74%.

The final column of tables A.4–A.6 indicates whether the difference between the observed values for the hospital sample and the hostel sample is statistically significant. For example if an observed difference is significant at the 99% level this means that there are 99 chances in a 100 that this is a valid difference and not attributable to sampling errors.

---

[2]Kish L and Hess I, "On variances of ratios and their differences in multi-stage samples", *Journal of the American Statistical Association* Vol 54 (1959).

[3]The formulae which were used to calculate the sampling errors and the sample design effects (comparing the results with those which would be achieved with a simple random sample) are shown in a separate paper available from Denise Lievesley, Sampling Division, OPCS, St Catherine's House, London WC2.

155

Table A.4 Sampling errors of selected values for nurses and hostel staff (percentages)

Description of variable	HOSPITAL NURSES			HOSTEL STAFF			Significance level of difference between nurses and hostel staff
	Value %	Sampling error	95% confidence interval	Value %	Sampling error	95% confidence interval	
% of nurses/hostel staff who are female (table 2.2)	70%	2%	66%–74%	82%	2%	78%–86%	99·9%
% of ward sisters/officers in charge aged 40 or over (table 2.2)	43%	3%	37%–49%	71%	4%	63%–79%	99·9%
% of nurses/hostel staff who have "A" levels or 5 "O" levels (table 2.8)	23%	2%	19%–27%	24%	2%	20%–28%	NS*
% of nurses born in a developing country (table 2.15)	14%	2%	10%–18%	not calculated			
% of nurses/hostel staff in children's wards and hostels who spent over an hour on a "social task" (table 4.4)	35%	5%	25%–45%	55%	7%	41%–69%	95%
% of day nurses/hostel staff (excluding trainees) who had worked in their ward or hostel for less than 2 years (table 5.3)	61%	3%	55%–67%	49%	3%	43%–55%	99%
% of nursing officers who had attended a case conference in previous 3 months (table 6.5)	68%	8%	52%–84%	not applicable			
% of nurses/hostel staff in children's wards and hostels who had previously worked with normal children for 4 weeks or longer (table 12.5)	24%	5%	14%–34%	56%	5%	46%–66%	99·9%
% of ward sisters/officers in charge who had attended a case conference in previous 3 months (table 6.5)	40%	5%	30%–50%	55%	5%	45%–65%	95%

*NS—not significant at 95% level of confidence.

Table A.5   Sampling errors of selected values for nurses and hostel staff (averages)

Description of variable	HOSPITAL NURSES			HOSTEL STAFF			Significance level of difference between hospitals wards and hostel
	Value average	Sampling error	95% confidence interval	Value average	Sampling error	95% confidence interval	
Age of nurses/hostel staff (table 2.2)	37·4	0·7	36·0–38·8	39·5	0·8	37·9–41·1	NS*
Number of restrictions in all wards and hostels (table 5.2)	3·4	0·1	3·2– 3·6	2·1	0·1	1·9– 2·3	99·9%
Number of restrictions in children's wards and hostels (table 5.2)	3·9	0·2	3·6– 4·2	3·0	0·2	2·5– 3·5	99%
Score on participation scale for ward sisters/officers in charge (table 6.8)	3·3	0·2	2·9– 3·7	4·9	0·2	4·6– 5·2	99·9%
Score on participation scale for nursing officers (table 6.8)	4·2	0·4	3·3– 5·1	not applicable			
Score on scope for development scale for day nurses/hostel staff (table 7.2)	19·3	0·1	19·0–19·6	20·2	0·2	19·8–20·6	99·9%
Score on community orientation scale for day nurses/hostel staff (table 7.6)	17·9	0·2	17·6–18·2	21·1	0·2	20·8–21·4	99·9%

*NS—not significant at 95% level of confidence.

Table A.6 Sampling errors of selected values for the sample of wards and hostels

Description of variable average values of:	HOSPITAL WARDS			HOSTELS			Significance level of difference between hospital wards and hostels
	Value average	Sampling error	95% confidence interval	Value average	Sampling error	95% confidence interval	
% of residents able to wash and dress themselve in all wards/hostels (table 3.8)	44%*	2%	39%–48%	77%*	3%	71%–83%	99·9%
% of residents able to wash and dress themselves in children's units (table 3.8)	20%*	5%	10%–30%	54%*	6·5%	42%–67%	99·9%
% of residents in care of staff throughout the day in all wards/hostels (table 4.1)	50%*	2%	46%–54%	15%*	3%	10%–20%	99·9%
Number of residents in all wards/hostels (table 3.4)	27·9	1·2	25·6–30·2	18·5	0·9	16·6–20·4	99·9%
Staff ratio in the high ability wards/hostels (table 3.10)	10·9†	0·9	9·1–12·7	6·2†	0·4	5·5– 6·9	99·9%
Staff ratio in the children's units (table 3.10)	4·2†	0·3	3·6– 4·8	3·2†	0·3	2·6– 3·8	95%

*These figures are averages based on the number of wards/hostels whereas the percentages in tables 3.8 and 4.1 are based on the total number of residents.
†These figures are average values which were used to calculate the sampling errors whereas table 3.10 shows the median values.

158

APPENDIX B—CLUSTER ANALYSIS

Summary

Cluster analysis was used in this survey with the aim of providing a classification of the wards and hostels according to the abilities of the residents in a way that would reflect the basic workload for the staff. Two clustering techniques were used, both with the RELOC method described in *Clustan* (Wishart 1970), with the error sum of square coefficient and the average distance coefficient. These produced similar classifications into 4 clusters which contained patients or residents who were respectively mainly high ability, average ability, low ability or non-ambulant with very low ability. The two classifications were combined to form a final classification into 4 groups which was thought to provide the most useful framework for assessing the relationship between the staff's role and the abilities of their residents.

B.1 Introduction

Cluster analysis is a statistical technique which produces a classification into groups (known as clusters) containing cases with similar characteristics. In general the cases in each cluster are more closely similar to one another than to the cases in any other cluster. The clusters are formed in order to optimize, or attempt to optimize, various specified statistical criteria. Classifications can be produced with the number of clusters varying, at one extreme, from the original number of cases, to the other extreme, of a single cluster containing all the cases. The use of different statistical criteria may lead to different classifications with the same number of clusters. Fuller details of cluster analysis and its applications are given in Everitt (1974) and Andeberg (1973).

One general problem with cluster analysis is deciding which of several possible classifications should be used. The associated statistical tests can only give vague indications as to which classification is the most suitable and the classifications can only be optimal in a very limited, statistical sense. In general greater confidence can be placed on classifications replicated by different techniques and consequently in this application two techniques were used. The selection of the final classification partly depends on the judgment of the researchers and in this case the adopted classification was considered to be the most suitable way of describing the types of wards and hostels for this survey although other classifications would be preferable for other purposes.

The main object of the cluster analysis was to produce a classification of the type of residents which would reflect the basic work load. This classification was required to provide a way of relating the staff's roles and views to the type of residents with whom they were working. As it seemed likely that hostel residents would be generally more capable than hospital patients, the classification was also needed so that comparison could be made between staff in hostels and staff in hospitals working with a similar type of patient. It was anticipated that a classification with 2, 3 or 4 clusters would be of most value and it was expected that some or all of the clusters would be equivalent to high grade units, mixed or medium grade and low grade. Pilot work had shown that the staff could not be expected to assign their own ward or hostel to one of these categories in a standard way.

Previous research had not produced a technique for classifying wards or hostels using the type of questions included in this survey. It is possible to classify wards or hostels using scales developed by Kushlick et al (1973) but in order to use their method it would have been necessary to have obtained detailed information on each resident in the selected wards and hostels. This would have been too time consuming and complex to have been used in this survey. However, several of the questions included on the abilities of the residents were based on the questions developed by Kushlick et al and also on questions used by Morris (1969) and Bone et al (1973).

159

B.2 Sample

The complete sample of wards and hostels was used in the cluster analysis except for acute sickness wards, hostels which had three or more residents who were not mentally handicapped and 10 units which were excluded because the self-completion questionnaires on their residents' longstanding physical disabilities had not been returned to us. The children's wards and hostels were included with the adults' as the main purpose of the analysis was to classify the wards and hostels according to the basic workload for the staff. In wards or hostels where some of the staff worked with only one group of the residents who were different from the other residents (eg a non-ambulant group), each group was included as a separate residential unit (up to a maximum of three groups per ward or hostel). This led to a total sample size of 383 units which were used without reweighting because this is not essential for producing a framework for classification.

B.3 Variables

The variables used in the cluster analysis are shown in table B.1 with their means and standard deviations.[1] The similarity between two units was measured as the sum of the squares of the differences in percentages between the units on each variable (ie Euclidean distance squared). The standard deviations can be considered to indicate the relative weight placed on each variable because the differences between the units are generally smaller on variables with small deviations. It was felt that this procedure would give a reasonably realistic reflection of the basic workload for staff as, for example, a difference of 28% in the proportion of residents able to feed themselves (one standard deviation) was felt to make a greater difference to the basic workload than a difference of 7% in the proportion of deaf residents (also one standard deviation).

B.4 Clustering methods

The cluster analysis was carried out with the Clustan 1B set of computer programmes developed by Wishart (1970) using the following techniques:—

(a) The RELOC method described in *Clustan* with the error sum of squares coefficient.

RELOC is an iterative method which, working from an initial classification (of 7 or 8 clusters in this case), examines each case to see whether it should be relocated in one of the other clusters. Once a stable solution has been reached for a given number of clusters, the method then merges the two most similar clusters and uses this as the starting solution for a new cycle of relocating. With the error sum of squares coefficient, a case is relocated and clusters are merged according to a criterion which aims to minimise the total variance within clusters. The stable solution obtained at each stage of RELOC is only locally optimal and may vary with a different initial classification. RELOC with the sum of squares coefficient was carried out with two initial classifications which were:—

(i) A completely random classification into 8 clusters with equal numbers in each cluster.

(ii) A classification which used seven units selected at random, as kernel points and then assigned the remaining cases to the cluster containing the kernel point to which they were most similar.

(b) The RELOC method with the average distance coefficient. This uses the same basic RELOC process as in (a) but with a criterion for relocating or merging which aims to minimise the average distance between cases in the

---

[1]In units where a single question had not been answered the answer was estimated from a similar question (for example if necessary the number of daytime incontinents was used to estimate the number incontinent at night).

160

Table B.1   Variables used in the cluster analysis

	Mean	Standard deviation
	%	%
Percentage who are able to walk by themselves (possibly using walking aids but without assistance from any one)	85	27
Percentage who are able to feed themselves without any assistance	82	28
Percentage who are able to wash and dress themselves without any assistance	51	38
Percentage who have behaviour problems, for example being aggressive, destructive or overactive	27	33
Percentage who are doubly incontinent at least twice a week during the day	21	29
Percentage who are singly incontinent at least twice a week during the night	30	32
Percentage who are allowed to go out of hospital or hostel grounds alone	32	39
Percentage who had at least one epileptic fit in the previous week	10	11
Percentage who are blind or partially sighted	5	8
Percentage who are deaf (excluding any who can hear using a hearing aid)	4	7
Percentage who suffer from cerebral palsy (or arthritis) and who are bedridden or have difficulty in walking up stairs	12	22
Percentage who suffer from any respiratory illness or heart condition and are bedridden or have difficulty walking upstairs	4	8
Percentage who need a special diet because they must not eat a certain type of food for health reasons	7	14

Totals	
Number of adult wards	251
Number of adult hostels	72
Number of children's wards	35
Number of children's homes	25
Number of units *(base for the means and standard deviations)*	383

same cluster. There is only a fairly subtle, statistical difference between this criterion and the error sum of squares criterion but where the clusters are not clearly defined these criteria are likely to produce different classifications. The average distance criterion was used with an initial classification based on 8 kernel points which were selected to ensure that they included units with residents of high, medium and low abilities.

The three types of starting solution which were used are illustrated in fig (i) for a hypothetical clustering of two variables.

B.5   Results

The classifications produced by the RELOC method with the error sum of squares coefficient with initial classifications (i) and (ii) were almost identical with 5 clusters and completely identical with 4, 3 and 2 clusters. The RELOC method with the average distance coefficient generally produced a different classification except that its 4 cluster solution, though not identical with, was very similar to the classification with 4 clusters produced with the error sum of squares coefficient. The means for each variable are

161

Fig (i) AN ILLUSTRATION OF THE THREE INITIAL CLASSIFICATIONS USED WITH RELOC

The diagrams show a hypothetical classification based on 2 variables.

a(i)   Random allocation to eight clusters

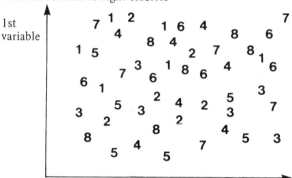

2nd variable

a(ii)   Cluster formed by allocating each point to the closest of 7 kernel points ($k_1 - k_7$) which were randomly selected

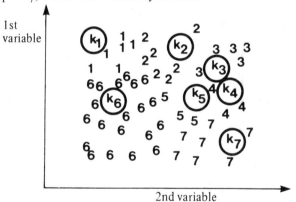

2nd variable

b   Clusters formed by allocating each point to the closest of 8 kernel points ($k_1 - k_8$) which were selected to ensure that they included units with residents of high, medium and low ability

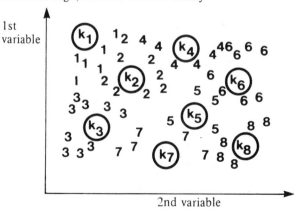

2nd variable

Table B.2 The means for the classifications into 4 clusters produced by (a) RELOC with the error sum coefficient and (b) RELOC with the average distance coefficient

	High ability		Average ability		Low ability		Non-ambulant with very low ability	
	(a)	(b)	(a)	(b)	(a)	(b)	(a)	(b)
Percentage who are able to walk by themselves (possibly using walking aids but without assistance from anyone)	99	99	94	92	83	74	23	17
Percentage who are able to feed themselves without any assistance	99	98	91	86	64	58	27	25
Percentage who are able to wash and dress themselves without any assistance	88	85	52	38	12	9	7	7
Percentage who are allowed to go out of the hospital or hostel grounds alone	84	67	12	8	9	8	1	1
Percentage who have behaviour problems for example being aggressive, destructive or overactive	6	0	30	41	51	47	35	31
Percentage who are doubly incontinent at least twice a week during the day	1	2	8	12	48	59	77	79
Percentage who are singly incontinent at least twice a week during the night	5	7	19	25	67	79	81	80
Percentage who had at least one epileptic fit in the previous month	4	5	9	10	16	19	22	22
Percentage who are blind or partially sighted	2	2	3	4	8	10	16	17
Percentage who are deaf (excluding any who can hear using a hearing aid)	3	3	3	4	5	5	6	7
Percentage who suffer from cerebral palsy (or arthritis) and are bedridden or have difficulty in walking up stairs	3	3	5	6	13	19	62	70
Percentage who suffer from any respiratory illness or heart condition and are bedridden or have difficulty walking upstairs	2	2	3	3	3	4	12	13
Percentage who need a special diet because they must not eat a certain type of food for health reasons	5	5	6	5	8	9	17	20
Number of adult wards in the cluster	52	85	119	103	51	41	29	22
Number of adult hostels in the cluster	63	68	8	4	1	0	0	0
Number of children's wards in the cluster	0	0	9	12	14	12	12	11
Number of children's homes in the cluster	0	6	19	15	4	3	2	1
Total number of units in the cluster (base for the means)	*115*	*159*	*155*	*134*	*70*	*56*	*43*	*34*

shown in table B2 for the classifications into 4 clusters with each method. The 4 clusters with either coefficient can be described as high ability, average ability, low ability and non-ambulant with very low ability. It can be seen that comparable clusters almost always have similar means and it was found that the means were always less than one standard deviation apart. This was not the case for the classifications into 3 or 5 clusters.

Statistical comparisons were made between the various classifications based on the average variance within clusters (see table B.3) which, in general, should be minimised. The classifications produced by RELOC with the error sum of squares coefficient always had a lower average variance within clusters when compared with classifications with the same number of clusters produced with the average distance coefficient. This was to be expected, as the error sum of squares coefficient directly aims to reduce the variance. However, this difference is only very slight for the classifications into 4 clusters. One statistical test suggested by several authors (for example Friedman and Rubin 1967) depends on examining a plot of the number of clusters against the average variance within clusters. It is stated that a sharp decrease in the average variance from n–1 clusters to n clusters would indicate that the n cluster solution is correct. When applied to the data in table B.3 for 2 or more clusters, no sharp decrease can be identified and so this test does not indicate a preference for any of the classifications.

Another statistical test, described by Beale (1969), was used to compare the average variance in the 3, 4, 5 and 8 cluster classifications produced by RELOC with the error sum of squares coefficient. This indicated that in each comparison, the classification with the larger number of clusters was a statistically significant improvement (at a 1% significance level). The classification into 8 clusters was far too detailed to be adopted for this application and consequently this statistical test was also of little practical value.

In both classifications into 4 clusters (Table B.2) each variable (apart from behaviour problems) consistently increases or decreases from the high ability cluster to the non-ambulant with very low ability cluster. The high ability adult wards contained patients who were generally of similar ability levels to the residents of the adult hostels and were likely to contain most of the patients who could be moved from a hospital to a hostel. A lower proportion of the patients in the average ability wards, than in the high ability wards, were able to wash and dress themselves and it was thought that the staff in these wards may need to place relatively more emphasis on teaching or encouraging their patients to do these tasks. The low ability wards contained the highest proportion

Table B.3   Average variance on each variable within clusters for each cluster solution

	(a) RELOC with error sum of squares coefficient with initial classification		(b) RELOC with average distance coefficient
Number of clusters	(i)	(ii)	
8	166	Not applicable	178
7	177	184	197
6	191	191	223
5		210	242
4		243	258
3		290	310
2		389	396
1		650	

164

of patients with behaviour problems and so it was thought that these staff may need to place relatively more emphasis on a custodial role. The fourth cluster contained most of the non-ambulant patients and a much higher proportion of patients who had an associated physical handicap or illness. It was thought that staff working in these wards may need to place relatively more emphasis on a clinical nursing role. For these reasons it was felt that either of these classifications would be useful in assessing the relationship between the staff's role and the abilities of their residents.

B.6   The final classification

It was decided to adopt a classification into 4 clusters because a similar 4 cluster classification was found with both clustering techniques and because it was felt that the 4 cluster classification would be useful in assessing the relationship between the staff's role and their residents' abilities. The final classification was formed by combining the classifications into 4 clusters produced by the 2 clustering techniques. The main difference between these classifications was in the high ability cluster which contained more adult wards and a lower average proportion of residents allowed to go out alone in the average distance classification than in the error sum classification. The former was adopted in this respect because it enabled more adult wards to be compared with the adult hostels and because the proportion of residents allowed to go out alone may partly reflect the policy of the ward or hostel rather than the ability of the residents. There were also minor differences in the number of units assigned to the low ability cluster and the non-ambulant with very low ability cluster. The classification from the error sum coefficient included slightly more units in both these lower ability clusters and was therefore adopted. This had the advantage that the final classification allocated almost exactly one-third of the adult wards to the high ability cluster, one-third to the average ability and one-third to the two lower ability clusters. The relationship between the final classification and the two classifications into 4 clusters is shown in a simplified way in figure (ii). Each unit is ranked on a hypothetical single dimension of ability on which the three classifications are shown. The means and standard deviations are shown for each variable for the final classification in table B.4.

For the analysis in section 3.3 and the remainder of the report the 10 units which were excluded from the cluster analysis because their self-completion questionnaires had not been returned, were assigned to a cluster based on their residents' abilities which had been assessed in the ward or hostel questionnaires. In order to simplify the computing procedures 5 units with separate groups of residents which were allocated to different clusters were reallocated to a single cluster based on the average ability of the residents in all the groups. This altered the way that 5 staff members in the individual sample were allocated to clusters.

165

Fig (ii) AN ILLUSTRATION OF THE FINAL CLASSIFICATION

The final classification (shown with arrows) is based on the four cluster classifications produced with error sum of squares coefficient (solid lines) and average distance coefficient (dotted lines). The units are shown ranked on a hypothetical single dimension representing ability.

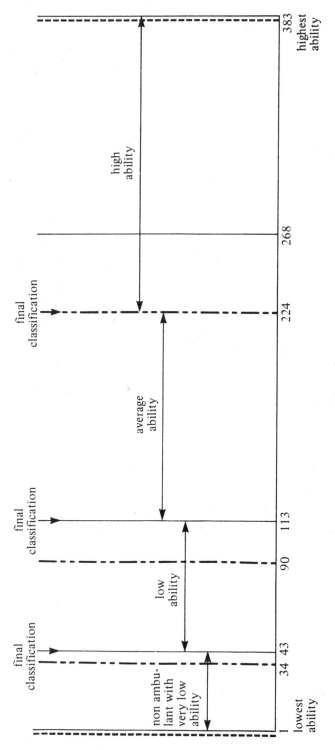

Table B.4 Means and standard deviations for the variable used in the cluster analysis for the final classification

	High ability		Average ability		Low ability		Non-ambulant with very low ability	
	Mean	SD	Mean	SD	Mean	SD	Mean	SD
	%	%	%	%	%	%	%	%
Percentage who are able to walk by themselves (possibly using walking aids but without assistance from anyone)	99	3	92	17	83	18	23	17
Percentage who are able to feed themselves without any assistance	98	8	90	16	64	24	27	19
Percentage who are able to wash and dress themselves without any assistance	85	21	42	26	12	15	7	14
Percentage who have behaviour problems, for example being aggressive, destructive or overactive	8	15	37	34	51	34	35	38
Percentage who are doubly incontinent at least twice a week during the day	2	6	9	10	48	23	77	23
Percentage who are singly incontinent at least twice a week during the night	7	9	22	13	67	24	81	22
Percentage who are allowed to go out of the hospital or hostel grounds alone	68	34	8	16	9	24	1	4
Percentage who had at least one epileptic fit in the previous month	5	6	9	8	16	14	22	11
Percentage who are blind or partially sighted	2	4	4	5	8	10	16	10
Percentage who are deaf (excluding any who can hear using a hearing aid)	3	8	4	5	5	7	6	7
Percentage who suffer from cerebral palsy (or arthritis) and are bedridden or have difficulty in walking up stairs	3	5	6	10	13	14	62	28
Percentage who suffer from any respiratory illness or heart condition and are bedridden or have difficulty walking up stairs	2	5	3	8	3	5	12	14
Percentage who need a special diet because they must not eat a certain type of food for health reasons	5	9	6	10	8	15	17	28

	Number	Number	Number	Number
Number of adult wards in the cluster	84	87	51	29
Number of adult hostels in the cluster	68	3	1	0
Number of children's wards in the cluster	0	9	14	12
Number of children's hostels in the cluster	6	13	4	2
Total number of units in cluster (base for means and standard deviations)	*158*	*112*	*70*	*43*

167

APPENDIX C QUESTIONNAIRES

Social Survey Division
St Catherines House
10 Kingsway
London WC2B 6JP

CARE OF THE MENTALLY HANDICAPPED

INDIVIDUAL SCHEDULE

SS 1085

July 1976

Serial No.

Interviewer's Name ....   Hospital/hostel

Number ....   Ward

Date of interview ....   Individual

Time of start of interview ....

Sampled grade ....

RECRUITMENT AND JOB HISTORY

1. What was your first paid job that involved caring for the
    mentally handicapped that is the grade or level at which you
    started?

    Q3(a)

Nursing assistant	1	1
Pupil nurse	2	2
Student nurse	3	3
Other nursing grade (specify)	4	4
Care assistant	5	5
Senior care assistant/assistant warden	6	6
Deputy warden	7	7
Warden/matron/officer in charge	8	8
Any domestic grade	9	9
Other (specify)	10	10

PROMPT AS NECESSARY

2. Was this in a hospital for the mentally handicapped
    or was it in some other kind of hospital or hostel?

    Q3(a)

Hospital for the mentally handicapped	1	1
Psychiatric hospital	2	2
Hostel for mentally handicapped adults	3	3
Home for mentally handicapped children	4	4
Other (specify)	5	5

PROMPT AS NECESSARY

3. Was this job in England, Scotland, Wales or Northern
    Ireland, or was it abroad?

England, Scotland, Wales or Northern Ireland	1	GO TO Q4
Abroad	2	ASK (a)

    (a) What was your first paid job in England, Scotland,
        Wales or Northern Ireland that involved caring for
        the mentally handicapped,

        RECORD GRADE AND TYPE OF HOSPITAL/HOSTEL IN COLUMNS
        Q3(a) ABOVE

1

4. When you originally applied for this first job
    (in England, Scotland, Wales or Northern Ireland),
    were you ....

    RUNNING PROMPT
    ... living within daily travelling distance
    of the (hospital/hostel) you applied to 1

    or elsewhere in England, Scotland, or Wales
    or Northern Ireland 2

    or Abroad (specify country)? 3

5. How long altogether have you worked in a job or jobs caring
    for the mentally handicapped, not counting any breaks in
    employment?

    PROMPT AS NECESSARY

    Less than 6 months .... 1 ⎤
    6 months but less than 2 years .... 2 ⎥
    2 years but less than 4 years .... 3 ⎥ ASK Q6
    4 years but less than 6 years .... 4 ⎦
    6 years but less than 10 years .... 5 ⎤
    10 years but less than 20 years .... 6 ⎥ GO TO Q7
    20 years or more .... 7 ⎦

HAND INFORMANT RED CARDS

6. These cards describe some reasons people have given for
    taking a job caring for the mentally handicapped. Can you
    pick out the cards that describe your reasons, if any,
    for taking your first paid job caring for the mentally
    handicapped (in England, Scotland, Wales or Northern
    Ireland)?

    RECORD IN BOX BELOW

REASON	Q4 RING REASON(S)	(a) RING MAIN REASON
A. I wanted to do (or continue doing) a nursing job	1	1
B. I wanted a job that involved caring for people.	2	2
C. I wanted to work with children aged under 16 ..	3	3
D. I was bored or fed up with other kinds of work.	4	4
E. I was interested because I had a relative who was mentally handicapped	5	5
F. I had been a voluntary worker with the mentally handicapped	6	6
G. I had a relative who worked with the mentally handicapped	7	7
H. I was attracted by the pay levels	8	8
I. The hours and shifts were convenient for me ...	9	9
J. A hospital or hostel for the mentally handicapped was close to my home	10	10
K. I wanted a job which provided accommodation ...	11	11
L. I was looking for any job	12	12
NONE OF THE ABOVE REASONS APPLIED	X	

2

ASK ALL WHO GAVE MORE THAN ONE REASON

NONE OR ONLY ONE REASON GIVEN DNA ....　1　GO TO Q7

(a) Which of these was your main reason for taking your
first paid job with the mentally handicapped?

RECORD IN BOX ON PREVIOUS PAGE

TO ALL

7. What were you doing immediately before you took this
(first) job caring for the mentally handicapped?

SINGLE
CODE

CODE
FIRST
THAT
APPLIES

Unemployed and actively seeking work	1
Paid work for more than 10 hrs a week	2
Full time education	3
Housewife	4
Other (specify)	5

8. (A) TO HOSPITAL STAFF
(Can I check) have you ever done any paid work in a
hostel or home for the mentally handicapped run by a
local authority or voluntary organization?

Yes 1
No .... 2 } GO TO Q9

(B) TO HOSTEL STAFF
(Can I check) have you ever worked as a nurse in a
hospital caring for the mentally handicapped?

Yes 1
No 2

9. Have you at any time worked as a nurse in a hospital
caring for patients who are not mentally handicapped -
for example in general or psychiatric or geriatric
nursing?

Yes ...... 1　ASK (a)
No .... 2　GO TO Q10

(a) Which other types or nursing have you done?

CODE ALL
THAT
APPLY

psychiatric	1
geriatric	2
sick children	3
general	4
other (specify)...	5

3

10. (Can I just check) what is your current grade or level?

    PROBE FOR EQUIVALENT GRADE IF NECESSARY

    CODE INFORMANTS IN THEIR ACTING GRADE IF THEY HAVE BEEN
    "ACTING UP" FOR AT LEAST A WEEK

RECORD GRADE
ON FLAP ABOVE
*
CODES 1 & 2
SIGNPOSTED AS 3

CODE 6
SIGNPOSTED AS 7

CODE 8
SIGNPOSTED AS 9

CODE 13
SIGNPOSTED AS 12

CODE 17
SIGNPOSTED AS 18

HOSPITAL

Divisional nursing officer	1*	GO TO Q38 ON PAGE 14
Principal nursing officer	2*	
Senior nursing officer	3	GO TO Q16 ON PAGE 6
Nursing officer	4	
Ward sister/charge nurse	5	
Deputy ward sister/charge nurse	6*	
Staff nurse	7	
Senior enrolled nurse	8*	
Enrolled nurse	9	GO TO Q11
Student nurse	10	
Pupil nurse	11	
Nursing assistant/auxiliary	12	
Cadet nurse	13*	
Other nursing staff (specify)	14	

HOSTEL

Warden/Matron/Officer in charge	15	
Deputy warden/matron/officer in charge	16	
Assistant warden/senior care assistant	17	GO TO Q12
Care assistant	18*	
Other hostel/home staff (specify)	19	

11. At present are you working on a ward or more than one
    ward, or are you studying full time or are you working
    in another kind of unit?

RECORD
ON
FLAP
ABOVE

PROMPT
AS
NECESSARY

On one ward	1	ASK (b)
On two wards	2	
On three wards or more	3	GO TO Q16
Working on a general ward/as part of training/secondment	4	GO TO Q81 ON PAGE 34
Studying full time	5	GO TO Q78 ON PAGE 31
Other kind of unit	6	ASK (a)

4

(a) What kind of unit do you work on?

In a hostel/home/other residential
unit .... 1 | ASK (b)

In a recreational/occupational
therapy unit .... 2 ⎤
                                     ⎥ GO TO Q16
In the patients school .... 3 ⎦

Teaching nurses in the
nurses training school . ... 4 | GO TO Q81
                                        ON PAGE 34
Other (specify) . . .. 5 | GO TO Q16

RECORD
ON
FLAP
ABOVE

PROMPT
AS
NECESSARY

(b) Can you give me the name of the (ward(s)/residential
unit) you work on at present?

IF 2 WARDS:- UNDERLINE AND REFER TO SAMPLED WARD
             OTHERWISE UNDERLINE AND REFER TO
             WARD LAST WORKED ON.

12. How many (patients/residents) are in your (ward/hostel)?

Number ⟶

At present do you work with all the (patients/residents)
in the (ward/hostel) or only with a group of them?

All   ..... 1 | GO TO Q13

Group .... . 2 | ASK (a) & (b)

(a) Can you give me the name of your group and the
type of (patients/residents) in the group?

(b) I should like you to think about the (patients/
residents) in your group and answer the following
questions about only them.

How many (patients/residents) are in your group?

Number ⟶

13. How many of the (patients/residents) are children aged
under twenty-one?

None | X | SEE (a)

All . . | Y | SEE Q14

Number ⟶ | GO TO Q15

RECORD
ON
FLAP
ABOVE

ASK NURSING STAFF WORKING WITH ADULTS

HOSTEL STAFF DNA ..	1	GO TO Q16

(a) Did you choose to work with adults or were you
  allocated to work with them by the hospital?
O

Chose to work with adults	1	GO TO Q16
Allocated to work with adults ...	2	
DNA-no children in the hospital..	3	

ASK NURSING STAFF WORKING WITH CHILDREN

HOSTEL STAFF DNA ..	1	GO TO Q15

14. Did you choose to work with children or were you
  allocated to work with them by the hospital?
O

Chose to work with children	1
Allocated to work with children..	2

15. Have you ever spent four weeks or longer working with
children who are not handicapped mentally or physically,
for example in a nursery, or a school or a children's
home?

Yes	1
No	2

HOURS AND SHIFTS

16. Can I check at present do you work during the day time or
on nights?

RECORD
IN FLAP
ABOVE

Daytime ...	1	ASK (b)
Nights	2	ASK (a)&(b)
Both	3	ASK (b)

(a) Do you always work on night shifts in this (ward/
hostel)?

RECORD
IN FLAP
ABOVE

Yes - always nights	1
Not always nights	2

(b) How many hours, on average, do you normally work per
week excluding any overtime and mealbreaks?

RECORD NUMBER OF HOURS →

ASK ALL EXCEPT STAFF CURRENTLY WORKING NIGHTS

WORKING NIGHTS DNA	1	GO TO Q18

6

17. In addition to these hours are you ever on call during the night?

Yes	1	ASK (a)
No	2	GO TO Q18

(a) How many nights, on average, are you on call per week?

Less than one night a week ..	X
One or more nights a week- record number of nights ⟶	

18. Did you do any paid or voluntary overtime during your last working week excluding any full week of absence through holidays or sickness?

Yes	1	ASK (a)
No	2	GO TO Q19

(a) How many hours paid or voluntary overtime did you do during your last working week, including any time in lieu that you will be taking?

Paid overtime - RECORD NUMBER OF HOURS ⟶

Unpaid overtime - RECORD NUMBER OF HOURS ⟶

Time in lieu - RECORD NUMBER OF HOURS ⟶

19. How far in advance do you know your off duty rota?

PROMPT AS NECESSARY	Always work the same shifts	X	SEE Q20
	Less than 2 weeks	1	
	2 weeks but less than 4 weeks	2	
	4 weeks but less than 2 months	3	SEE (a)
	2 months but less than 6 months ...	4	
	6 months or longer	5	

ASK ALL EXCEPT NURSING OFFICERS

NURSING OFFICERS DNA	1	GO TO Q36 ON PAGE 13

(a) Are the (nursing/care) staffs' preferences for off-
O   duty times taken into account when the rota is worked out?

Yes	1
No	2
D.K.	3
Other (specify).	4

7

NURSING OFFICERS DNA	1	GO TO Q36 ON PAGE 13

JOB DESCRIPTION

20. I would like to ask you about the tasks you carried out on your last day at work, excluding today. Could I just check, which day would that be?

Monday	1
Tuesday	2
Wednesday ..	3
Thursday ...	4
Friday	5
Saturday ...	6
Sunday	7
	(a)

21. At what times were you on duty on ....
excluding any meal-breaks?

(b)
(c)
(d)

22. Can I check how many hours did you work altogether on .... apart from meal breaks?

RECORD NUMBER OF HOURS ──────▶

HAND INFORMANT ORANGE CARDS

23. These cards describe some of the tasks which (nursing/care) staff might do. Can you pick out the cards that describe tasks that you did on ....?

TAKE BACK CARDS AND RECORD IN GRID

HAND INFORMANT THE CARDS DESCRIBING TASKS HE HAD CARRIED OUT

(a) On which of these tasks did you spend 15 minutes or less on ....?

CODE AS 3 IN GRID AT (a)

(b) On which of the other tasks did you spend an hour or less?

CODE AS 4 IN GRID AT (b)

(c) Could you look through the remaining cards and check that you spent more than an hour on each one?

IF YES - CODE AS 5 IN GRID AT (c)

INTERVIEWER CHECK:- WAS TASK N CARRIED OUT?

Yes ..	1	ASK Q24
No ...	2	GO TO Q25

8

TASKS	Tasks carried out		(a) 15 minutes or less	(b) An hour or less	(c) More than an hour
	Yes	No			
A ENCOURAGING OR TEACHING RESIDENTS/ PATIENTS TO DO DOMESTIC TASKS, OR TEACHING READING, WRITING OR UNDERSTANDING MONEY	1	2	3	4	5
B TAKING RESIDENTS/PATIENTS OUT OF THE HOSTEL/WARD e.g. taking them for a walk, shopping or on outings	1	2	3	4	5
C PLAYING GAMES OR SUPERVISING ART OR HANDICRAFT	1	2	3	4	5
D ENCOURAGING RESIDENTS/PATIENTS TO ORGANISE THEIR OWN ACTIVITIES INSIDE OR OUTSIDE THE WARD/HOSTEL	1	2	3	4	5
E MAKING BEDS OR PUTTING OUT CLOTHES	1	2	3	4	5
F PREPARING OR CLEARING AWAY MEALS, TIDYING THE WARD/HOSTEL, MENDING OR WASHING CLOTHES	1	2	3	4	5
G ROUTINE ADMINISTRATIVE WORK	1	2	3	4	5
H GIVING MEDICAL ATTENTION OR TREATMENT e.g. giving out drugs or injections, looking after patients/residents who are physically ill.	1	2	3	4	5
I MAKING ASSESSMENTS OR REPORTS ON INDIVIDUAL PATIENTS/RESIDENTS	1	2	3	4	5
J BRIEFING OR TRAINING OTHER NURSING/ CARE STAFF OR DISCUSSING PATIENTS/ RESIDENTS WITH OTHER NURSING/CARE STAFF	1	2	3	4	5
K ADVISING OR DEALING WITH PARENTS OR RELATIVES OF THE MENTALLY HANDICAPPED	1	2	3	4	5
L DEALING WITH BEHAVIOUR PROBLEMS e.g. restraining aggressive, destructive or noisy patients/residents.	1	2	3	4	5
M GETTING PATIENTS/RESIDENTS OUT OF BED OR PUTTING THEM TO BED	1	2	3	4	5
N ASSISTING WITH FEEDING, WASHING, DRESSING, BATHING OR TOILETING PATIENTS/RESIDENTS	1	2	3	4	5

24. You said that you spent some time assisting with feeding,
    washing, dressing or bathing (patients/residents).
  O For most of the time were you .....

RUNNING PROMPT	...... actually feeding, washing, dressing or bathing them	1
	or were you encouraging them to do this for themselves	2
	or were you supervising them while they did this themselves?	3
	Other (specify)	4

HAND INFORMANT PINK CARDS

25. (a) These cards describe some parts of the work carried out
  O   by (nursing/care) staff. Would you pick out the card
        that describes the part of the work that you like best?

        RECORD AT (a) IN GRID

    (b) Would you pick out the card that describes the part of
        the work that you like second best?

        RECORD AT (b) IN GRID

	(a) LIKED BEST	(b) SECOND BEST
A PLAYING OR TAKING PART IN ACTIVITIES WITH THE PATIENTS/ RESIDENTS	1	1
B PROVIDING MORE COMFORT OR BASIC CARE FOR THE PATIENTS/ RESIDENTS for example by keeping them tidy or nicely dressed	2	2
C TRAINING OR TEACHING THE PATIENTS/RESIDENTS TO DO THINGS FOR THEMSELVES for example feeding, dressing or domestic tasks..	3	3
D ENCOURAGING THE RESIDENTS/PATIENTS TO MAKE MORE DECISIONS FOR THEMSELVES	4	4
E LOOKING AFTER PATIENTS/RESIDENTS WHEN THEY ARE ILL OR NEED SOME MEDICAL ATTENTION	5	5
F TAKING PART IN DISCUSSIONS WITH MEMBERS OF OTHER PROFESSIONS	6	6
G ADVISING OR DEALING WITH RELATIVES OF THE MENTALLY HANDICAPPED	7	7
H TRAINING OTHER NURSING/CARE STAFF	8	8

10

ASK ALL WHO WORK ON ONE OR TWO WARDS

HOSTEL STAFF DNA	1	GO TO Q27
NURSING STAFF IN OTHER RESIDENTIAL UNITS DNA	2	
NURSING STAFF IN 3 OR MORE WARDS DNA	3	GO TO Q78 ON PAGE 31
NURSING STAFF IN NON-RESIDENTIAL UNIT DNA	4	GO TO Q77 ON PAGE 30

26. (Can I check) is your ward an acute sickness ward?

Yes ...	1	GO TO Q77 ON PAGE 30
No	2	ASK Q27

27. How long have you been working in your present (ward/hostel)?

	Less than 3 months	1	GO TO Q78 ON PAGE 31
PROMPT AS NECESSARY	3 months but less than 6 months..	2	SEE Q28
	6 months but less than 1 year ...	3	
	1 year but less than 2 years	4	
	2 years but less than 4 years ...	5	
	5 years but less than 10 years ..	6	
	10 years or more	7	

ASK ALL, EXCEPT STUDENTS/PUPILS, WHO HAVE BEEN IN THEIR
PRESENT WARD/HOSTEL FOR AT LEAST 3 MONTHS

STUDENTS/PUPILS DNA ..	1	GO TO Q 78 ON PAGE 31

WARD/HOSTEL ROUTINE

REFER INFORMANT TO THE SELECTED WARD AND TO HIS GROUP (IF ANY)
OF PATIENTS/RESIDENTS

28. Do all the .....

O

RUNNING PROMPT	... (patients/residents) get up at the same time at weekends as on weekdays	1
	or do any get up at a different time at the weekends?	2
	D.K.	3

29. If one of your (patients/residents) wanted to watch a
O late television programme at the weekend would he or she
usually be allowed to watch it?

Yes	1
No	2
D.K. ...	3

11

ALWAYS WORKS NIGHTS DNA	1	SEE Q41 ON PAGE 16

30. Do any of the (patients/residents) go into the (ward) kitchen, for example, to help with the clearing up or to get a drink?

Yes ...	1
No	2

31. Do the staff in your (ward/hostel) ever ask the (patients/residents) about what they would like for their meals?

Yes	1	ASK Q32
No	2	GO TO Q33
Other (specify) ..	3	

32. How often are the (patients/residents) asked about what they would like for their meals?

	Daily	1
PROMPT AS NECESSARY	At least once a week	2
	At least once a month	3
	Other (specify)	4

33. Does your (ward/hostel) ever have meetings with the (patients/residents) to discuss topics such as meals or bedtimes or other rules?

Yes ...	1	ASK (a)
No	2	GO TO Q34

(a) How often do you have these meetings?

	At least once a month	1
CODE FIRST THAT APPLIES	At least twice a year	2
	At least once a year	3

34. When you are on duty do you usually wear a uniform or overalls?

Yes - uniform ...	1	ASK (a)
Yes - overalls ..	2	
No - neither ..	3	GO TO Q35

(a) Are you obliged to wear a (uniform/overalls) by the (hospital/hostel) or is it voluntary?

Obliged to	1
Voluntary	2

12

35. What rules, if any, are there about the days or times
O   that relatives can come to visit the (patients/residents)
in your (ward/hostel)?

SEE
Q41
ON
PAGE 16

PROMPT AS NECESSARY	Can only come on fixed visiting days or times 1
	Should come on fixed visiting days or times but exceptions are made 2
	Can come when they like if they ring first 3
	Can come at any time during the day or evening 4
	D.K. 5
	Other (specify)... 6

TO NURSING OFFICERS

36. Are you responsible for a group of wards or are you
working in a different type of unit?

RECORD
IN FLAP
ABOVE

Group of wards	1	ASK (a)-(g)
Other unit	2	GO TO Q37

(a) How many wards are you responsible for?

Number ⟶

(b) Are all the patients in your wards children or are they
all adults, or do you have children and adults?

All children	1
All adults	2
Some children and some adults ..	3

(c) Are all the patients in your wards severely mentally
handicapped or all mildly handicapped, or do you have
some severely and some mildly handicapped patients?

All severely handicapped	1
All mildly handicapped	2
Some severely and some mildly handicapped..	3

13

(d) What are the shift systems for the full-time day
    nursing staff on your wards?

(e) At what times if any do the day shifts overlap
    excluding any overlap with the night shifts?

No overlap	1
Other (specify) ..	2

(f) How happy do you think the full-time day nursing
  O staff are with the shift system? Do you think they
    are ...

	... very happy	1
RUNNING	fairly happy	2
PROMPT	a little unhappy..	3
	or very unhappy?..	4

(g) How satisfied are you with the extent that this
  O shift system can provide the best care possible
    for the patients. Are you ....

	... very satisfied	1	
RUNNING	fairly satisfied	2	GO TO
PROMPT	a little dissatisfied..	3	Q38
	or very dissatisfied?..	4	

37. What type of unit are you working in?

ASK NURSING OFFICERS AND SENIOR NURSING OFFICERS

38. Do you have any responsibility for types of patients
    other than the mentally handicapped?

Only mentally handicapped patients	1
Some mentally handicapped and some other type of patients	2

14

ASK SENIOR NURSING OFFICERS

NURSING OFFICERS DNA	1	GO TO Q40

39. What are your **main** areas of responsibility and duties?

O

40. Do you think there are any tasks or responsibilities
O   which are currently carried out by staff in different
    professions which should be carried out by nursing
    staff?

Yes ...	1	ASK (a)-(c)
No	2	SEE Q41

(a) Which tasks are they?

(b) Which profession currently carries out this task?

(c) Which level of nursing staff do you think should carry
    out this task?

RECORD IN GRID

(a) Task/responsibility	(b) Profession	(c) Nursing Level	CODE ALL THAT APPLY	OFF USE
		Assistant/Auxiliary ...	1	(a)
		Student/pupil	2	
		Enrolled/staff nurse ..	3	
		Ward sister/charge	4	(b)
		Nursing officer	5	
		Other (specify)	6	
		Assistant/Auxiliary ...	1	(a)
		Student/pupil	2	
		Enrolled/staff nurse ..	3	
		Ward sister/charge	4	(b)
		Nursing officer	5	
		Other (specify)	6	
		Assistant/Auxiliary ...	1	(a)
		Student/pupil	2	
		Enrolled/staff nurse ..	3	
		Ward sister/charge	4	(b)
		Nursing officer	5	
		Other (specify)	6	

15

THE ROLE OF OTHER PROFESSIONS

REFER INFORMANT TO THE SELECTED WARD AND TO HIS GROUP
(IF ANY) OF PATIENTS/RESIDENTS.

ASK ALL HOSTEL STAFF

SENIOR NURSING OFFICERS DNA	1	GO TO Q64 ON PAGE 27
NURSING OFFICERS NOT RESPONSIBLE FOR WARDS DNA ...	2	GO TO Q77 ON PAGE 30
OTHER NURSING STAFF DNA	3	GO TO Q42

41. Do any of your residents attend a training centre or
sheltered workshop?

Yes ...	1	GO TO Q43
No	2	GO TO Q48
D.K. ..	3	

ASK HOSPITAL STAFF

42. Do any of your patients attend any kind of occupational
or recreational centre including for example a sheltered
workshop, a training centre or an occupational therapy
unit?

Yes ...	1	ASK (a)
No	2	GO TO Q48
D.K. ..	3	

(a) Are the centres they attend run by nursing staff or by
staff in other professions such as occupational
therapists?

Run by nurses	1
Run by other professions	2
Run by nurses and other professions	3
D.K.	4

43. Do you think the centre or centres that your (patients/
O residents) attend mainly aim to keep the (patients/
residents) occupied or do they mainly aim to provide
the (patients/residents) with some specific training?

Mainly aim to keep them occupied ...	1
Mainly aim to provide them with some specific training	2
D.K.	3

16

44. How valuable to your (patients/residents) who attend
O   these centres is the service provided by them? Would
    you say it is .....

RUNNING PROMPT ... very valuable	1
fairly valuable	2
or of little value?.....	3
D.K. ...	4

45. How do you feel about the amount of contact you have
O   with the staff of these centres? Would you like to have ..

RUNNING PROMPT ... less contact ....·	1
the same amount	2
or more contact with them? ...	3

46. How long is it since you last discussed a (patient's/
    resident's) progress with a member of the centre's staff?

PROMPT AS NECESSARY Less than four weeks	1
Four weeks but less than 3 months ...	2
3 months but less than 6 months	3
6 months or more	4
Never	5

47. During the past two years have you ever spent two hours
    or longer at one of these centres with the (patients/
    residents) from your (ward/hostel) either working with
    the staff or just observing what the (patients/residents)
    were doing?

Yes	1
No	2

ASK STAFF WITH ANY CHILDREN UNDER 21 IN THE WARD/HOSTEL

NO CHILDREN UNDER 21 DNA ...	1	GO TO Q49

48. Do any of the (patients/residents) in your (ward/hostel)
    go to school regularly or are regularly seen by a
    school teacher?

Yes	1	ASK (a)
No	2	
D.K. ...	3	GO TO Q49

    (a) How valuable for the children is the service provided
    O   by the school staff? Would you say it is ...

RUNNING PROMPT ... very valuable	1
fairly valuable	2
or of little value?	3
D.K.	4

17

(b) How do you feel about the amount of contact you have
with the school staff? Would you like to have ...
O

	RUNNING PROMPT	... less contact	1
		the same amount	2
		or more contact with them? ..	3

(c) How long is it since you last discussed a child's
progress with a member of the school staff?

PROMPT AS NECESSARY	Less than four weeks	1
	Four weeks but less than 3 months ...	2
	3 months but less than 6 months	3
	6 months or more	4
	Never	5

49. Do the (nursing/care) staff have their own informal or
formal meetings lasting at least a quarter of an hour to
discuss individual (patients/residents) in your (ward(s)/
hostel)?

	Yes ...	1	ASK (a)
	No	2	GO TO Q50
	D.K. ..	3	

(a) How long is it since you last attended one of these
meetings with (nursing/care) staff?

PROMPT AS NECESSARY	Less than four weeks	1	ASK (b)
	Four weeks but less than 3 months ...	2	
	3 months but less than 6 months	3	
	6 months or more	4	
	Never	5	GO TO Q50

(b) Do you usually attend these formal or informal meetings
with (nursing/care) staff?

| | Yes ... | 1 |
| | No .... | 2 |

(c) Do you think these meetings are ...
O

	RUNNING PROMPT	... very valuable	1
		fairly valuable	2
		or of little value?	3
		D.K. ..	4

18

ASK ALL EXCEPT WARDENS/WARD SISTERS/CHARGE NURSES OR
NURSING OFFICERS

WARDENS/WARD SISTERS/CHARGE NURSES/NURSING OFFICERS DNA.	1	GO TO Q50

(d) Do the staff at your level or grade usually contribute
O to these meetings or is most of the talking done by the
more senior staff?

They usually contribute to the meetings.	1	
Most of the talking is done by the more senior staff	2	
Other (specify)	3	

50. Are any of the patients in your wards at present being
trained using a behaviour modification programme?

Yes ...	1	ASK (a)&(b)
No	2	GO TO Q51
D.K. ..	3	

(a) Are any of the nursing staff from the ward regularly
involved in carrying out the behaviour modification
programme?

Yes ...	1	
No	2	

(b) How valuable do you think these behaviour modification
O programmes are for the patients? Would you say they
are ....

RUNNING PROMPT	... very valuable	1	
	fairly valuable	2	
	or of little value? ..	3	
	D.K. ..	4	

51. Have you ever been given any advice or training on ways
of carrying out or designing behaviour modification
programmes?

Yes ...	1	
No	2	
D.K. ..	3	

ASK ALL WHO WORK ON (SOME) DAY SHIFTS

ALWAYS WORKS NIGHT SHIFTS DNA	1	GO TO Q78 ON PAGE 31

52. Are there any voluntary workers who talk to or take part
in any activities with any of your (patients/residents)?

Yes ..	1	
No ...	2	

53. Do/would you encourage voluntary workers to take part
O   in activities with the (patients/residents) or do/would
     you prefer this to be left to the (ward/hostel) staff?

                Encourage voluntary workers   1   ASK (a)

                Prefer this to be left to the staff   2   SEE Q54

    (a) Does/would your (ward/hostel) give voluntary workers
        any advice or training on the sort of things they
        could do with the (patients/residents)?

                                              Yes ..   1

                                              No ...   2

ASK ALL EXCEPT NURSING/CARE ASSISTANTS

                      NURSING/CARE ASSISTANTS DNA ..   1   GO TO Q78
                                                             ON PAGE 31

54. How long is it since you last talked to a social worker
    about one of your (patients/residents)?

                        ┌ Less than four weeks   1   ┐
            PROMPT   │ Four weeks but less than 3 months ...   2   │ ASK (a)
            AS   │ 3 months but less than 6 months   3   │ & (b)
            NECESSARY   │ 6 months or more   4   ┘
                        └ Never   5   GO TO (b)

    (a) How valuable for your (patients/residents) is the
        service provided by social workers? Would you say
      O it is ....

                        ┌ ... very valuable   1
            RUNNING   │   fairly valuable   2
            PROMPT   │ or of little value? ...   3
                        └   D.K. ..   4

    (b) How do you feel about the amount of contact you have
        with social workers? Would you like to have ...
      O

                        ┌ less contact   1
            RUNNING   │ the same amount   2
            PROMPT   └ or more contact with them?   3

20

55. How long is it since a consultant psychiatrist or a
consultant for the mentally handicapped last talked to
you about a (patient's/resident's) progress?

PROMPT AS NECESSARY	Less than four weeks	1	⎤
	Four weeks but less than 3 months...	2	ASK (a)
	3 months but less than 6 months	3	
	6 months or more	4	⎦
	Never	5	GO TO (d)

(a) In general how valuable for your (patients/residents)
O are recommendations made by consultants about the
medical treatment for (patients/residents)? Would you
say they are .....

RUNNING PROMPT	.... very valuable	1
	fairly valuable	2
	or of little value?.......	3
	D.K. ...	4

(b) Do consultants ever make any recommendations about
training or social care for the (patients/residents)?

	Yes ..	1	ASK (c)
	No ...	2	GO TO (d)

(c) In general how valuable for your (patients/residents)
O are recommendations made by consultants about the
training or social care for your (patients/residents)?
Would you say they are ....

RUNNING PROMPT	.... very valuable	1
	fairly valuable	2
	or of little value?.......	3
	D.K. ...	4

(d) How do you feel about the amount of contact you have
O with consultants? Would you like to have ....

RUNNING PROMPT	.... less contact	1
	the same amount	2
	or more contact with them?	3

21

56.   frequently (is/are) your (ward(s)/hostel) visited
        (ward doctor/GP)?

        PROMPT
        AS
        NECESSARY

        At least 5 times a week   1

        At least once a week   2

        At least once a month   3

        Less frequently than once a month   4

57. How long is it since a (ward doctor/GP) last talked to
    you about a (patient's/resident's) progress?

        PROMPT
        AS
        NECESSARY

        Less than four weeks   1

        Four weeks but less than 3 months   2

        3 months but less than 6 months   3   ASK (a)

        6 months or more   4

        Never   5   GO TO (d)

(a) In general how valuable for your (patients/residents)
  O are recommendations made by (ward doctors/GPs) about
    the medical treatment for (patients/residents)? Would
    you say they are .....

        RUNNING
        PROMPT

        ... very valuable   1

        fairly valuable   2

        or of little value?   3

        D.K..   4

(b) Do (ward doctors/GPs) ever make recommendations
    about training or social care for the (patients/
    residents)?

        Yes ..   1   ASK (c)

        No ...   2   GO TO (d)

(c) In general how valuable for your (patients/residents)
  O are recommendations made by (ward doctors/GPs) about
    the training or social care for your (patients/
    residents)? Would you say they are ....

        RUNNING
        PROMPT

        ... very valuable   1

        fairly valuable   2

        or of little value?   3

        D.K..   4

i) How do you feel about the amount of contact you have
  with (ward doctors/GPs)? Would you like to have ...

RUNNING PROMPT	... less contact	1
	the same amount	2
	or more contact with them?	3

58. How long is it since you last talked to a psychologist
about one of your (patients/residents)?

PROMPT AS NECESSARY	Less than four weeks	1	ASK (a)
	Four weeks but less than 3 months ..	2	
	3 months but less than 6 months	3	
	6 months or more	4	
	Never	5	ASK (c)

(a) Do psychologists ever make recommendations about
training or social care for your (patients/residents)?

Yes ..	1	ASK (b)
No ...	2	GO TO (c)

(b) In general how valuable for your (patients/residents)
  are recommendations made by psychologists about the
training or social care for the (patients/residents)?
Would you say they are ....

RUNNING PROMPT	... very valuable	1
	fairly valuable	2
	or of little value?	3
	D.K...	4

(c) How do you feel about the amount of contact you have
  with psychologists? Would you like to have ...

RUNNING PROMPT	... less contact	1
	the same amount	2
	or more contact with them?	3

59. Are any case conferences or discussions held with members
of other professions on individual (patients/residents)
in your (ward(s)/hostel)?

Yes ...	1	ASK (a)
No	2	SEE Q60
D.K. ..	3	

23

(a) How long is it since you last attended a case
conference or discussion with members of other
professions?

	Less than four weeks	1	
PROMPT	Four weeks but less than 3 months ...	2	ASK (b)
AS	3 months but less than 6 months	3	
NECESSARY	6 months or more	4	
	Never	5	SEE Q60

(b) Do you think these case conferences or discussions
with members of other professions are ....

O

RUNNING	.... very valuable	1	
PROMPT	fairly valuable	2	
	or of little value?	3	
	D.K. ..	4	

(c) Do you usually attend these case conferences or
discussions?

	Yes	1	SEE (i)
	No	2	SEE Q60

ASK ALL EXCEPT NURSING OFFICERS

	NURSING OFFICERS DNA	1	GO TO Q60

(i) Do the staff at your level or grade usually
O contribute to these discussions or is most of
the talking done by the more senior staff or
other professions?

Their level/grade usually contribute to the discussions	1
Most of the talking is done by the more senior staff or other professions	2
Other (specify)	3

TO WARD SISTERS/CHARGE NURSES, NURSING OFFICERS AND WARDENS

OTHERS DNA .... | 1 | GO TO Q78 ON PAGE 31

60. I should like to ask you about how much influence you
O   have over the way some decisions are made. The answers
  I would like you to choose from are written on this card.

HAND INFORMANT INFLUENCE ON DECISION CARD

How much influence
do you have over:

		A	B	C	D	E	F
1	Whether a new (patient/resident) should be admitted to your (ward(s)/hostel)?	1	2	3 ASK (a)	4 ASK (a)	5 ASK (a)	6
2	Whether a (patient/resident) should be allowed to go home with relatives for the weekend?	1	2	3 ASK (a)	4 ASK (a)	5 ASK (a)	6
3	Whether a (patient/resident) should be transferred out of your (ward(s)/hostel)?	1	2	3 ASK (a)	4 ASK (a)	5 ASK (a)	6
4	Whether a (patient/resident) should attend a school	1	2	3 ASK (a)	4 ASK (a)	5 ASK (a)	6
5	Whether a (patient/resident) should attend a training centre or occupational therapy unit?	1	2	3 ASK (a)	4 ASK (a)	5 ASK (a)	6

FOR EACH ITEM CODED 3, 4 or 5, ASK:

(a) You said you do not take part in making the final
  decision on .... (WHETHER A (PATIENT/RESIDENT) .....
  etc). Who makes the final decision?

CODE ALL THAT APPLY

	ITEM 1	2	3	4	5
Consultant psychiatrist or consultant for the mentally handicapped	1	1	1	1	1
Nursing Officer	2	2	2	2	2
Psychologist	3	3	3	3	3
Other (specify nursing grade or profession)	4	4	4	4	4

25

ASK WARDENS

| WARD SISTERS/CHARGE NURSES/NURSING OFFICERS DNA ... | 1 | GO TO Q78 ON PAGE 31 |

61. Do you have one person or a group of people who are immediately in charge of you?

| One person .... | 1 | ASK (a) |
| Group of people .. | 2 | ASK (b) |

(a) Is this person only responsible for staff working with the mentally handicapped or is he or she also responsible for staff working with other types of residents or clients?

| Only responsible for staff working with the mentally handicapped .... | 1 | GO TO Q62 |
| Also responsible for staff working with other types of clients .... | 2 | |

(b) Are any of these people only responsible for staff working with the mentally handicapped or are they all also responsible for staff working with other types of residents or clients?

| At least one is only responsible for staff working with the mentally handicapped .... | 1 | |
| They are all also responsible for staff working with other types of clients .... | 2 | |

62. If you wanted to be promoted within your local authority
O would this be possible if you only had experience of working with the mentally handicapped or would your authority insist that you had worked with another type of resident or client?

Possible if only had experience of working with the mentally handicapped	1	
Authority would insist you had also worked with another type of resident/client	2	
Don't know	3	

63. If you wanted to be promoted within your local authority
O would this be possible with your present qualifications or would your authority insist that you obtained an additional qualification?

Possible with present qualifications..	1	GO TO Q78 ON PAGE 31
Authority would insist on an additional qualification	2	ASK (a)
Don't know	3	GO TO Q78 ON PAGE 31

26

(a) Which additional qualifications would your authority
    insist that you obtained before you could be promoted?

    Professional social worker
    qualification 1   ] GO TO Q78
    Other (specify) 2   ] ON PAGE 31

ASK SENIOR NURSING OFFICERS

64. Are there any children in your wards who attend a school
    or who are regularly seen by teachers?

                                Yes ... 1   ASK (a)&(b)
                                No 2   GO TO Q65

    (a) How valuable for the children is the service provided
     O by the school staff? Would you say it is ...

                        .... very valuable 1
            RUNNING   fairly valuable 2
            PROMPT   or of little value? ... 3
                                       D.K. .. 4

    (b) How do you feel about the amount of contact your
     O nursing staff have with the school staff. Do you
        think your nursing staff should have ...

                        .... less contact 1
            RUNNING   the same amount 2
            PROMPT   or more contact with
                               them? 3
                                       D.K. .. 4

65. Do any of your patients attend any kind of occupational
    or recreational centre including for example a sheltered
    workshop, a training centre or an occupational therapy
    unit?

                                Yes 1   ASK (a)&(b)
                                No 2   GO TO Q66

    (a) How valuable to these patients is the service provided
     O by these centres? Would you say it is.....

                        .... very valuable 1
            RUNNING   fairly valuable 2
            PROMPT   or of little value? ... 3
                                       D.K. ... 4

27

(b) How do you feel about the amount of contact your
nursing staff have with the staff from these centres?
O Do you think your nursing staff should have ...

RUNNING PROMPT	.... less contact	1
	the same amount	2
	or more contact with them?	3
	D.K. ..	4

66. Do/would you encourage voluntary workers to help with
O   the patients or do/would you prefer this to be left to
the ward staff?

Encourage voluntary workers.	1
Prefer this to be left to the staff	2

67. Are any behaviour modification programmes being carried
out with any of the patients in your wards?

Yes	1	ASK (a)
No	2	
D.K. ...	3	GO TO Q68

(a) How valuable do you think behaviour modification
O   programmes are? Do you think they are ....

RUNNING PROMPT	... very valuable	1
	fairly valuable	2
	or of little value?...	3
	D.K. ...	4

68. Have you ever been given any formal training on ways of
designing or carrying out behaviour modification
programmes?

Yes	1
No	2

69. How valuable are consultants' recommendations about the
medical treatment for patients? Do you think they are ...
O

RUNNING PROMPT	... very valuable	1
	fairly valuable	2
	or of little value? ...	3
	D.K. ...	4

70. How valuable are consultants' recommendations about the
O training or social care for patients? Do you think they
are ....

> RUNNING
> PROMPT

.... very valuable 1

fairly valuable 2

or of little value? ... 3

D.K. .. 4

71. How do you feel about the amount of contact your staff
O have with consultants? Would you like them to have ....

> RUNNING
> PROMPT

.... less contact 1

the same amount 2

or more contact with
them? 3

D.K. .. 4

72. How valuable are recommendations from ward doctors or
O GPs about the medical treatment for patients? Do you
think they are ...

> RUNNING
> PROMPT

.... very valuable 1

fairly valuable 2

or of little value? ... 3

D.K. .. 4

73. How valuable are recommendations from ward doctors or
O GPs about training or social care for patients? Do you
think they are ....

> RUNNING
> PROMPT

.... very valuable 1

fairly valuable 2

or of little value? ... 3

D.K. .. 4

74. How do you feel about the amount of contact your
O staff have with ward doctors or GPs? Would you like
them to have ....

> RUNNING
> PROMPT

.... less contact 1

the same amount 2

or more contact with
them? 3

D.K. ... 4

29

75. How valuable are the recommendations from psychologists
O about training or social care for the patients? Do you
think they are ...

RUNNING PROMPT	... very valuable	1
	fairly valuable	2
	or of little value? ..	3
	D.K. ..	4

76. How do you feel about the amount of contact your staff
O have with psychologists? Would you like them to have ...

RUNNING PROMPT	... less contact	1
	the same amount	2
	or more contact with them?	3
	D.K. ..	4

GO TO Q78

SATISFACTION/DISSATISFACTION

ASK ALL NURSING STAFF IN ACUTE SICKNESS WARDS OR
NON-RESIDENTIAL UNITS

SENIOR NURSING OFFICERS DNA 1   GO TO Q78

77. I should like to ask you some questions about how
O satisfied or dissatisfied you are with certain aspects
of your work. The answers I would like you to choose
from are written on this card.

HAND INFORMANT SATISFACTION CARD

How satisfied are you with ...	Very satis-fied	Fairly satis-fied	A little dis-satis-fied	Very dis-satis-fied	Does not apply
(a) The facilities that are available for patients in your (unit/wards)?	1	2	3	4	5
(b) The co-operation you get from the other staff in your (unit/wards)?	1	2	3	4	5
(c) The staffing level in your (unit/wards), that is the ratio of staff to patients?	1	2	3	4	5
(d) The cooperation you get from the nursing staff in your patients' (unit/wards)?	1	2	3	4	5
(e) Your hours and shift arrangements?	1	2	3	4	5
(f) Your pay?	1	2	3	4	5
(g) Your chances of promotion?	1	2	3	4	5
(h) The administrative side of your work?	1	2	3	4	5
(i) The domestic side or your work?	1 GO TO Q80	2 GO TO Q80	3 GO TO Q80	4 GO TO Q80	5 GO TO Q80

30

78. I should like to ask you some questions about how satisfied
O or dissatisfied you are with certain aspects of your work.
   The answers I would like you to choose from are written
   on this card.

HAND INFORMANT SATISFACTION CARD

How satisfied are you with ...	Very satis-fied	Fairly satis-fied	A little dis-satis-fied	Very dis-satis-fied	Does not apply
(a) The toys, games and similar facilities that are available for (patients/residents) in your (ward(s)/hostel)?	1	2	3	4	5
(b) The cooperation you get from the other (nursing/care) staff in your (ward/hostel)?	1	2	3	4	5
(c) The staffing level in your (ward(s)/hostel) that is the ratio of staff to (patients/residents)?	1	2	3	4	5
(d) Your hours and shift arrangements?	1	2	3	4	5
(e) Your pay?	1	2	3	4	5
(f) Your chances of promotion?	1	2	3	4	5
(g) The domestic side of your work?	1	2	3	4	5
(h) The cooperation you get from the staff in the childrens school?	1	2	3	4	5
(i) The cooperation you get from the staff in the training centre or occupational therapy unit?	1	2	3	4	5

31

TO ALL EXCEPT PERMANENT NIGHT STAFF OR NURSING/CARE
ASSISTANTS OR STUDENTS/PUPILS

PERMANENT NIGHT STAFF DNA	1	GO TO Q79
DAY STAFF-NURSING/CARE ASSISTANTS DNA	2	GO TO Q80
STUDENTS/PUPILS STUDYING FULL TIME DNA	3	GO TO Q81
STUDENTS/PUPILS NOT STUDYING FULL TIME DNA ...	4	GO TO Q80

How satisfied are you with ...	Very satis-fied	Fairly satis-fied	A little dis-satis-fied	Very dis-satis-fied	Does not apply
(j) The administrative side of your work?	1	2	3	4	5
(k) The cooperation you get from consultants?	1	2	3	4	5
(1) The cooperation you get from GPs or ward doctors?	1	2	3	4	5
(m) The cooperation you get from social workers?	1	2	3	4	5
(n) The cooperation you get from psychologists?	1	2	3	4	5

TO WARDENS, WARD SISTERS/CHARGE NURSES, NURSING OFFICERS AND
SENIOR NURSING OFFICERS

DEPUTY WARDENS, STAFF NURSES OR ENROLLED NURSES DNA	1	GO TO Q80

How satisfied are you with					
(o) The amount of influence you have over which (patients/residents) should be admitted to or transferred out of your (ward(s)/ hostel)?	1	2	3	4	5
(p) The support you get from the person or people in charge of you?	1	2	3	4	5

ASK ALL PERMANENT NIGHT STAFF

OTHERS DNA	1	GO TO Q80

79. How do you feel about the amount of contact you have
with the day staff in your (ward(s)/hostel). Would
you like to have ....

RUNNING PROMPT	... less contact	1
	the same amount	2
	or more contact with them?	3

32

AIMS

80. (a) These cards describe some things that staff might be aiming to do for the
    O   (patients/residents) in their (ward(s)/hostel/unit) within the next few years.
         Could you tell me which of these is the most important aim of your
         (ward(s)/hostel/unit) given your present resources and the type of
         (patients/residents) you have?

    (b) And which is the second most important aim?

    (c) And which is the third most important aim?

AIMS	(a) most important	(b) second most important	(c) third most important
A ENABLE SOME OF THE PATIENTS/RESIDENTS TO LIVE OUT OF THE HOSPITAL/HOSTEL WITHIN THE NEXT FEW YEARS. e.g. prepare patients to move from a hospital to a hostel, or prepare residents to move from a hostel to a group home.	1	1	1
B PROVIDE THE PATIENTS/RESIDENTS WITH PROPER MEDICAL ATTENTION	2	2	2
C PROVIDE BASIC CARE FOR THE PATIENTS/RESIDENTS e.g. ensuring that they are washed, fed and clothed etc.	3	3	3
D PROVIDE A HOMELIKE ATMOSPHERE e.g. provide an informal atmosphere, try to minimise routines.	4	4	4
E PROVIDE A MORE SHELTERED ATMOSPHERE FOR THE PATIENTS/RESIDENTS	5	5	5
F TEACH THE PATIENTS/RESIDENTS HOW TO FEED, WASH, TOILET AND DRESS THEMSELVES	6	6	6
G ENABLE THE RESIDENTS/PATIENTS TO LIVE MORE INDEPENDENTLY IN SOCIETY e.g. preparing them to go to work, enabling them to go out of the hospital/hostel alone, teaching them to read, write or understanding money.	7	7	7
H ENABLE THE RESIDENTS/PATIENTS TO DEVELOP EMOTIONALLY AND PSYCHOLOGICALLY AND HELP THEM TO MAKE MORE CHOICES FOR THEMSELVES e.g. make them aware of opportunities, develop their self awareness.	8	8	8
I PREVENT THE PATIENTS/RESIDENTS FROM BECOMING AGGRESSIVE OR DESTRUCTIVE	9	9	9
J TO PROVIDE EMOTIONAL SUPPORT FOR THE PARENTS OF THE PATIENTS/RESIDENTS	10	10	10

HAND INFORMANT NURSING AND CHILDREN OR SOCIAL WORK
QUALIFICATION CARD

1. Do you have any of the qualifications listed on this card?

Yes ...	1	ASK (a)
No	2	SEE INTERVIEWER CHECK A

(a) Which ones have you obtained,

RECORD IN GRID OPPOSITE

FOR EACH QUALIFICATION OBTAINED, ASK:

(b) In which year did you obtain this qualification?

RECORD IN GRID OPPOSITE

FOR EACH QUALIFICATION OF TYPE A-C, ASK:

NO QUALIFICATIONS TYPE A-C DNA	1	SEE (d)

(c) Did you obtain this by experience or after being a
pupil nurse?

RECORD IN GRID OPPOSITE

FOR EACH QUALIFICATION OF TYPE B OR E ASK:

NO QUALIFICATIONS TYPE B OR E DNA ..	1	SEE INTERVIEWER CHECK A

(d) Can I check did you obtain your SEN/SRN in general
nursing while you were working with the mentally
handicapped or while you were working with a different
type of patient?

RECORD IN GRID OPPOSITE

INTERVIEWER CHECK A

HAS INFORMANT OBTAINED ANY OF THE QUALIFICATIONS MARKED *

Yes	1	SEE INTERVIEWER CHECK B
No — IF STUDENT/PUPIL NURSE	2	GO TO Q82
IF NURSING OR CARE ASSISTANT	3	GO TO Q89 ON PAGE 40
IF NURSING OFFICER	4	GO TO Q87 ON PAGE 39
IF SENIOR NURSING OFFICER	5	GO TO Q87 ON PAGE 39
OTHERS	6	GO TO Q91 ON PAGE 41

INTERVIEWER CHECK B

HAS INFORMANT OBTAINED ANY OF THE QUALIFICATIONS MARKED *
FROM 1971-1976?

YES - IF STUDENT/PUPIL NURSE	1	GO TO Q82
YES - OTHERS	2	GO TO Q84
NO	3	GO TO Q85

34

	NURSING AND CHILDRENS OR SOCIAL WORK QUALIFICATIONS	(a) Record if obtained Yes	(b) Record last two digits of year 19	(c) By experience	After being pupil nurse	(d) With the ment. hand.	With different type
A	SEN Enrolled nurse in Subnormality/Deficiency nursing	1	19→	1	2*		
B	SEN Enrolled nurse in General nursing	2	→	1	2	1*	2
C	SEN Enrolled nurse in Mental Illness nursing	3	→	1	2		
D	SRN Registered nurse in Subnormality/Deficiency nursing	4*	→				
E	SRN Registered nurse in General nursing	5	→			1*	2
F	SRN Registered nurse in Mental Illness nursing	6	→				
G	SRN Registered nurse in Sick Children nursing	7	→				
H	SRN Registered nurse in Fever nursing	8	→				
I	Any equivalent foreign nursing qualification (SPECIFY)	a	→				
J	Any other nursing qualification	a	→				
K	Certificate in the residential care of children and young persons	9*	→				
L	Senior certificate in the residential care of children and young persons	10*	→				
M	Certificate in residential social work	11*	→				
N	Certificate of qualification in social work	12*	→				
O	Central Training Council's Diploma for teaching the mentally handicapped (T.C.T.M.H.)	13*	→				
P	Any equivalent foreign children's or social work qualifications (SPECIFY)	a	→				
Q	Any other children's or social work qualifications (SPECIFY)	a	→				

82. Can I check at present are you working on a general ward with patients who are not mentally handicapped on secondment as part of your training?

Yes ...	1
No	2

83. For how long have you been a (student/pupil) nurse?

PROMPT AS NECESSARY.	Less than 6 months	1	GO TO Q91 ON PAGE 41
	6 months but less than 1 year	2	
	1 year but less than 2 years	3	ASK Q84
	2 years or more	4	

REFER STUDENTS/PUPILS TO THEIR PRESENT TRAINING

REFER INFORMANTS WITH MORE THAN ONE * QUALIFICATION OBTAINED IN 1971-1976 TO THE ONE OBTAINED MOST RECENTLY

HAND INFORMANT YELLOW CARDS

84. These cards refer to some of the areas which are covered in training courses for staff working with the mentally handicapped. Would you tell me which of these areas (were/have been) included in your training to (obtain/ become) ....?
                    (NAME QUALIFICATION)

RECORD IN GRID

HAND ALL THE CARDS TO THE INFORMANT

Some people find that it would have been better if their training had placed more emphasis on certain areas and less emphasis on other areas.

(a) If more emphasis could have been placed on two of these areas, on which two would you have preferred more emphasis?

   RECORD IN GRID AT (a)

(b) If less emphasis could have been placed on two of these areas, on which two would you have preferred less emphasis?

   RECORD IN GRID AT (b)

36

TRAINING AREAS	WHETHER INCLUDED		(a) RING TWO AREAS FOR MORE EMPHASIS	(b) RING TWO AREAS FOR LESS EMPHASIS
	YES	NO		
A KNOWLEDGE OF CLINICAL NURSING e.g. ways of looking after patients/residents with a physical illness, giving injections, treating bedsores.	1	a	1	1
B KNOWLEDGE OF THE CAUSE OF MENTAL HANDICAP AND OF GENETICS	2	a	2	2
C WAYS OF DEALING WITH DIFFICULT BEHAVIOUR IN PATIENTS/RESIDENTS e.g. aggressive or destructive behaviour	3	a	3	3
D BASIC WAYS OF CARING FOR PATIENTS/RESIDENTS e.g. how to wash, bath, dress, toilet them.	4	a	4	4
E THE EDUCATIONAL AND TRAINING SIDE OF YOUR WORK e.g. teaching patients/residents to wash or feed themselves, or teaching reading or writing, preparing them to go to work	5	a	5	5
F WAYS OF PROVIDING A HOMELIKE ATMOSPHERE FOR PATIENTS/RESIDENTS	6	a	6	6
G THE SORT OF GAMES AND OTHER RECREATIONAL ACTIVITIES YOU COULD DO WITH THE PATIENTS/RESIDENTS	7	a	7	7
H WAYS OF ENABLING PATIENTS/RESIDENTS TO DEVELOP EMOTIONALLY AND PSYCHOLOGICALLY AND HELPING THEM TO MAKE MORE CHOICES FOR THEMSELVES e.g. ways of making them aware of opportunities or developing their self awareness	8	a	8	8
I KNOWLEDGE OF THE USE OF PERSONAL RELATIONSHIPS e.g. the use of group dynamics or staff-patient/resident relationships	9	a	9	9
J WAYS OF TRAINING OR SUPPORTING OTHER NURSING OR CARE STAFF	10	a	10	10
K WAYS OF HELPING PARENTS TO CARE FOR THE MENTALLY HANDICAPPED IN THEIR OWN HOMES	11	a	11	11
L KNOWLEDGE OF THE MENTAL HEALTH ACTS AND THE LEGAL RIGHTS OF PATIENTS/RESIDENTS	12	a	12	12
M THE SORT OF WORK CARRIED OUT BY STAFF IN OTHER PROFESSIONS	13	a	13	13
N THE DEVELOPMENT AND GROWTH OF NORMAL CHILDREN	14	a	14	14

ASK ALL EXCEPT STUDENT/PUPIL NURSES

STUDENT/PUPIL NURSES DNA .. | 1 | GO TO Q91
ON PAGE 41

85. Since you (became/obtained ....
   (NAME MOST RECENT QUALIFICATION)
   have you attended any refresher courses or been given any
   further training?

Yes ... | 1 | ASK (a)

No .... | 2 | GO TO Q86

(a) Which subjects were covered in your refresher courses
    or further training?

(b) Are courses of further training continuing education
    available for qualified staff from your present
    (hospital/hostel)?

Yes ... | 1 |
No .... | 2 | SEE Q87
D.K. .. | 3 |

86. Are any courses of further training or continuing education
    available for qualified staff from your (hospital/hostel)?

Yes ... | 1 | ASK (a)
No .... | 2 | SEE
D.K. .. | 3 | Q87

(a) What are the reasons why you have not attended any of
  O these courses of further training or continuing
    education?

38

ASK NURSING OFFICERS AND SENIOR NURSING OFFICERS

OTHERS DNA .... | 1 | GO TO Q91
                          ON PAGE 41

87. I should now like to ask you about the present syllabus
    for student nurses training to become registered in
    subnormality nursing. Are there any subject areas which
    you think should be given more emphasis in the training
    of student nurses?

Yes ... | 1 | ASK (a)

No .... | 2 |
                  GO TO Q88
D.K. .. | 3 |

(a) Which subject areas do you think should be given
    more emphasis?

88. Are there any subject areas which you think should be
    given less emphasis in the training of student nurses?

Yes ... | 1 | ASK (a)

No .... | 2 |
                  GO TO Q91
D.K. .. | 3 | ON PAGE 41

(a) Which subject areas do you think should be given less
    emphasis?

NOW GO TO Q91
ON PAGE 41

39

ASK NURSING ASSISTANTS AND CARE ASSISTANTS

89. Have you been given any training or advice on ways of
O   feeding, washing or dressing patients or ways of changing
    incontinent patients?

Yes ...	1	ASK (a)
No	2	GO TO Q90

(a) Was this training or advice given ...

PROMPT EACH	Yes	No	Very val.	Fairly val.	Little val.
... on an induction course?	1	2	3	4	5
by the (sister or charge nurse/ warden or matron) in your (ward/hostel)?	1	2	3	4	5
or in some other way? (if yes specify)	1	2	3	4	5

FOR EACH CODED 1 IN GRID ASK:

(i) In practice have you found that this training or
    advice given .... was .....
              (SPECIFY WAY)

RUNNING   ⌈ very valuable
PROMPT | fairly valuable
               ⌊ or of little value? RECORD IN BOX ⟶

90. Have you been given any training or advice on ways of
O   dealing with difficult behaviour in patients - for
    example aggressive or destructive behaviour?

Yes	1	ASK (a)
No	2	GO TO Q91

(a) Was this training or advice given ...

	Yes	No	Very val.	Fairly val.	Little val.
... on an induction course?	1	2	3	4	5
by the (sister or charge nurse/ warden or matron) in your (ward/hostel)?	1	2	3	4	5
or in some other way? (if yes specify)	1	2	3	4	5

FOR EACH CODED 1 IN GRID ASK:

    (i) In practice have you found that this training or
         advice given .... was ....
             (SPECIFY WAY)

RUNNING
PROMPT

    very valuable
    fairly valuable
    or of little value? RECORD IN BOX

ASK ALL

91. Do you have any views on the sort of work that staff
caring for the mentally handicapped should do in the
future?

Yes ... 1   ASK (a)

No 2   GO TO Q92

(a) What are your views on the sort of work staff caring
for the mentally handicapped should do in the future?

41

SELF COMPLETION

92. Here is a list of statements which some people have made about mentally
handicapped people. Can you read through each statement and put a tick in
one of the boxes to show whether you agree strongly, agree slightly, neither
agree nor disagree, disagree slightly or disagree strongly with each statement.

	I AGREE STRONGLY 1	I AGREE SLIGHTLY 2	I NEITHER AGREE NOR DISAGREE 3	I DISAGREE SLIGHTLY 4	I DISAGREE STRONGLY 5
A Hardly any mentally handicapped adults who are at present in hospitals are capable of living in local authority hostels					
B Residential homes or hospitals for the mentally handicapped should be sited as close as possible to the community they serve					
C Low grade patients can make considerable progress with a carefully designed training programme					
D Adult patients/residents should be treated like young children					
E Mentally handicapped patients/ residents appreciate attractive surroundings					
F More mentally handicapped patients/residents should be sterilized					
G We cannot expect to understand the odd behaviour of patients/residents					
H Hardly any severely mentally handicapped children could be properly looked after at home by their parents.					
I A carefully designed training programme for a patient is more important than kindness					
J Mentally handicapped adults should be discouraged from developing sexual relationships					
K Mentally handicapped patients who have been discharged from hospitals are often not properly cared for in hostels					
L More mentally handicapped adults could benefit from being in paid employment (apart from in a hospital job or a sheltered workshop)					
	1 I AGREE STRONGLY	2 I AGREE SLIGHTLY	3 I NEITHER AGREE NOR DISAGREE	4 I DISAGREE SLIGHTLY	5 I DISAGREE STRONGLY

42

FUTURE INTENTIONS

93. I'd now like to talk to you about any future plans you
O may have concerning your own job or career. Are you
   seriously thinking of leaving your present job within
   the next 6 months?

Yes ...	1	ASK (a)
No	2	GO TO Q94

(a) Are you thinking of taking a different job caring for
    the mentally handicapped or are you thinking of doing
    something else?

Different job caring for mentally handicapped...	1	GO TO Q94
(SPONTANEOUS) Retiring	2	GO TO Q100
Other (specify).	3	SEE Q95

94. In 5 years time do you think you will still be working
O with the mentally handicapped or do you think you will
   be doing something else?

Working with the mentally handicapped	1	ASK (a)
(SPONTANEOUS) Retiring	2	
Other (specify).	3	SEE Q95
D.K.	4	

(a) What grade or level do you think you will be in 5
    years time?

Same grade/level	1
Other (specify)	2

ASK ALL NURSING STAFF

HOSTEL STAFF DNA	1	GO TO Q98

95. In the future, do you think you would ever like to
O transfer to a different type of nursing that is other
   than with mentally handicapped patients in a hospital?

Yes ...	1	ASK (a)
No	2	GO TO Q96

43

(a) In the future, do you think you might like to
transfer to nursing ....

	psychiatric patients	1	⎤
	geriatric patients	2	CODE
INDIVIDUAL	sick children	3	ALL
PROMPT	general nursing	4	THAT
	community nursing	5	APPLY
	or another type of		
	nursing? (specify)	6	⎦

96. In the future, would you ever seriously think of working
   O in a hostel or home for the mentally handicapped run by
   a local authority or voluntary society?

Yes ...	1
No	2
D.K. ..	3

97. Have you ever visited a hostel or home for the mentally
handicapped run by a local authority or voluntary
society?

Yes ...	1	GO TO Q100
No	2	ASK (a)

(a) Have you ever been told about the sort of work that
is carried out in a hostel or home for the mentally
handicapped run by a local authority or voluntary
society?

Yes ...	1	⎤ GO TO Q100
No	2	⎦

TO ALL HOSTEL STAFF

98. In the future, would you ever seriously think of working
   O in a hospital for the mentally handicapped?

Yes ...	1
No	2
D.K. ..	3

99. Have you ever visited a hospital for the mentally
   O handicapped?

Yes ...	1	GO TO Q100
No	2	ASK (a)

(a) Have you ever been told about the sort of work
that is carried out in a hospital for the
mentally handicapped?

Yes ...	1
No	2

44

BACKGROUND INFORMATION

HAND INFORMANT EDUCATIONAL QUALIFICATIONS CARD

100. Have you passed any of the examinations listed on
this card?

Yes ...	1	ASK (a)
No	2	GO TO Q101

    (a) Which of the examinations have you passed?

        RECORD IN GRID BELOW

    ASK FOR QUALIFICATIONS 1-7

    (b) In how many subjects have you passed this examination?

        RECORD IN GRID BELOW

		(a) Passed	(b) No. of subjects
ENGLISH/ WELSH/ N.IRISH SCHOOL EXAMS	G.C.E. 'O' Level or School Certificate or Matric ... (NOT LOCAL OR REGIONAL RSA CERTIFICATES)	1	
	G.C.E. 'A' Level or Higher School Certificate	2	
	CSE (Certificate of Secondary Education) Grade 1 ...	3	
	CSE Other grades or ungraded	4	
SCOTTISH SCHOOL EXAMS	Scottish Certificate of Education (SCE) Ordinary Grade, or .... Scottish Leaving Certificate (SLC) Lower Grade, or .... Scottish Universities Preliminary Exam (SUPE) Ordinary or Lower Grade	5	
	SCE or SLC or SUPE Higher Grade	6	
	Certificate of Sixth Year Studies	7	
UNIVER- SITY OR TEACHING	University Diploma	8	
	University Degree	9	
	Teaching qualification (other than mentally handicapped teaching)	10	
	Any foreign qualifications	11	

101. How old were you when you completed your continuous
full time education?

GAPS OF ANY LENGTH DUE TO ILLNESS, AND OF A YEAR OR LESS FOR ANY OTHER REASON SHOULD BE IGNORED		
15 or younger	1
16	2
17 or 18	3
19 or older	4

45

102. In which country were you born?

England	1	
Scotland	2	
Wales	3	
N. Ireland	4	
Outside UK (specify country)	5	ASK (a)

    (a) In what year did you first arrive to live permanently
        in the United Kingdom?

Year 19→

103. Are you living in accommodation provided by the
      (hospital/hostel)?

Yes ...	1	ASK (a)
No	2	GO TO Q104

    (a) Is your accommodation within the (hospital/hostel)
        grounds?

Yes ...	1	ASK (b)
No	2	GO TO Q104

    (b) Do the (patients/residents) ever come to your
        accommodation except when you have invited them?

Yes	1
No	2
Other (specify).	3

ASK HOSTEL STAFF

HOSPITAL STAFF DNA	1	GO TO Q104

    (c) Does your accommodation have a separate entrance
        from the entrance used by the residents?

Yes	1
No	2
Other (specify).	3

104. What was your age on your last birthday?

Age ⟶

105. INTERVIEWER:-   (a)

W	1
C	2

      (b) Sex -

male	1
female	2

46

106. Are you married, single, widowed, divorced or
     separated?

M	1	ASK (a)
S	2	GO TO Q109
W/D/Sep	3	ASK (a)

    (a) Do you have any children?

Yes ...	1	SEE (b)
No	2	SEE Q107

ASK FEMALE INFORMANTS

MALES DNA	1	GO TO Q107

    (b) Do you have any children aged under 16 who are
     living with you?

Yes ...	1	ASK (i)&(ii)
No	2	GO TO Q108

        (i) How many of these are aged under 5?

None	X
Number ⟶	

        (ii) How many of your children are aged from 5
     to 15?

None	X	GO TO
Number ⟶		Q 108

ASK MARRIED MALE INFORMANTS

OTHERS DNA ...	1	GO TO Q108

107. Does your wife regularly do any paid work?

Yes ...	1	ASK (a)
No	2	GO TO Q108

    (a) Does she usually work for 10 hours or more
     per week?

10 hours or more ...	1	ASK (i)
Less than 10 hours..	2	GO TO Q108

        (i) Does she usually work for 30 hours or more
     per week?

30 hours or more ...	1
Less than 30 hours..	2

47

108. Do you do any other paid work, apart from this job?

Yes ...   1   ASK (a)-(c)

No   2   GO TO Q109

(a) What other type of work do you do?

(b) How many hours a week on average do you carry out this additional job?

Less than one hour   X   GO TO Q109

One hour or more record
nearest number of hours →   ASK (c)

(c) What is your gross pay before any deductions in this additional job?

Weekly £ →

Monthly £→

109. Is there anything else you would like to say about
O   any aspect of your work?

END OF INTERVIEW   TIME INTERVIEW ENDED ....

INTERVIEWER:-	Less than 30 mins	1
	30 mins but less than 40 mins	2
	40 mins but less than 50 mins	3
TIME INTERVIEW TOOK	50 mins but less than 65 mins	4
	1 hr 5 mins but less than 1 hr 20 mins ...	5
	1 hr 20 mins but less than 1 hr 40 mins ..	6
	Over 1 hr 40 mins (specify)	7

Social Survey Division
St Catherines House
10 Kingsway
London WC2B 6JP

July 1976

CARE OF THE MENTALLY HANDICAPPED

WARD/HOSTEL SCHEDULE

Interviewer's Name .... Hospital/hostel

Number .... Ward

Date of interview .... Individual

Time of start of interview ....

---

1. (Can I just check) how many (patients/residents) are in
   your (ward/hostel)?

   Number ———————▶

   ASK HOSPITAL STAFF

   HOSTEL STAFF DNA   1   GO TO Q3

2. Is this a sick ward, or a predischarge ward or hostel,
   or a ward that is mainly for short stay patients, or some
   other type of ward?

   Sick ward   1   END
                                         INTERVIEW

   Predischarge ward/hostel ......   2 ⎤
                                         ⎥
   Mainly short stay patients ....   3 ⎬ GO TO Q6
                                         ⎥
   Other (specify) ....   4 ⎦

   ASK HOSTEL STAFF

3. Are your residents all mentally handicapped or do you have
   any other type of residents?

   All mentally handicapped ......   1 ⎤
                                         ⎥
   Only 1 or 2 residents who are   ⎬ ASK Q4
   not mentally handicapped ......   2 ⎦

   3 or more residents who are
   not mentally handicapped   3   END
                                           INTERVIEW

4. Is this hostel mainly for short stay residents who you
   expect will spend two months or less in the hostel?

   Yes   1

   No   2

1

5. How long has this hostel been open for the care of
residents who are mentally handicapped?

PROMPT AS NECESSARY	Less than 6 months	1	
	6 months but less than 1 year	2	
	1 year but less than 5 years	3	
	5 years or more	4	

6. Do all the (nursing/care) staff in your (ward/hostel) work
with all the (patients/residents) or do any of the staff
only work with a group of (patients/residents)?

All the staff work with all the (patients/residents)	1	GO TO Q9
At least one of the staff only works with a group	2	ASK (a)

(a) Does each group have roughly the same type of (patients/
residents) or do any of the groups have a different
type of patient?

Each group has roughly the same type	1	GO TO Q9
At least one group has a different type	2	ASK (i)

(i) How many groups of (patients/residents) are there?

2 ..	2	ASK Q7
3 ..	3	
4 or more ...	4	GO TO Q9

7. Can you give me the name of each group and the type of
(patient/resident) in each group?

1st GROUP _

2nd GROUP _

3rd GROUP _

8. How many (patients/residents) are in each group?

1st group Number ⟶	
2nd group Number ⟶	
3rd group Number ⟶	

2

REPEAT QUESTIONS 9-17 FOR EACH GROUP FOR INFORMANTS WHO
ANSWERED Q7 OTHERWISE THE QUESTIONS REFER TO ALL THE
PATIENTS/RESIDENTS

9. Are the (patients/residents) all (males/boys) or (females/
girls) or are they mixed?

<table>
<tr><td rowspan="3">ALL THE
PATIENTS/
RESIDENTS</td><td>All males/boys ......</td><td>1</td></tr>
<tr><td>All females/girls ...</td><td>2</td></tr>
<tr><td>Mixed sexes ....</td><td>3</td></tr>
</table>

	1st group	2nd group	3rd group
All males/boys	1	1	1
GROUPS All females/girls ...	2	2	2
Mixed sexes	3	3	3

10. How many of your (patients/residents) are able to walk by
themselves possibly using walking aids but without
assistance from anyone?

<table>
<tr><td rowspan="3">ALL THE
PATIENTS/
RESIDENTS</td><td>None ......</td><td>X</td></tr>
<tr><td>All ....</td><td>Y</td></tr>
<tr><td>Number ⟶</td><td></td></tr>
</table>

	1st group	2nd group	3rd group
None	X	X	X
GROUPS All	Y	Y	Y
Number ⟶			

11. How many of your (patients/residents) are incontinent
at least twice a week during the daytime?

<table>
<tr><td rowspan="3">ALL THE
PATIENTS/
RESIDENTS</td><td>None ......</td><td>X</td><td>GO TO Q12</td></tr>
<tr><td>All ....</td><td>Y</td><td rowspan="2">ASK (a)</td></tr>
<tr><td>Number ⟶</td><td></td></tr>
</table>

	1st group	2nd group	3rd group
None	X	X	X
GROUPS All	Y] ASK (a)	Y] ASK (a)	Y] ASK (a)
Number ⟶			

3

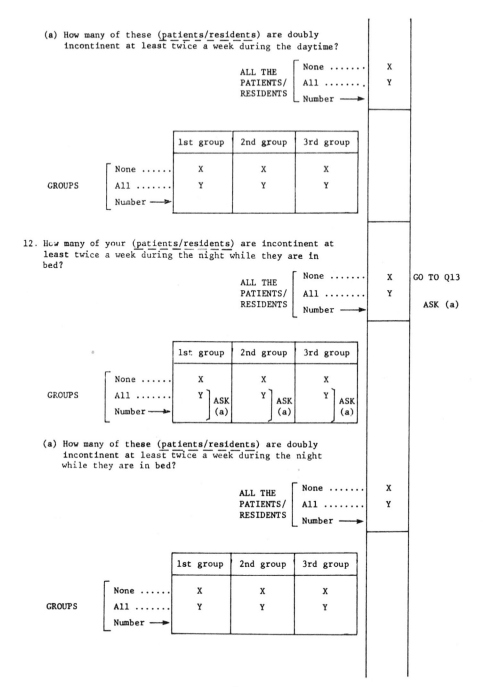

(a) How many of these (patients/residents) are doubly
incontinent at least twice a week during the daytime?

		None	X
ALL THE PATIENTS/ RESIDENTS		All	Y
		Number →	

		1st group	2nd group	3rd group
GROUPS	None	X	X	X
	All	Y	Y	Y
	Number →			

12. How many of your (patients/residents) are incontinent at
least twice a week during the night while they are in
bed?

		None	X	GO TO Q13
ALL THE PATIENTS/ RESIDENTS		All	Y	
		Number →		ASK (a)

		1st group	2nd group	3rd group
GROUPS	None	X	X	X
	All	Y ⎤ ASK (a)	Y ⎤ ASK (a)	Y ⎤ ASK (a)
	Number →			

(a) How many of these (patients/residents) are doubly
incontinent at least twice a week during the night
while they are in bed?

		None	X
ALL THE PATIENTS/ RESIDENTS		All	Y
		Number →	

		1st group	2nd group	3rd group
GROUPS	None	X	X	X
	All	Y	Y	Y
	Number →			

4

13. How many of your (patients/residents) have other behaviour problems, for example, being aggressive, destructive or overactive, which means that you could not leave them on their own for more than five minutes, unless you had to?

ALL PATIENTS/ RESIDENTS	None	X
	All	Y
	Number ⟶	

GROUPS		1st group	2nd group	3rd group
	None	X	X	X
	All	Y	Y	Y
	Number ⟶			

14. How many of your (patients/residents) are able to feed themselves without any assistance?

ALL PATIENTS/ RESIDENTS	None	X
	All	Y
	Number ⟶	

GROUPS		1st group	2nd group	3rd group
	None	X	X	X
	All	Y	Y	Y
	Number ⟶			

15. How many of your (patients/residents) are able to wash and dress themselves without any assistance?

ALL PATIENTS/ RESIDENTS	None	X
	All	Y
	Number ⟶	

GROUPS		1st group	2nd group	3rd group
	None	X	X	X
	All	Y	Y	Y
	Number ⟶			

5

16. How many of your (patients/residents) are allowed to go
    out of the (hospital/hostel) grounds alone if they want to?

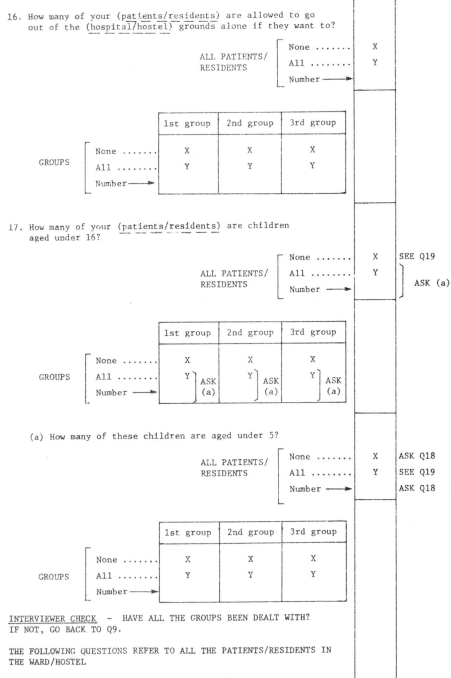

	1st group	2nd group	3rd group

ALL PATIENTS/RESIDENTS

- None X
- All .... Y
- Number ——→

GROUPS

- None .... X X X
- All .... Y Y Y
- Number ——→

17. How many of your (patients/residents) are children
    aged under 16?

ALL PATIENTS/RESIDENTS

- None X   SEE Q19
- All .... Y
- Number ——→   ASK (a)

	1st group	2nd group	3rd group

GROUPS

- None .... X X X
- All .... Y⎤ASK Y⎤ASK Y⎤ASK
- Number ——→   (a)   (a)   (a)

(a) How many of these children are aged under 5?

ALL PATIENTS/RESIDENTS

- None X   ASK Q18
- All .... Y   SEE Q19
- Number ——→   ASK Q18

	1st group	2nd group	3rd group

GROUPS

- None .... X X X
- All .... Y Y Y
- Number ——→

INTERVIEWER CHECK — HAVE ALL THE GROUPS BEEN DEALT WITH?
IF NOT, GO BACK TO Q9.

THE FOLLOWING QUESTIONS REFER TO ALL THE PATIENTS/RESIDENTS IN
THE WARD/HOSTEL

6

ASK ALL WITH ANY CHILDREN AGED 5-15

NO CHILDREN AGED 5-15 DNA	1	SEE Q19

18. How many of the children aged from 5 to 15 in your (ward/ hostel) go to school regularly or are regularly seen by a teacher?

None	X	ASK (a)
All	Y	SEE Q19
Number ———➤		ASK (a)

(a) Why do (some of) these children not go to school and
O are not seen by a teacher?

ASK ALL HOSPITAL STAFF WITH ANY PATIENTS AGED 16 OR OVER

HOSTEL STAFF WITH ANY RESIDENTS AGED 16 OR OVER DNA ..	1	GO TO Q20
NO PATIENTS/RESIDENTS AGED 16 OR OVER DNA	2	GO TO Q22

19. How many of your patients regularly attend any kind of occupational or recreational centre including for example a sheltered workshop or a training centre or an occupational therapy unit?

None	X	
All	Y	GO TO Q2
Number ———➤		

20. How many of your residents regularly attend a training centre or sheltered workshop?

None	X
All	Y
Number ———➤	

21. How many of your (patients/residents) regularly do any paid work outside the (hospital/hostel)?

None	X
All	Y
Number ———➤	

7

22. During your last working week how many of the (patients/ residents) in your (ward/hostel) had a relative come to visit them or to take them out?

None	X	
All	Y	
Number ⟶		

23. Do any relatives take part in activities with the (patients/residents) apart from taking out their own relatives?

Yes	1	
No	2	

24. Did any voluntary workers spend half an hour or longer talking to or taking part in any activities with your (patients/residents) during the past two weeks?

Yes	1	
No	2	

25. How many of the (patients/residents) have their own individual lockers or cupboards?

None	X	
All	Y	
Number ⟶		

26. Is your (ward/hostel) ever kept locked between 8am and 8pm?

Yes	1	ASK (a)
No	2	GO TO Q27

(a) For how many hours between 8am and 8pm was your (ward/ hostel) kept locked during the last weekday that you were on duty?

Not at all	X	
Less than an hour ...	Y	
One hour or more record nearest number of hours ⟶		

8

STAFF: PATIENT RATIO

2 . would like to ask you for some information so that we
can work out the ratio of staff to (patients/residents) in
your (ward/hostel) on your previous weekday at work during
the time that the day staff were on duty.

    (a) Could I just check, at what time did the first day
        staff come on duty (yesterday/previous weekday)?

                Time ....

    (b) At what time did the last of the day staff go off-
        duty (yesterday/previous weekday)?

                Time ....

    (c) (Yesterday/previous weekday) what were the total
        number of hours worked by the day (nursing/care)
        staff, including yourself, between ....
                        TIME AT (a)
    and ....?
       TIME AT (b)

NUMBER OF STAFF	Office use	NO. HOURS EACH WORKED	Office use

28. (Yesterday/previous weekday) how many of the (patients/
residents) were in the care of your staff for all the time
between .... and ....?
            TIME AT (a)   TIME AT (b)

EXCLUDE ANY PATIENTS/RESIDENTS WHO LEAVE THE WARD/HOSTEL GROUNDS UNACCOMPANIED BY A STAFF MEMBER	None X	GO TO Q29
	All .... Y	ASK (a)
	Number ⟶	

    (a) How many of these (patients/residents) stayed indoors,
    inside the (ward/hostel), all the day?

	None X	GO TO Q29
	All .... Y	ASK (i)
	Number ⟶	

       (i) How many of these (patients/residents) had a
           physical illness (yesterday/previous weekday)
           which meant that they had to stay inside?

None	X
All	Y
Number ⟶	

TO ALL NOT CODED Y AT Q28

IF Q28 CODED Y = ALL DNA	1	GO TO Q30

29. (Yesterday/previous weekday) what was the total number of
hours that each (patient/resident) was away from the (ward/
hostel) grounds and not in the care of your (nursing/care)
staff?
INCLUDE ANY PATIENTS/RESIDENTS WHO LEAVE THE WARD/HOSTEL
GROUNDS UNACCOMPANIED BY A STAFF MEMBER

NUMBER OF PATIENTS	Office use	NO. OF HOURS EACH WAS NOT IN THE CARE OF STAFF	Office use

10

30. How many of the daytime (<u>nursing/care</u>) staff in your (<u>ward/</u><u>hostel</u>), including yourself and including part-time staff, have worked there continuously for more than a year?

Number ⟶

END OF INTERVIEW

INTERVIEWER

Time of end of interview ....

Length of interview

Less than 10 mins	1
10 mins but less than 20 mins	2
20 mins but less than 30 mins	3
30 mins or more (specify)	4

OFFICE USE ONLY

Office

Total in ward/hostel ⟶

Total answering routines ⟶

1st group	2nd group	3rd group

11

CARE OF THE MENTALLY HANDICAPPED

SURVEY OF STAFF ATTITUDES FOR THE JAY COMMITTEE

Social Survey Division
St Catherines House
10 Kingsway
London WC2B 6JP

SELF-COMPLETION QUESTIONNAIRE

SS 1085

Serial Number

Hospital/hostel

(Ward/hostel)

We would be very grateful if you would complete the following questions about the extent to which the patients or residents in your ward or hostel suffer from certain physical handicaps and illnesses. These questions will provide us with some background information on the extent to which you are working with patient or residents who have these additional disabilities. We are asking these questions separately from the main interviews because we realise that you will often need to refer to your ward or hostel records to complete them.

After you have completed the questionnaire could you hand it to our interviewer while she is working in your hospital or hostel, or if this is not convenient please post it to me at the above address.

Our interviewer will be happy to assist, if you have any difficulty in answering these questions.

Most of the questions can be answered either by entering the number of patients or residents in the column provided, or by ringing the X. Beside some of the boxes and the Xs you will find instructions about which questions to answer next. If there are no instructions please go straight to the next question.

Thank you very much for your help.

Yours sincerely

Paul Wilson

Paul Wilson
Research Officer

NOTES   In answering these questions –
         Include any patients or residents who are –

         (a) temporarily on holiday

         (b) on home visits

         (c) short stay i.e. only expected to be in the ward/hostel for a short
             period

         (d) day patients/residents who come to the ward/hostel at least 4 days a week.

         Exclude any patients/residents who at present are away at boarding school
         during term time.

1

1. What is the name of your ward or hostel? ....

    ....

    ....

2. How many patients/residents are in your ward/hostel?

                        Please record the number ———▶

3. How many of your patients/residents are blind or
    partially sighted? Do not count any who could see
    with spectacles.

                        Please record the number ———▶   . . . .
                                If none ring ———▶   X

4. How many of your patients/residents are deaf?
    Do not count any who can hear using a hearing aid.

                        Please record the number ———▶   . . . .
                                If none ring ———▶   X

5. How many of your patients/residents are epileptics
    (including any controlled epileptics)?

                        Please record the number ———▶   . . . . | Answer Qn 6
                                If none ring ———▶   X | Answer Qn 8

6. How many of these epileptics had at least one fit in
    the previous year?

                        Please record the number ———▶   . . . . | Answer Qn 7
                                If none ring ———▶   X | Answer Qn 8

7. How many of these epileptics had at least one fit in
    the previous month?

                        Please record the number ———▶   . . . .
                                If none ring ———▶   X

8. How many of your patients/residents suffer from
    asthma, bronchitis or any other respiratory illness?

                        Please record the number ———▶   . . . . | Answer (a)
                                If none ring ———▶   X | Answer Qn 9

    (a) How many of the patients/residents with any of
        these respiratory illnesses are bedridden or
        have difficulty in walking up stairs?

                        Please record the number ———▶   . . . .
                                If none ring ———▶   X

2

9. How many of your patients/residents suffer from a heart condition?

Please record the number ──▶   . . . .   Answer (a)

If none ring ──▶   X   Answer Qn 10

(a) How many of the patients/residents with a heart condition are bedridden or have difficulty in walking up stairs?

Please record the number ──▶   . . . .

If none ring ──▶   X

10. How many of your patients/residents suffer from arthritis?

Please record the number ──▶   . . . .   Answer (a)

If none ring ──▶   X   Answer Qn 11

(a) How many of the patients/residents with arthritis are bedridden or have difficulty in walking up stairs?

Please record the number ──▶   . . . .

If none ring ──▶   X

11. How many of your patients/residents suffer from cerebral palsy (spasticity)?

Please record the number ──▶   . . . .   Answer (a)

If none ring ──▶   X   Answer Qn 12

(a) How many of the patients/residents with cerebral palsy (spasticity) are bedridden or have difficulty in walking up stairs?

Please record the number ──▶   . . . .

If none ring ──▶   X

12. How many of your patients/residents need to have a special diet because they must not eat a certain type of food for health reasons?

Please record the number ──▶   . . . .

If none ring ──▶   X

3

Printed in England for Her Majesty's Stationery Office by Oyez Press Limited
Dd 294799   K120   2/79